# 3D Game Animation For Dummies®

## 3D Community Web Sites

To get the latest news, forums, tutorials, galleries, and job listings, check out these 3D community Web sites.

| | |
|---|---|
| 3D.ARTISTS | www.raph.com |
| Highend3D | www.highend3d.com |
| CG Channel | www.cgchannel.com |
| 3D Total | www.3dtotal.com |
| Renderosity | www.renderosity.com |
| Ultimate 3D Links | www.3dlinks.com |
| 3D Café | www.3dcafe.com |
| 3D Commune | www.3dcommune.com |
| 3D Up | www.3dup.com |
| 3D Gate | www.3dgate.com |
| 3D Ring | www.3d-ring.com |
| CG Focus | www.cgfocus.com |
| 3D Ark | www.3dark.com |
| CG Talk | www.cgtalk.com |

## Common Maya Hotkeys

### Navigation Hotkeys

| Command | Hotkey |
|---|---|
| Tumble or Spin view | Alt (Option)+left mouse button drag |
| Track or Pan view | Alt (Option)+middle mouse button drag |
| Dolly or Zoom view | Alt (Option)+right mouse button drag |
| Fit Selected object in view | F |
| Single view/Four views toggle | Spacebar |

### Display View Hotkeys

| Command | Hotkey |
|---|---|
| Rough, Medium, and High resolution NURBS view | 1, 2, and 3 |
| Wireframe view | 4 |

(continued)

# 3D Game Animation For Dummies®

Cheat Sheet

## Display View Hotkeys *(continued)*

| | |
|---|---|
| Shaded view | 5 |
| Texture view | 6 |
| Lighting view | 7 |
| Access Paint Effects panel | 8 |
| Undo View Change | [ |
| Redo View Change | ] |

## Menu Hotkeys

| Command | Hotkey |
|---|---|
| Access Hotbox | Press and hold spacebar |
| Access Marking Menus | Right click on object |
| Access Animation menu set | F2 |
| Access Modeling menu set | F3 |
| Access Dynamics menu set | F4 |
| Access Rendering menu set | F5 |

## Object Select and Transform Hotkeys

| Command | Hotkey |
|---|---|
| Select Objects tool | Q |
| Move Objects tool | W |
| Rotate Objects tool | E |
| Scale Objects tool | R |
| Object mode/Component mode toggle | F8 |
| Grow polygon selection | > |
| Shrink polygon selection | < |

## Animation Hotkeys

| Command | Hotkey |
|---|---|
| Set Animation key | s |
| Previous key | , (comma) |
| Next key | . (period) |
| Play Animation toggle | Alt+V |

**For Dummies: Bestselling Book Series for Beginners**

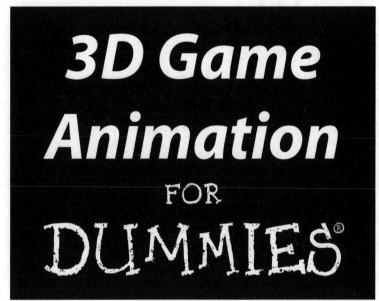

# 3D Game Animation

## FOR

# DUMMIES®

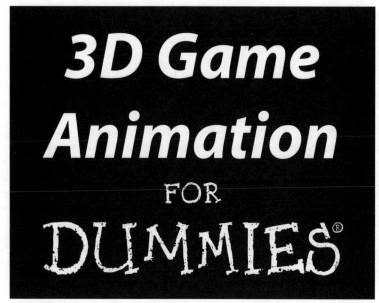

# 3D Game Animation

## FOR DUMMIES®

by Kelly L. Murdock

Wiley Publishing, Inc.

**3D Game Animation For Dummies**®

Published by
**Wiley Publishing, Inc.**
111 River Street
Hoboken, NJ 07030-5774

WILEY

# About the Author

**Kelly L. Murdock** is a gamer who loves to play video games. Occasionally, he takes a break from playing games to author a computer book or two. His book credits include various Web, graphics, and multimedia titles, including five editions of the *3ds max Bible* (up to version 7), *Maya 6 Revealed, Lightwave 3D 8 Revealed, Poser Revealed, gmax Bible, Master VISUALLY HTML and XHTML, JavaScript: Your visual blueprint for building dynamic Web pages, Adobe Atmosphere Bible,* and coauthoring duties on two editions of the *Illustrator Bible* (versions 9 and 10) and the *Adobe Creative Suite Bible.*

With a background in engineering and computer graphics (and games), Kelly has been all over the 3D (and games) industry and still finds it fascinating (along with games). He's used high-level CAD workstations for product design and analysis (but not for games), completed several large-scale visualization projects (while he was thinking about games), created 3D models for feature films (that were made into games), worked as a freelance 3D artist (which meant more time for games), and even done some 3D (and game) programming. And, yes, Kelly has even created a series of games for the non-defunct Animabets Web site including Knockout, Treasure Bones, and Middle Skip.

In his spare time, Kelly enjoys the outdoors while rock climbing, mountain biking, or skiing. He has recently formed a design company with his brother, Chris, called Logical Paradox Design.

# Dedication

I've created a monster, a gaming fool,

And playing video games is all he wants to do.

He has Mario for breakfast, and Donkey Kong for lunch,

And yellow dots for dinner is all he wants to munch.

His best friends are Kirby, Sonic and Link,

These friends give him puzzles that make him think.

But, I'm worried that he's becoming a slouch,

Because he only sees these friends while sitting on the couch.

So, I've encouraged him to go play outside,

Only if I can take my Game Boy, he cried.

I'll show him who's boss, I'll challenge him to a game.

But, after ten rounds with no wins, I was feeling quite lame.

He has two computers, a GameCube and more,

And he plays on his Game Boy till his fingers get sore.

Buying presents are easy, just a game or two,

But they should take him longer than a week to get through.

I've lost my son, these games have gone to his head,

So for my newest game, I'll challenge his brother instead.

To Eric and Thomas, 2005

# Author's Acknowledgments

This acknowledgment gives me a chance to thank all the great game designers and creators that have made many of the games that I've enjoyed so much through the years. First, thanks to the good people at Atari for all the great early original arcade games, including Battlezone, Tempest, Dig Dug, and Marble Madness, some of my favorite games. Thanks also to Atari for creating one of the first available consoles, the Atari 2600. Yes, the games all stunk, but it really gave us a chance to suspend our disbelief.

Secondly, thanks to Nintendo, Midway, Namco, Sega, Taito, Williams, Exidy, and Capcom for their early video games. I loved to play original games including Robotron and Crazy Climber, for proving that two joysticks are better than one; Ice Climber, for letting me pick the level to complete; Donkey Kong and Congo Bongo, for introducing games with a storyline; and Defender, for the best hyperspace sound out there. I spent way more quarters than I should have on these and other games, but it was worth it.

Kudos go to the early console makers of Nintendo, Sega, and Sony, and to the early computer game computers, Apple and Commodore. These systems showed us that original games for the home could be just as fun as the expensive arcade games. Hours of playing Super Mario and Sonic kept my pockets full of quarters and gave me a glimpse of what the future held.

Finally, to the current console, arcade, computer, and web game creators, I salute you in your endeavor to create unique original games in all their forms. Thanks for sharing your vision and for making computing more than just spreadsheets and flowcharts.

I'd also like to acknowledge my dear family, especially my sons Eric and Thomas for all the hours of research playing games. Now off the GameCube, it's your dad's turn to play Pikmin. Thanks also to Angela for her patience and support and for allowing the kids' games to take over her computer instead of mine.

Huge thanks goes out to Tom Heine, who was the mastermind behind this title and who kept me on track to complete it in this century. Tom, are you sure you don't want a brain surgery *For Dummies* book?

I'd also like to thank Carmela Bourassa at Alias for Maya support in writing this book. Maya was selected as the 3d software for this book because they are one of the most popular packages for creating games and because they offer a freely available version of their software called Maya, Personal Learning Edition. With this software, you can gain the valuable skills needed to obtain a job in the game industry.

Finally, thanks to Sarah Hellert, the project editor on this book and to Chris Murdock for his technical editing. I'm sure they are both gamers at heart.

## Publisher's Acknowledgments

We're proud of this book; please send us your comments through our online registration form located at `www.dummies.com/register/`.

Some of the people who helped bring this book to market include the following:

*Acquisitions, Editorial, and Media Development*

**Project Editor:** Sarah Hellert

**Acquisitions Editor:** Tom Heine

**Copy Editor:** Gwenette Gaddis Goshert

**Technical Editor:** Chris Murdock

**Editorial Manager:** Robyn B. Siesky

**Permissions Editor:** Laura Moss

**Media Development Manager:** Laura VanWinkle

**Media Development Supervisor:** Richard Graves

**Editorial Assistant:** Adrienne D. Porter

**Cartoons:** Rich Tennant (`www.the5thwave.com`)

*Composition Services*

**Project Coordinator:** Adrienne Martinez

**Layout and Graphics:** Carl Byers, Kelly Emkow, Denny Hager, Joyce Haughey, Jennifer Heleine, Barry Offringa, Lynsey Osborn, Julie Trippetti

**Proofreaders:** Laura Albert, Leeann Harney, Susan Moritz, Joe Niesen, TECHBOOKS Production Services

**Indexer:** TECHBOOKS Production Services

*Special Help:* Rebecca Huehls

**Publishing and Editorial for Technology Publishing**

**Richard Swadley,** Vice President and Executive Group Publisher

**Barry Pruett,** Vice President and Publisher, Visual/Web Graphics

**Andy Cummings,** Vice President and Publisher, Technology Dummies

**Mary Bednarek,** Executive Acquisitions Director, Technology Dummies

**Mary C. Corder,** Editorial Director, Technology Dummies

**Publishing for Consumer Dummies**

**Diane Graves Steele,** Vice President and Publisher

**Joyce Pepple,** Acquisitions Director

**Composition Services**

**Gerry Fahey,** Vice President of Production Services

**Debbie Stailey,** Director of Composition Services

# Contents at a Glance

# Table of Contents

# Introduction

● ● ● ● ● ● ● ● ● ● ● ● ● ● ● ● ● ● ● ● ● ● ● ● ● ● ● ● ● ● ● ● ● ● ● ● ● ● ● ● ● ● ● ● ● ● ● ● ● ●

*V*ideo games, we love 'em. The challenge, the cool graphics, the gameplay, the next level, the enemies, the bosses, the high score, multi-player mode, just time to kill — whatever the reason, games to gamers are worth the time.

Each game is an investment costing time. Time required to learn the controls, time needed to become familiar with the interface, time to pass each level, time to beat each boss, and time to find each secret in the game. Is the reward worth this time investment? It must be because we keep coming back. This phenomenal growth of the game industry is a testament of its appeal.

So, what makes video games so appealing? Why have we as consumers made gaming a billion-dollar-a-year industry? Part of the answer is that games have become much more engaging and interesting. We've moved beyond the times when two paddles would hit a dot back and forth and when a simple yellow character would move about a maze avoiding floating ghosts. The games of today allow a character to relive a battle in the Second World War, fight aliens on a distant planet using futuristic weapons, and undertake covert missions as a super spy.

A huge part of the answer lies in the evolution of games from 2D to 3D. A majority of games released this year will include 3D graphics. 3D adds a level of realism and depth to a game that wasn't possible in the side-scrolling world. It also enables games to be more immersive. If you're curious about how 3D games are made, then prepare for your journey.

## About This Book

If you love playing video games, then you probably love talking about games, reading about games, thinking about games, and even creating games. Think of your favorite games. What is it about these games that make them your favorites? What do you look for in your next game? If you can define the qualities of a successful game, then you're beginning to think like a game creator. Game creators are extremely creative and often have a really unique way of looking at the world. Just think of the minds that have brought us Pacman, Mario, Donkey Kong, Pikmin, Kirby, and Sonic.

If you have an ambition to do this for a career, then there are two paths you can follow. One path is programming, which includes a lot of math, a lot of code, and nifty topics like Artificial Intelligence. The other path is creating game content, which includes the graphics, animations, and visuals. Both paths are in high demand, and both are extremely fulfilling when the final product is shipped, but the choice is yours.

This book focuses on the second path and teaches the skills needed to create game content, specifically 3D animations. To gain these valuable skills, you need to learn the concepts, but you also need to learn the actual 3D software used to create games. Throughout this book, the concepts are presented in a generic manner in order to be applicable to any 3D software, but the examples are taught using the free version of Maya.

Alias' Maya is one of the most powerful, robust 3D animation packages available today. Learning Maya skills will give you the experience that you need to make it in the gaming industry or to create your own games. The Maya, Personal Learning Edition that is used for the examples in this book can be downloaded for free from the Alias Web site, www.alias.com. This version of Maya is not a limited trial version, nor is it a feature-disabled version. It includes all the features of the actual shipping version of Maya, except that the images are rendered with a watermark and the saved files are limited to this version.

After downloading Maya, Personal Learning Edition, you can cruise on over to the For Dummies Web site and download the example files used throughout this book. These examples can be found at www.dummies.com/go/3dgamefd. Be aware that the file format used by Maya, Personal Learning Edition are incompatible with the commercial version of Maya and vice versa.

Creating games is a broad topic to cover in a single book, and Maya is an amazing piece of software with hundreds of features. I won't be able to cover either topic comprehensively, but I hope that some of the concepts, techniques, and insight provided in these pages are helpful to you in your task.

# Conventions Used in This Book

Each 3D software package has its own unique way of referring to different features, which can be confusing when you're first starting out. For example, 3ds max calls the center window viewports, but Maya calls them the workspace. I try to use generic descriptions for the concept portions of the book and specific Maya definitions in the examples, but keep in mind that each feature may have a different name in a different 3D package.

# Foolish Assumptions

Gone are the days when one individual could handle every aspect of game production. Nowadays, even in the animation department you'll find animators specializing in character, vehicles, buildings, and so on. My first assumption is that you don't know it all, and my second assumption is that you aren't quite sure what area you want to specialize in.

Based on these assumptions, you may find that the topics tend to jump all over the place because I'm trying to cover all the bases. If this book were more focused on a particular aspect, then its title might have been something like *Animating a Futuristic Armored Vehicle with Only Three Wheels and Seven Different Weapons For Dummies*.

# How This Book Is Organized

If you look closely at the table of contents, you'll notice that the chapters roughly follow the same order that a game is created, starting with storyboards, moving to the UI and background elements, and then on to characters, and finishing with cut scenes. The final part, The Part of Tens, includes some good information that will help you on your path.

## Part I: Creating 3D Content for Games

The chapters in this part get the ball rolling, covering some of the background animation concepts, including the critical task of storyboarding.

## Part II: Creating Interfaces, Modeling Scenery, and Texturing Backgrounds

These chapters define the environment that the game will take place in. This can include the user interface, scenery and props, backgrounds, and lighting.

## Part III: Designing, Modeling, and Animating Game Characters

Characters often represent the pinnacle of the animation pipeline because they are the models that will be seen the most in the game. This part covers many of the tricks used to make your characters look their best.

## Part IV: Animating Game Cut Scenes

Cut scenes are used to introduce the game and to tell a story. Because they are static animations streamed from the CD, they don't have the limitations that other game assets have.

## Part V: The Part of Tens

The Part of Tens includes several lists along with a discussion of the tools, jobs, and tricks for getting a gaming job. This part also includes a glossary and a directory of animation schools.

# Icons Used in This Book

This icon provides a tip that helps you save some time or reduce some frustration.

This icon reminds you of a topic or feature that was covered previously. Rather than repeat myself, I use this icon to highlight some fact that you should keep in mind.

This is a book geared for beginners, but even beginners want to find out about some complex topics. A sampling of advanced topics and more detailed explanations are explained with these icons.

This icon warns you of certain actions or features that can cause considerable frustration if done incorrectly. Watch for these icons to keep your stress level down.

# Part I
# Creating 3D Content for Games

The 5th Wave          By Rich Tennant

"Well, shoot – I know the animation's moving a mite too fast, but <u>dang</u> if I can find a 'mosey' function anywhere in the toolbox!"

# In this part . . .

Before jumping headfirst into the specifics of animation, an overview of the game creation process is in
order. This part covers the various animation pieces in
the context of the game production pipeline.

Animation sequences created without storyboards often
end up lost. A storyboard gives the animation a purpose
and a goal and actually saves time. This part covers the
creation of storyboards and offers some good tips for
using them.

This part also delves into some of the basics of traditional
animation. Understanding the basics that animators at
Disney, Hanna-Barbera, and Warner Bros. have used over
the years will ground your work in the best practices of
the day.

# Chapter 1

# Getting Started with 3D Game Animation

*B*efore embarking on the journey of building game animations, you need to have a good idea of the task at hand. You also need to take some time to set up your system with the proper hardware and software needed to accomplish the task. This chapter gets you started on your journey by taking you through these preparatory tasks.

One of the first things to do is to look for all the various game elements that use 3D animations. 3D graphics and animations are used pervasively in games, and new uses are appearing all the time. As you play games, start looking for the places where 3D animations are used, and think about how you can use 3D animations in a similar way within your game.

After you have a good idea of all the various places within a game where 3D graphics are used, you need to familiarize yourself with the tools used to create these 3D graphics and the required hardware.

Finally, this chapter looks at the process of developing 3D games, so you'll have a good idea of what you're getting yourself into.

# This Whole Place Is Full of 3D — Identifying 3D Game Elements

When 3D games first stated to appear, they were easy to identify because the word, 3D, appeared in either the game title or its subtitle. Over time, 3D has affected every type of game, as if including a 3D aspect added some new element to the game. But I'm afraid that 3D Tetris has about the same game play as normal Tetris.

So, if 3D graphics don't add anything to the playability of a game, what is the benefit? The answer lies in making it visually appealing. Remember those Magic Eye stereogram posters that appeared everywhere several years ago. Why did people spend hours of time staring at those strange lines on the page? It was the 3D aspect that intrigued people and fed the frenzy.

In an increasingly competitive gaming market, a visually appealing game can make the difference between one that sells and one that doesn't, so 3D graphics have become an obvious choice for many game elements. If you begin to dissect many popular games, you find that 3D graphics are used all over the place. Figure 1-1 shows a sample 2D Tetris piece next to the same piece in 3D. Which would you rather see?

If your game idea is unique, look for additional ways to use 3D graphics to give your game added appeal.

## User interfaces

One of the first places where you may notice 3D graphics in a game and probably the easiest 3D element to create is the user interface. This can range from something as simple as a menu with 3D text to a raised surface with some gradient variation to a complex fully-animated machine-like interface.

Creating and using a 3D user interface help accentuate the 3D action on the screen and do much to immerse the user within the game. A good example of this type of interface is found in the game Descent, where the interface surrounds the action like windows of the ship that you are controlling. This interface adds to the game play by helping you to think you're actually within a ship.

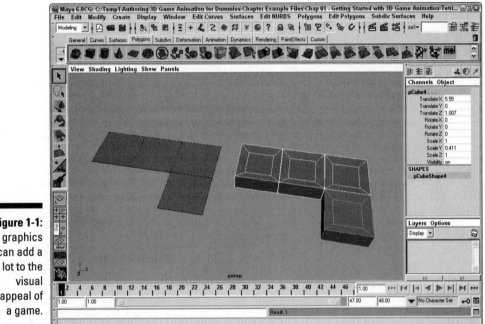

**Figure 1-1:**
3D graphics
can add a
lot to the
visual
appeal of
a game.

The key to an effective interface is one that enhances and doesn't distract from game play. The adventure game Myst is a great example of an interface that doesn't interfere with the game play. It allows players to navigate between the different scenes using only the mouse cursor, which changes for the different commands. This simple solution doesn't require annoying buttons or a menu bar to get in the way of the gorgeous images. For more details on building effective 3D user interfaces, check out Chapter 4.

## Backgrounds

3D backgrounds can provide a realistic sense of depth to the game. Backgrounds are typically rendered images that exist behind all the scene objects. Backgrounds differ from scenery and props in that they typically are not accessible to the game player.

Think of the background in the old Battlezone arcade game. The mountains in the distance were never accessible no matter how long you drove your tank toward them, yet they provided a reference that you could use to orient your rotations.

Creating background images typically involves texturing, which is covered in Chapters 6 and 7.

## Scenery and props

Scenery and props are game elements with which the player can interact directly. They typically are specific objects placed in specific positions for a special purpose. However, sometimes the special purpose is only to adorn the game.

Scenery consists of objects that are used to populate the actual environment that the player is placed within such as the actual 3D environments in which the player can move around. Scenery is used as obstacles, shields, or goals and defines the boundaries of the environment, thereby limiting and channeling the range of motion for the player.

Doom is a good example of how scenery is used to create an environment. It includes an environment of 3D rooms, corridors, and halls through which the player can move. You could move through these rooms and see what was beyond, and they formed a nice barrier that kept you within a given area.

Props do more than just define the environment, but they are objects placed in the scene for a purpose tied to game play such as a weapon, a health unit, or a key for moving to other levels.

By using 3D graphics for scenery and props, you can use these objects to provide visual feedback to players that helps them as they play, such as a switch that gets indented or a door that slides open.

Scenery and props are actual 3D objects that populate the game environments. The process of modeling scenery and prop objects is covered in Chapter 5.

## Characters

Perhaps the most visible aspects of a 3D game are the characters. These characters can be either the player itself or the game enemies. Using 3D graphics and the technical tools available in most 3D packages today, you can give your characters realistic lifelike motion that further embeds the player within the game.

The gaming world is replete with popular characters from the amorphous blobs like Pacman and his posse to the dangerous adventurer, Laura Croft.

The key to making memorable characters is to endow them with abilities, weaknesses, and personalities that make them unique from all other game characters. This also makes them likely to have sequels and even movie deals.

Working with 3D characters is also the most difficult aspect of 3D game animation creation and presents the most challenges. To address this difficult aspect of game animation, an entire part has been dedicated to characters. You can find details on designing, modeling, and animating characters in Part III.

## Cut scenes

Although cut scenes aren't involved in game play, they serve an important purpose by providing a welcome break, a chance to add some narrative and explanations, and the ability to further engross the player in the game.

Although Pacman was one of the first video games to include cut scenes after so many levels as a reward for the successful player, most of the console games available today include cut scenes woven together to tell a story. The Nintendo console games featuring Mario are a great example of how cut scenes are used to tell an engrossing story to hold the game players as they progress through the game.

Cut scenes are typically static and aren't limited in the number of polygons required for real-time display. This gives you a chance to work with high-resolution 3D graphics that show the player what the characters and scenes could really be and should represent a visually appealing high point.

Cut scenes are also more flexible in their format. They could include cartoon segments, video, or any number of different techniques. Cut scenes are used for many different means, but remember that they should be a reward for the successful player and, like the interface, shouldn't interfere with the game play. More on creating cut scene animations is covered in Part IV.

# Opening the Toolbox — the Tools Used to Create 3D Game Animations

Way back when video games first appeared, the graphics were less than appealing. Think of Pong with its single-pixel ball and four-pixel-wide paddles. The game programmers didn't use any external tools to create these graphics. They simply turned the pixels on.

Over time, these simple pixel representations were replaced with 2D images that can move about the screen (called sprites) like those found in the early video games such as Donkey Kong, Pacman, and Centipede. These sprites evolved from simple pixels to clever designs produced by an artistic department and delivered to the programmers who made the designs move about the scene. The art and design department used some type of 2D drawing package to create their designs.

With the introduction of 3D games, a whole new level of programming was introduced along with the tools used to create the 3D animations. These complex tools have come a long way from the simple 2D drawing packages.

Currently, several different software packages are used to create 3D game animations, and several other software packages work in conjunction with the 3D animation packages to create the finished results.

The software products mentioned in this section are professional-level tools and take some time to learn to use.

## Modeling, rendering, and animation software

The main software tool that is used to create 3D game animations is a package that can model, render, and animate 3D scenes. Several different packages are available to do this for all the major operating systems. You can find a more in-depth list of these various software packages in Chapter 17.

Below is a short list of the most popular and capable 3D modeling, rendering, and animation packages:

- **Maya:** Used extensively to create both movies and games, Maya is especially good at modeling and animating organic-based objects.

- **3ds max:** Perhaps the most-popular modeling, rendering, and animation package for games, 3ds max includes a host of features for animating characters.

- **SoftImage XSI:** As part of the Avid line-up, SoftImage XSI includes an amazing collection of additional tools in its base package.

- **Lightwave:** Used in many television series, Lightwave consists of two separate interfaces for modeling and animating.

Follow these steps to download and install Maya, Personal Learning Edition:

1. **Open a Web browser and type the following address,** www.alias.com.

   This is the home page for Alias, the company that creates Maya.

2. **On the home page, locate and click the product page for Maya. Then look for and click the link to download the Maya, Personal Learning Edition product.**

   Be aware that Alias makes several other popular products, but you can find Maya in the Products page. Maya, PLE is available for both Windows and Mac. The entire file is around 150 MB.

   If you don't have access to download the entire file, then you can also purchase a CD containing the software directly from Alias for a minimal cost. Information on purchasing a CD can also be found on the Alias Web site.

3. **Before you can download the software, you need to enter your e-mail address.**

   Alias uses this address to e-mail you a software key that you need to run the software. You'll also have to fill out a form with your name, address and phone number.

   In addition to the software, Alias also has several other resources available for download including shaders, models, and scenes.

4. **After the download is complete, locate and double-click the downloaded executable file.**

   This begins the installation wizard. During the installation, you'll need to enter the software key number that was e-mailed to you (see Figure 1-2). If you check your e-mail right after initiating the download, you should be able to find the software key number.

**Figure 1-2:**
Maya,
Personal
Learning
Edition,
requires a
software
key in order
to be
installed.

> **Maya 6.0 Personal Learning Edition Installation**
>
> **Software Key**
>
> A software key is required to unlock this installer. The software key would have been e-mailed to you if you registered and downloaded Maya Personal Learning Edition from our web site.
>
> Enter your Maya Personal Learning Edition software key:
>
> **Need a software key?**
> Please register with us at our website for your software key to unlock the Maya Personal Learning Edition software installer.
>
> Register Now!
>
> InstallShield
>
> < Back    Next >    Cancel

**5. After Maya, PLE is installed, you can run the software by locating and clicking its icon on the desktop or in the Alias folder.**

When Maya, PLE is run, a title screen, shown in Figure 1-3, is shown while the program loads. A separate Output Window also loads. This window is used to display commands as text and can be closed if it gets in the way. Figure 1-4 shows the software when it is opened for the first time.

**Figure 1-3:** The Maya, Personal Learning Edition title screen appears while the software is loading.

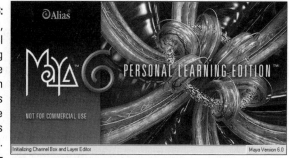

**Figure 1-4:** Maya, Personal Learning Edition is only available for non-commercial use.

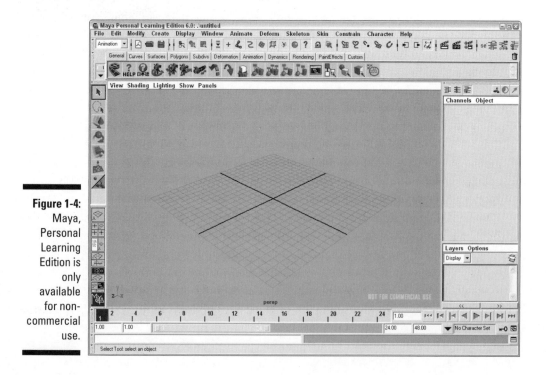

## Paint and texturing software

In addition to creating and animating objects that appear in the scene, 3D animators also paint and texture objects for added realism while keeping down the polygon count. These textures are typically painted in an image-editing package such as Photoshop, which provides tools for including transparency, texture, and surface treatments.

## Compositing software

Another important piece of the animation puzzle is compositing several separate rendered pieces together into a single image. Compositing software is typically used to accomplish this. This software is also used to edit animations and in some cases add special effects to the rendered animation sequence.

## Hardware requirements

In addition to the software, you need a pretty powerful computer to run this software. These are the minimum requirements for running the 3D packages mentioned above:

- A Pentium II, AMD Athlon, or Macintosh G4 processor
- Microsoft Windows XP, Windows 2000, or Mac OS 10.2.4
- 512 MB RAM
- CD-ROM drive
- A video graphics card that supports OpenGL and/or Direct3D
- A three-button mouse or a mouse with a scroll wheel
- 450 MB of hard drive space

Although the above hardware configuration makes animation possible, it also represents the minimum requirement, which means you'll be waiting often and dealing with memory issues. If available, you'll want to secure the following recommended system configuration:

- A dual-processor Pentium IV, AMD Athlon, or Macintosh G4 processor
- Microsoft Windows XP with the latest Service Pack, or Mac OS X Panther
- 1 GB RAM

   ✔ A video graphics card with 256 MB that supports OpenGL and Direct3D

   ✔ A mouse with a scroll wheel

   ✔ A pressure-sensitive graphics tablet

# Creating 3D Games — Slightly More Complicated Than a Connect-the-Dots Puzzle

Creating a 3D game involves many different aspects, but at the most basic level, you can think of two separate pipelines — programming and artwork. The programming aspect involves defining how the objects move, and the artwork aspect creates the look and feel of the objects involved.

This book focuses on the artwork aspect of 3D game creation, but it doesn't really touch on the programming aspect.

A good companion book to this one that covers the game programming aspect is *Windows Game Programming For Dummies,* 2nd Edition, by André LaMothe.

For the artwork aspect of game development, a simplified approach includes the following four steps. However, at no point along the way is the artwork considered final and complete: You may need to make adjustments during each phase.

## Game design

The process for the artwork aspect of game creation begins with a design. In most game companies, this task is accomplished by a single person known as a Game Designer, but it typically involves the input from many members of the game development team. The design is the high-level plan for the game and deals with the playability of the game. This design has a direct impact on both the artwork and the programming aspects.

Having a solid design up front is critical to the success of the game. If the design has flaws, these will be discovered later in the game development, causing artwork and programming to be redone. Chapter 2 covers most of the design documents that you need to create during this critical phase.

# Art design

After the game design is completed and approved, the art team can start with the art design. This task defines how the game will look and should adhere closely to the game design blueprint. During this phase, the programmers can work in parallel using simple representations that can be swapped out later with the actual art pieces. The Art Design phase is where most of a 3D Game Animator's time is spent.

Chapter 2 also covers the art design elements that you'll be working on.

# Integration

As the artwork is completed, it is delivered to the programmers who combine it with their program code. This integration phase may require some rework of the various art pieces.

While the programmers are integrating the artwork with the game code, game animators are free to work on the cut scenes along with any rework that is necessary.

# Testing

After the artwork and the code are combined into a cohesive game, the process of testing is essential to reveal any potential problems. Although a separate team of testers is typically used to complete this phase, the art department needs to take a close look at the final results to see how their colors and shading are affected by the real-time lighting.

# Learning the Big Picture

The big picture is that this book is teaching you how to create 3D animations. These animations and the skills you learn can be applied toward a game, but they can also be used to create artistic images and movies. The goal is to teach you 3D animation skills, but exactly how you use them is up to you.

# Chapter 2

# Game and Art Design, and Creating Storyboards

● ● ● ● ● ● ● ● ● ● ● ● ● ● ● ● ● ● ● ● ● ● ● ● ● ● ● ● ● ● ● ● ● ● ● ● ● ● ● ● ● ● ● ● ● ●

## *In This Chapter*

▶ Documenting the game design

▶ Beginning the art design phase

▶ Creating storyboards

▶ Adding dialogue

● ● ● ● ● ● ● ● ● ● ● ● ● ● ● ● ● ● ● ● ● ● ● ● ● ● ● ● ● ● ● ● ● ● ● ● ● ● ● ● ● ● ● ● ● ●

*I*f you sat down with the entire game team and explained in intricate detail what the game should look like, the chances are good that the follow-up meeting the next week would be mass confusion. However, if you presented a coherent set of design documents, everyone would have a reference to help stay on track.

The first two phases involved in creating game artwork are the Game Design phase and the Art Design phase. Each of these phases has specific documents that must be produced.

The Game Design phase can include some artwork, but it mainly involves text documents and flowcharts. The Art Design phase, on the other hand, includes detailed drawings of all the objects, characters, and environments that make up the game. The documents produced during the Art Design phase can include drawings, storyboards, and visual representations.

A *storyboard* is a series of connected images that shows the motion of an animated sequence. For depicting game play, the storyboard can show several possible game paths. Storyboards are just one of the Art Design documents, which can also include concept art and dialogue tracks. This chapter covers the important tasks involved in creating the design documents that drive the entire project.

# Documenting the Game Design: What Exactly Does This Game Do?

To get the whole ball running, you first need to define exactly what kind of game you are creating. If you have access to a Game Designer that can deliver a detailed game design to you, then you can move directly into the Art Design phase. But if you don't have a Game Designer readily available, then start by jotting down any rough game ideas you have.

As you describe the game concept, you may want to use other games to help describe your game concept. For example, consider the following game concept: a game in which a first-person shooter (as in Quake) has enemies descending from the top of a staircase; as the enemies get shot with my freezing ray, they freeze solid allowing me to move them like Tetris blocks into position within a cage, and the more enemies I can pack into a single cage, the higher my bonus score.

The above example is fairly simple, yet using the game references, you should already have several good ideas on how to proceed.

## Brainstorming

To get the creative juices flowing, you can invite a group of individuals for a brainstorming session. For these sessions, everyone is encouraged to throw out ideas, which in turn inspire other ideas. When conducting a brainstorming session, be sure to invite several individuals who can record all the ideas that are discussed.

## Gathering feedback

Another good way to gather game ideas is to run your game ideas past several others and get their feedback. Be sure to get the feedback from sources whom you trust. Over time, you'll find that certain individuals provide excellent feedback.

I've found that programmers, who have analytical minds, are excellent sources of feedback.

# Writing a Game Design Document

A Game Design Document is a detailed explanation of the game's concept. The more details you include in this document, the better starting point the game has. It should cover the game details and include sections covering the following:

- ✔ **Basic premise of the game:** What is the concept behind the game? What kind of game is it: an adventure game, a first-person shooter, a puzzle game, etc.?

- ✔ **Victory and progress criteria:** How does a player progress through the game, and what must be done to win the game?

- ✔ **Failure criteria:** How does a player lose a life, or what obstacles can halt the player's progress?

- ✔ **Difficulty assessment:** How does the game get harder?

- ✔ **Game controls:** How does the player control the character or its environment?

- ✔ **Rough game storyline:** What is the story behind the game?

- ✔ **Game introduction and controls training:** How is the game first introduced, and how are the controls explained to the player?

- ✔ **Game conclusion:** How does the game end?

- ✔ **Game events:** What events take place during the game, and how are they resolved by the player?

- ✔ **Basic user interface:** What is the basic user interface, how do the interface elements impact the game, and what information is needed?

- ✔ **Scoring and other game measurements:** Will the game keep score? What is the value of different objects such as weapons, health, and damage?

- ✔ **Multiplayer and online modes:** Will the game include a multiplayer or online mode, and how will those modes differ from normal game play?

## Adding flowcharts

In addition to the textual explanation, the Game Design Document should also include a flowchart. Flowcharts, such as the one shown in Figure 2-1, can show quickly how the game flows from beginning to end.

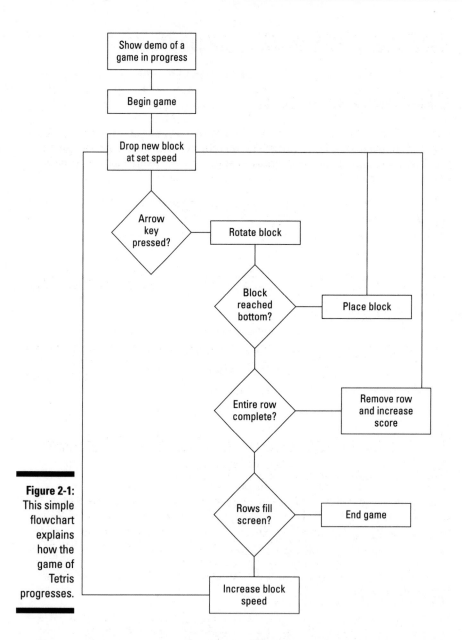

**Figure 2-1:**
This simple
flowchart
explains
how the
game of
Tetris
progresses.

As you begin to build flowcharts for the game design, you must realize that the entire game may not be expressed in a single flowchart. More than likely, you'll need to compile several different flowcharts to represent the game.

If you're having trouble building flowcharts, get some help from a programmer. They're generally very good at understanding game flows.

## Obtaining approval

After the Game Design Document and its flowcharts are completed, you need to get them approved by the game development team before proceeding to the next phase. All issues that are identified and addressed in the Game Design phase save lots of rework later in the process.

Be sure to include team members from every team in the game design approval.

# Growing Ideas into Design — Beginning the Art Design Phase

After the game design is complete and approved, you can move on to the Art Design phase. This phase, like the Game Design phase, also produces a number of documents that are used as reference pieces throughout the game development cycle.

## Sketching inspirations: You didn't throw away your pencils, did you?

You may be tempted by a powerful piece of animation software so that you want to jump right in and start creating stuff. Playing around with the software is fine, but before you begin working on game animations, you need to have a clear set of art design documents, so that the entire team starts to get an idea of how this game should look. As a first step, you need to discipline yourself to sit down away from the computer and think about how you want the game to look.

The process of designing game artwork relies on a portion of inspiration, a whole lot of creativity, and a little bit of clever thinking. The Game Design Document may provide some of the details that you can use to guide you, but it really shouldn't include much in the way of describing the look of the game objects. For example, the Game Design Document may mention that the game includes eight different types of weapons that cause different amounts of damage, but that is about all you can expect.

Sketching early ideas on paper as ideas come gives an outline that you can refer to at a later time. Sketching ideas also provides crucial references that you can use to flesh out later.

The first round of sketches should be broad and open without limiting the design of the game. They should be intended to inspire others as you go through brainstorming sessions with members of the team.

Many game designers keep a sketch notebook with them at all times in order to record any new inspired ideas that they get.

After you have several good ideas and design concepts, you need to begin to focus on the ideas that you have made the most progress with. Start with your best and most concrete ideas and flesh them out into finished art pieces.

## Compiling reference materials

When the animators at Disney worked on *The Lion King,* they actually brought a couple of lions into the studio for the animators to study. By watching these kingly animals prancing about their studio, they were able to grasp the nuances that helped them to make their animations realistic.

As you begin to sketch and draw art designs, using reference materials can help a great deal. These reference materials can include the following:

- ✔ **Pictures:** Images taken from books, encyclopedias, magazines, and so on can really help as you begin the art design process. Typically, the more images you have, the better. Games such as Call of Duty use reference material extensively to accurately create period models such as warcraft airplanes, tanks, and weapons.

- ✔ **Common objects:** If the object you're modeling really exists, then obtaining the object and being able to handle it can make a big difference.

- ✔ **Locations:** When modeling buildings or locations, going on site can help. Be sure to take your digital camera to capture the details for later.

When using reference materials, remember that images, movies, and even certain objects may be copyrighted and cannot be used without permission from the copyright holder.

## Fleshing out details, and producing final designs

Work with the rough sketches, and flesh them into finished artwork by redrawing lines, adding some color, and drawing in the details. At this point, you can move from paper sketches to a computer using a paint or drawing software that you are comfortable with. Completing the finished artwork on a computer makes distributing the design art to others for feedback easy, and duplicating as needed is equally easy.

Completed art design documents can include several different mediums, including the following:

- ✔ **Hand-drawn artwork:** Many artists are most comfortable working with traditional media like charcoal or pen and ink. Such artwork can be easily scanned into a computer.

- ✔ **Clay sculptures:** Another popular medium for visualizing art designs is clay. Building models from clay provides an actual 3D model that you can hold and rotate. It also provides an object that you can digitally scan using a 3D scanning tool.

- ✔ **3D models:** For some objects, it is easiest to cut to the chase and build the object in a 3D modeling package.

Before counting a specific object completed, be sure that you get feedback from the rest of the team and approval before continuing.

## Labeling details

The phrase "a picture is worth a thousand words" is really true. That's why they call it art design, but don't forgo words entirely. A paragraph of text along with some labels pointing to specific items can help prevent some questions. Labeling the details also gives you a chance to name the various creations, which gives the team a context to refer to when talking about the object.

# Creating Storyboard Documents

Another key design element is the storyboard. Art design is good for presenting the look and feel of game objects and characters, but the storyboard is used to define the movement of these objects within the scene.

Remember to give each storyboard a title and/or number so you can reference it in other storyboards.

## Types of storyboards

Storyboards are a documentation tool used to explain how a game progresses. To convey this information, several different types of storyboards can be used, including the following:

- **Cartoon frame storyboard:** This type of storyboard includes multiple frames on a single page much like a cartoon.

- **Index card storyboard:** Another storyboarding technique is to place each drawing on a separate index card. These cards can then be pinned to a bulletin board in order to establish a sequence. Using this method allows you to easily add, remove, and reorder drawings.

- **Pre-visualization animation:** This type of storyboard is a rough-cut animation that shows objects moving between predefined locations without any details such as secondary motion.

- **Motion Layout Diagram:** A Motion Layout Diagram shows a top view of a particular level and marks the motions of enemies in the level.

Remember that storyboards, like the other art design elements, need approval before continuing.

## Specifying logical flow paths

When storyboarding a movie, the storyboards are linear, progressing from one scene to another. But storyboarding a game is slightly different because the game player controls how the action progresses.

Before storyboarding a game flow, you need to think about all the possible directions the game can take; each of these directions will be a separate storyboard flow. As you put together a list of flows that need to be storyboarded, consider the following possible flows:

- **Goal flow:** The player reaches his goal destination.

- **Failure flow:** The player fails in his attempt to move forward.

- **Wait flow:** The player is left waiting before continuing.

- **Start flow:** The player begins a new level.

- **End flow:** The player ends a level and continues; may be similar to the goal flow.

- **Event flow:** An event happens that impacts the game; this can be events such as an enemy appears, a disaster occurs to which the player needs to respond, or a bonus round is reached.

- **Interface notification:** The interface notifies the player that an event has happened; may be similar to the event flow.

- **Multiplayer flow:** This includes any special events that occur as part of multiplayer mode.

- **Story (cut scene) flow:** This details how the story progresses based on the player's achievements.

- **Communication flow:** The player communicates with another character in the game.

## Storyboarding cut scenes

Storyboarding cut scenes can be linear just like a movie. Keep in mind that you'll probably need to divide the entire storyboard into several smaller sections that can be played at the end or start of each new level. A separate storyboard should exist for each different cut scene.

## Creating a master storyboard

As you begin to complete the storyboards of the various game flows and cut scenes, you also need to complete a master storyboard that references each of the individual storyboards. This master storyboard should cover the entire game from beginning to end, including separate storyboards for all the sub-flows. For example, a separate storyboard may be played if the player passes the level or finds a secret, or if the player dies. It also gives you the big picture of the game.

# Who's Talking Now? Adding Dialogue

Another critical storyboard piece is the dialogue track. Think of a comic strip without the little word balloons above each panel. Without dialogue, many jokes wouldn't make sense.

Dialogue doesn't need to be added to a storyboard as word balloons. Typically, the text is written under the storyboard images along with any sound effects.

Dialogue is typically handed to you by a writer whose job it is to write the game story. But, as you add the dialogue to the storyboard, look for places where the text doesn't match the dialogue, such as with positions, right or left. Also, look for sound effects that aren't included in the write-up but that become apparent as you draw the storyboards.

Animation sound effects that are created using everyday, household objects are often called Foley Sound, named after Jack Foley, who created sound effects for many black-and-white films.

# Chapter 3

# Starting with Traditional Animation Basics

*B*efore diving headfirst into 3D animation, it would be prudent to cover some of the basics of traditional animation. Many of the same animation concepts used by the Disney animator 40 years ago still apply today.

Think of the scene in the animated feature *Snow White* where you first see the poisoned apple. Several animation techniques are used to draw your attention to the apple. It is painted with richer colors, a specular highlight sparkles in the light, and the background is slightly dimmed. Using these animation techniques draws the viewer's focus to the apple and emphasizes to the viewer that this apple is important to the story.

Now think of how health units are displayed in games like Quake or Half Life. They are typically animated spinning or floating in the air outlined with a bright white or green color that makes them clearly visible for anywhere within the level. Although the medium is different than traditional animations, the techniques are often the same.

By understanding and applying the basic animation concepts, you'll be a better animator.

One of the best places to learn new animation techniques is to watch and analyze animated features of all types. Look for the techniques mentioned in this chapter as well as other techniques that can be applied to game animation. So, the next time someone complains that you watch too many cartoons, tell him it's research.

# Layering Images — the Simplest Animation Technique

Animation is an illusion created by viewing a series of images that change slightly from image to image in rapid succession. As each of these images is shown in quick succession, the mind interprets the changes as motion.

Each separate image of an animation sequence is called a *frame*.

A simple manual example of this may be accomplished by drawing slightly changing images in the margins of a book and then flipping the pages quickly to see the motion. Although this is a rudimentary approach that we all probably did as kids in school, movies and 3D games use the same concept.

Movies have standardized the speed (called the *frame rate*) at which the images are flipped in front of a film projector. Film technicians have also standardized the resolution and dimensions of the film stock for many different media, including film, television, DVD, and even the Web.

The frame rate is the number of frames that are displayed to the viewer in one second. The standard frame rate for motion pictures is 24 frames per second. Next time you watch a film, see if you can count them all.

Animation on computers also uses the same concept, except that the computer figures out the images that need to be displayed, and that can change based on the user's input. When creating 3D animations, you have control over the number of frames, the frame rate, and the resolution of the animation that you are creating. Before beginning an animation project, be sure to check the animation settings that you are using. These settings are covered in more detail in Chapter 10.

# Look at the Birdie and Smile — Focusing the Audience's View

Just as a photographer wants to focus exactly where you are looking, an animator also wants to focus what the viewer is looking at. Several techniques can be used to focus and hold the viewer's attention. These techniques are subtle, but by using them, the animation flows smoothly, and the viewer is better able to grasp the intended story.

## Avoid complex motions

One of the first techniques to keep in mind is to avoid multiple, complex motions in a single scene. If too many things are happening at once, then the viewer gets confused as to which object she should focus on, and you risk losing her focus.

Imagine a scene where a character explains a specific key combination to accomplish a back flip, but at the same time a plane crashes in the background. The player obviously focuses on the plane crash and completely misses the instructions. This is an over-emphasized example, but the problem is clear.

Storyboarding helps prevent these extraneous motions, because each frame of a storyboard should include only a single motion. The background can include static animations such as the swinging pendulum of a clock or the ambient motion of cars on a street. Try to keep background motions subtle.

When a scene calls for more than one motion, try to make one of the motions linear. For example, if a character is supposed to jump on a car, show one scene with the character anxiously waiting for the car to approach, another showing the car in motion, and a final scene with the car's motion remaining linear while the character moves toward it. This sequence shows the moving character and car both separately before showing them together. This attracts the viewer's focus to the character and not the car for the last scene.

*Linear motion* occurs when an object travels in a straight line.

## Displaying anticipation of intended motion

Another good way to focus a viewer's attention is to include some visual clues that help the viewer to anticipate motion. Cartoons are very good at these visual clues. For example, when Bugs Bunny gets ready to run quickly, he raises his leg and pulls his arm back in preparation to run before zooming off.

Games include many examples of this, such as the radar in MechWarrior that warns of incoming robots, the flashing ghosts in Pacman when a power pellet has almost run out, the box in Tetris that indicates which block is appearing next, and the pained look of a character's face in Doom when he is almost out of health.

Anticipation clues don't have to be visual. Often, sounds are used to prepare the player for action. A revving engine sound can be used to indicate the motion of a vehicle before it moves or the creepy sound of an approaching enemy.

## Emphasizing motion with exaggeration

A sister technique to anticipation is exaggeration. Imagine that a character is punching another character in an exaggerated fashion, such as a motion you might see in Mortal Combat. The animation to make a character punch doesn't involve simple motion from the shoulder forward. No, for this type of punch, the character moves his entire body backward with his hand extended fully behind him and then swings the fist forward with a step and a crunching blow. The exaggerated motion displays the power that the character has.

Exaggerated motion often fails the realism test, but the viewer is quick to forgive the exaggerated motion. Games, in particular, often exaggerate certain actions for sensationalism. Think of the car wrecks that occur in Midtown Madness or Need for Speed. In real life, cars don't always flip, spin, and roll in this manner, even if they are traveling over 100 mph, but it makes the game much more fun.

## Making foreground objects stand out

Another common technique for helping the audience to focus on a particular object and motion is to highlight the object with brighter colors, add a glow about the object, or simply dim the background. Audio clues can also help emphasize the foreground object's motion.

# Do You Have a Good Stopwatch? Controlling Timing and Pacing

Think of how a good comedian tells a joke. Any good comedian would agree that a joke's timing and pacing are crucial to the joke's success. Correct timing delivers the punch line when it is expected, and proper pacing keeps the listener engaged while the joke is being delivered.

The same holds true for animation. Correct timing and proper pacing make a big difference in how smoothly the animation runs.

Lately, several commercials have begun using an entirely different timing and pacing technique that overloads the user with random images presented so quickly that the viewer doesn't have time to focus on them. The goal of these commercials is to excite the viewer by overloading his senses. This shouldn't be the goal of your animations.

## Establishing correct timing

Good animation timing is critical to how smoothly the sequence plays and is often one of the most serious problems that plagues game animations. Poor animation timing happens when subsequent motions happen too quickly or too slowly after the previous motion.

For animated television cartoons that are trying to create enough frames to fill a 30-minute time slot, the timing problems are typically related to having too many frames between motions, but for game animations that are trying to cram animation sequences onto a tight CD-ROM or DVD-ROM, the opposite problem occurs.

For correct game animation timing, be sure to allow sufficient time between actions for the motion to develop and be anticipated. This can be accomplished by adding an additional 20 to 40 frames at the beginning and end of each animated storyboard drawing. The extra time can then be edited during the editing phase if the animation is running too slow.

If you're animating real-life scenes such as a conversation between two characters, try acting it out and timing the scene with a stopwatch. This gives you a good idea on how many total frames you should use for the sequence.

Game timing is closely related to the interface controls. When the player presses a button, the animation needs to occur immediately or he may miss the enemy he is trying to hit. Most of the game play timing issues are addressed by the programmers, but several animation timing issues also exist.

Consider the game of Dungeon Siege. If you abandon the game temporarily to answer the phone, then the character cycles through some wait animations. These wait animations let you know that the character is still active and awaiting a command rather than being frozen while the game is paused or crashed. However, recovering from these wait states poses an interesting problem for animators. By inserting a two- or three-frame buffer during the split second, you can quickly interpolate a character's current pose back to its ready state, but be careful not to include any extreme body poses as part of the wait animations unless you have a larger number of frames to buffer.

## Establishing pacing

Each frame of the storyboard defines a single action that takes place, but it really doesn't give any information on the pacing of these motions, which is something you need to get a feeling for. When animating, don't be stingy with frames and don't be afraid to insert extra frames to separate the motions.

You want to allow enough time between motions so the viewer can anticipate the motion. Imagine the storyboard frames that call for a character to pick up a weapon, fire it, and react to the recoil. If these motions occur simultaneously with no pause between the different actions, then the sequence appears rushed and fake. Adding some frames between the actions gives the character time to aim the weapon, find the trigger, and have the projectile leave the weapon barrel, even if those details aren't shown.

Much of the pacing depends on the amount of action in the story. For fast-paced action sequences, you want the motions to occur quickly, but for slower conversations and building sequences, you want more pausing between motions.

Pacing should be dynamic between different sequences. Avoid using the same pacing throughout all animations. Use fast pacing to match the excitement level of the animation and slow pacing for a mellowing effect.

# Do I Need to Draw Every Frame? Accomplishing Efficient Animation Techniques

A standard 2D animation that plays for 2 seconds at 24 frames per second includes 48 frames of animation, and an animation that runs for 90 minutes requires 129,600 frames, which would be tons of animation for any animator to complete.

Luckily, animators use lots of tricks to make this overwhelming task easier to accomplish.

## Posing characters and in-betweening

A common practice among animators is to have your main animator draw the main character at one pose for the start of a shot and then another pose for the end of the shot. Then these two poses are taken by another animator, known as an In-Betweener, who draws all the frames between these two frames using the two created by the main animator as reference. Using this method, the main animator keeps busy while others do the work of creating the in-between frames.

Even quicker than using extra artists to create the in-between frames, several 2D animation packages exist that can create the in-between frames automatically, but these packages have some drawbacks. Often, they incorrectly alter lines while making the in-between frames, such as shortening an arm.

The solution to these 2D problems is to move into 3D. Objects in 3D have volumes associated with them, so the computer knows the precise location of all object surface points at all times. So, animating in 3D requires that you pose your characters or objects in their first and last positions, and then the software automatically computes all the in-between frames. This process of animating is called keyframing, and it is covered in Chapter 10.

## Using animation loops

Another common animation practice that reduces the number of new frames of required animation for a project is to create and use animation loops. If your storyboard calls for a character to walk ten steps, then you could simply animate the character taking two steps and repeat the loop five times.

This can work well if you keep the scrolling background separate from the character animation, so the background changes continuously while the character is walking.

Animation loops are particularly useful in games where the character acts out a specific action and then returns to the original stance, such as a Mortal Kombat fighting game or the wait animation of an inactive character.

The key to creating animation loops that don't skip or look erratic is to make the first pose exactly match the final pose.

## Panning images

Another way to reduce the total number of frames that you need to create is to avoid animating altogether. For example, if you draw a long image of a background, then you can simply move the background slowly while a character in the foreground moves through a walk cycle. The character appears to be walking, but it's actually just walking in place.

Japanese anime features use the panning image technique quite often, not only with backgrounds, but with foreground images also.

# Animating Realistic Motions

Cartoon-style animations often follow specific non-realistic motions for humorous reasons. Think of how a character running off a cliff pauses before falling or how a character running through a brick wall leaves a perfect outlined hole in the wall.

Realistic motion doesn't follow the rules of cartoons, and if you're striving for realism, you need to consider the physical properties of weight, friction, volume, and density.

## Animating physically realistic reactions

While animating realistic objects, you should get in the habit of assigning physical properties to objects. Then, as you animate, watch for collisions and reactions with the environment that don't look right. If a 300-pound fighter puts the smack down on a sexy 90-pound ninja, then the ninja realistically should go flying lots farther than the other way around. Also, a motorcycle wrecked on ice travels much farther than one wrecked on pavement.

To help produce realistic object animations between 3D objects, many 3D packages include dynamic modules that can numerically assign physical properties to objects and simulate real-world physical interactions. Dynamics are covered in Chapter 13, but be warned that a dynamics module won't do all the work for you.

## Making realistic motion with primary and secondary motion

Another aspect of realistic motion is adding secondary motion to scene objects. Imagine a female character, running at top speed, who suddenly stops. The primary motion is easy to identify: The character's body moves quickly and comes to an abrupt stop. Other primary motions could include her legs moving back and forth and her arms swinging opposite to her legs. For the more subtle primary motions, you may notice a slight twist in her torso and her body moving up and down with each stride.

But if you saw the action in real life, what other motions would you see? You'd probably see her hair and clothes surge forward as she stops. These motions are based on the movements of other parts in the scene. This type of motion is called secondary motion. Secondary motion plays a crucial role in producing realistic motion.

Perhaps the best way to learn to identify secondary motion is to watch objects colliding in everyday life, such as dropping objects on various surfaces. Another good place to see collisions is watching sports events; football, in particular, is a great display of secondary motion.

Dynamics can be used to add secondary motion, or you can add it by hand, but identifying secondary motion and making sure that it is included with an animation add an extra touch that makes the animation more realistic.

## Developing a Unique Style

I'll say just one final note on traditional animating: Work to establish your own unique style. If you look closely at the Hanna-Barbera cartoons, whether you watch Fred Flintstone or Yogi Bear, you notice their unique style.

When you first start to develop your own style, try mimicking several other styles and then work to vary them slightly. Over time, your style should start to feel natural to you.

Styles are established not only by the overall look and feel of a character, but also by the little details and flairs that you add to your characters. A style can become your calling card, distinguishing your work from the thousands of other animators out there.

# Part II

# Creating Interfaces, Modeling Scenery, and Texturing Backgrounds

The 5th Wave    By Rich Tennant

Jeez—that's impressive! Let's see that airbrush effect again.

# In this part . . .

One of the first tasks you'll take on once game production begins is to define and complete the game environment. There are several different aspects of the game environment, including a user interface, scenery and props, and backgrounds.

The user interface, or UI, is the means by which the game player interacts initially with the game. It can include menus to access the game features or the actual information feedback that tells the player how he's doing. Advanced UIs can include animations.

You'll jump into the modeling process, starting with simple scenery and prop elements before progressing to modeling examples in Maya.

Next, this part shows you the aspects of materials and textures that give you the chance to add detail to an object without changing its geometry.

Lighting is an important part of defining the environment's mood. Effective lighting interfaces with animation, as you'll find out in Chapter 10.

# Chapter 4

# Creating Game User Interfaces

*T*he main purpose of a game interface is to present information to the player. This information can tell the player the status of his character, such as current weapon, health, and items the character is carrying. It can also inform the player about the environment, such as which level he is on, a map of the current level, and whether any enemies are close. The interface also informs the user of his progress in the game, such as total number of enemies defeated, puzzles solved, or items that have been found.

Game interfaces can vary greatly from extremely simple, such as the interface for the popular adventure game Myst, to extremely complex like the multi-page interfaces found in role-playing games such as Everquest.

This chapter takes a close look at 3D game interfaces as one of the first and easiest 3D elements to create, including coverage of several design techniques for interface design, the process, and several 3D tricks for creating 3D interfaces.

## Understanding the Basics of Interface Design

When designing a game interface, you need to keep two key questions in mind. First, does the interface include all the information that the player needs and wants? Second, does the interface ever get in the way of the player, and if so, what can be done to prevent this?

If the game interface is designed to address these two questions, then it has a good chance of succeeding. You should ask these other design questions as well:

- ✔ How does the interface look?
- ✔ Is it organized effectively and pleasing to look at?
- ✔ Does it fit the game's look?
- ✔ Does the interface interfere with the game play?
- ✔ Can the game player get to the desired command with a minimum number of mouse clicks?
- ✔ Is the game designed for a PC or for a console game system?
- ✔ Does the interface use common, familiar controls, or does the player need to learn something new?

## *Identifying interface information*

One of the first steps in interface design is to identify the information that needs to be included. This information comes directly from the game design document; if you have any questions, you can ask the game designer.

After the information that is to be included on the interface is identified, you need to decide how the information is to be presented. You can present this information in many different ways, including these examples:

- ✔ **Text and numeric labels:** Text and numeric labels need to be clearly marked with a title that identifies the information.
- ✔ **Graphical icons and containers:** Collected items can be represented by a graphical icon such as a weapon, a flag, or a badge. The container for this item shows an empty outline that fits the object and shows whether the item has been collected.

Using graphical icons can also eliminate the need to translate text into different languages. These are some graphical elements you can use:

- ✔ **Menus:** Menus are common interface elements for games and software and present lists of commands.
- ✔ **Sliders:** Sliders provide a way to change a value in a given range by dragging with the mouse.
- ✔ **Bar graph:** Bar graphs are used to show how much of a total value is available, such as health or magic. Be sure to show the total value as a bar and include a numeric value with the bar graph.

✔ **3D maps:** A navigable 3D map is another common element. The keys within the environment should work the same as playing the game.

✔ **Help sections and tutorials:** Animation sections are helpful for showing how certain actions are executed and for explaining sections of the game.

✔ **Time lines:** Time lines are another helpful interface element for showing a game's progress.

## Defining interface backgrounds

Be sure to include details about the interface background as part of the design. The background should be of a high enough contrast that all text and labels are clearly legible. Image-based backgrounds aren't recommended unless the image is lightened or darkened while the interface elements are displayed.

## Using interface fade in and fade out

If the interface is a separate page or several pages that appear when requested, then you can make its appearance and disappearance smoother by animating the interface screen to zip in from the side and then zip out. By including this animation effect, the user isn't surprised by the interface's appearance, and he can also see the game paused behind the interface.

It's the programmer's job, but make sure that game play is paused while an external interface page appears. No one likes to be killed while he is checking his inventory.

## Making the interface easy to navigate

If the interface includes several different controls that can be selected, make sure that the current selection is clear by highlighting the object before a button is pressed.

For some serious commands, such as saving the game progress or exiting the game without saving its current state, you want to present a confirmation message to the player before executing the command. You can ask the user, "Are you sure you want to exit the game without saving?"

When an external interface is being used, make sure that the button to access the interface is clearly labeled, such as placing Right and Left buttons to switch between different interface pages.

## Including sounds

Every interface action should be associated with a sound. This auditory feedback lets the player know that he has selected a command or an item. A good example of this is the sound of bullet being loaded into a gun chamber when a new weapon is selected in the game of Doom.

## Making the game area as big as possible: Maximizing interface real estate

I really don't like handheld game systems such as the Game Boy Advance or Sony PlayStation Portable because they just feel too small. It's like playing a game on a 12" television screen. I realize that their benefit is that you can play while taking the bus to school or work, but for me, the bigger the game, the better.

A similar problem arises when the game interface encroaches on the game area. Of course, it is important to know how much health you have left and which weapon is currently active, but when I'm strafing around a corner, I'd prefer to have the sides of the screen showing me what nefarious enemy I may encounter than to see an interface element. I know I'm not alone in this request.

One of the first goals on interface design is to create an interface that doesn't get in the way of the game. Although this may seem like an easy request to meet, it can be challenging.

# Starting with a Layout: The Process of Interface Design

Perhaps the best place to start with an interface design is to draw it conceptually on paper. Quick sketches can be an easy way to get feedback on the design before ever moving into 3D.

Paper sketches can be easily scanned into a 2D drawing program such as Illustrator, where the design can be fleshed out in more detail by adding logos, text, and enhancements.

# Importing drawing files

Illustrator files can then be imported into a 3D program, where you can add depth to the design and render the finished look.

Follow these steps to import an interface design:

1. **Choose File ⇨ Import to open the Import dialog box.**

   The Import dialog box, shown in Figure 4-1, lets you select the directory and file that you want to import.

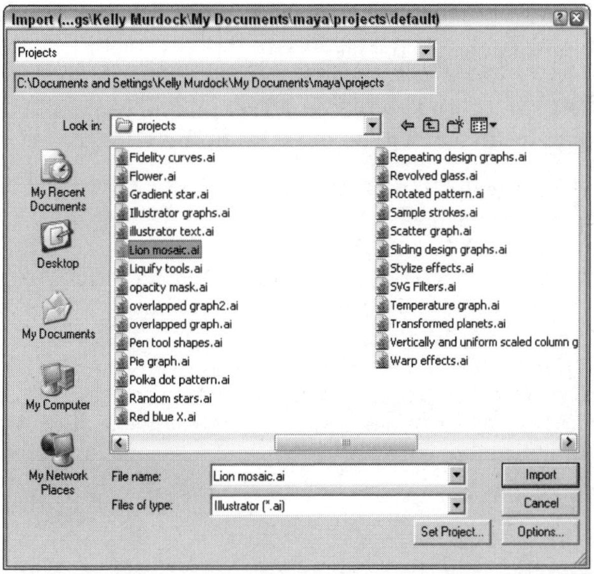

**Figure 4-1:**
The Import dialog box lets you select the directory and the file containing the Illustrator files.

2. **Select the Illustrator (.ai) option from the Files of Type drop-down list.**

   This selection filters the available files so that only files with the .ai file extension are visible.

3. **Select the interface design file to open, and click the Import button.**

   The imported file is added to the existing scene.

# Building a 2D layout

If you don't have access to a drawing package such as Illustrator, then you can use the features within your 3D package to create the interface layout. This is accomplished using curves and/or splines.

### Selecting an orthogonal view

Each 3D package can view the scene objects from different perspectives, including Front, Back, Left, Right, Top, and Bottom views. Each of these views is known as a special type of view called an orthogonal view. *Orthogonal views* look at the scene objects from the end of an axis, so all the objects are shown in 2D.

Views that aren't 2D (or orthogonal) are called Perspective views. *Perspective views* let you look at the scene objects from any point in space.

The default setup of Maya loads with a single Perspective view enabled, as shown in Figure 4-2. The title of each view is centered along the bottom edge of the view.

Follow these steps to change the viewport:

1. **Select the Panels ⇨ Orthographic ⇨ Front menu command from the panel menu located along the top edge of the view panel.**

   The Front view panel replaces the default Perspective view, as shown in Figure 4-3. You can change the view back to a Perspective view using the Panels ⇨ Perspective ⇨ Perspec menu command.

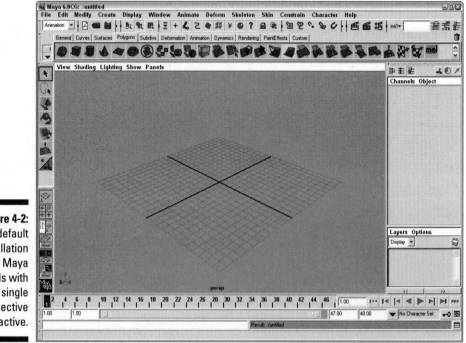

**Figure 4-2:** The default installation of Maya loads with a single Perspective view active.

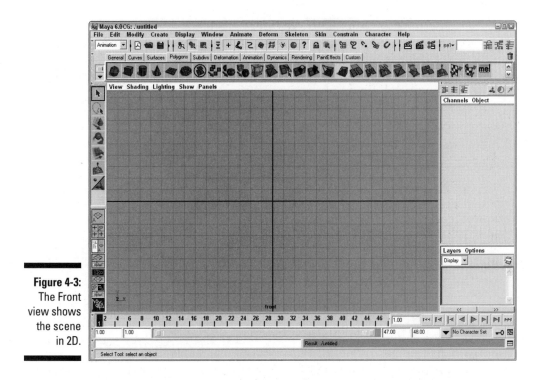

**Figure 4-3:**
The Front
view shows
the scene
in 2D.

2. **Click the Four View button in the Quick Layout Buttons, as shown in Figure 4-4, located under the Toolbox.**

**Figure 4-4:**
The Quick
Layout
Buttons
offer an
easy way to
change the
scene view.

Single Perspective View

Four View

The Four View button replaces the current view with four separate view panels, as shown in Figure 4-5.

You can switch between the single maximized view and the four separate view panels by pressing the spacebar.

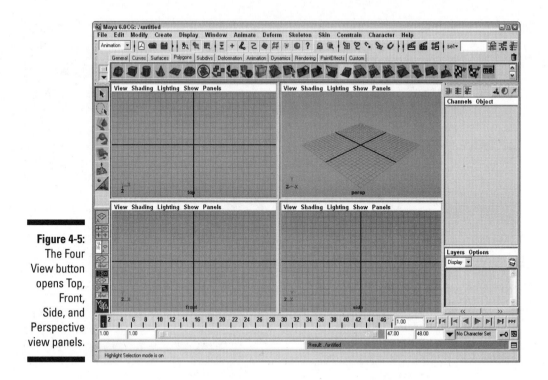

**Figure 4-5:**
The Four
View button
opens Top,
Front,
Side, and
Perspective
view panels.

## Loading a scanned image as a background

A scanned image can be loaded as a background image into the 3D view. This provides a reference that you can follow as you draw the splines that make up the interface.

Follow these steps to load a scanned image as a view background:

1. **Select the View ⇨ Image Plane ⇨ Import Image menu command from the panel menu located along the top edge of the view panel.**

   An Open dialog box appears in which you can select the image file to load as the view panel background.

2. **Locate the image that you want to load, and click the Open button.**

   The image appears as a background to the selected view panel, as shown in Figure 4-6.

3. **Select the File ⇨ Save Scene As menu command and save the file as Scene with interface background.mb.**

   The remaining examples in this chapter build from the previous one. By saving the file at the end of each example, you can continue the next example where this one left off.

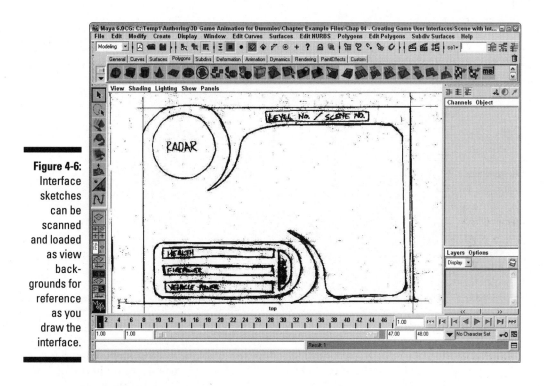

**Figure 4-6:**
Interface sketches can be scanned and loaded as view backgrounds for reference as you draw the interface.

### Drawing splines

3D packages such as Maya typically offer several different ways to draw curves and splines, but these curves are created by clicking and dragging in the view panel using a curve creation tool.

Maya includes tools for drawing Control Vertices (CV) curves, Edit Point (EP) curves, freehand curves with the Pencil tool, and arcs. These tools are found in the Create menu.

CV curves are created by clicking to place control vertices. Each CV is connected with a straight line that is called a hull. The curve bends within the defined hull to maintain a smooth curve.

EP curves are created by clicking to create Edit Points. The curve always moves through the center of these Edit Points. Figure 4-7 shows a sample CV curve with its hull and a sample EP curve with its Edit Points.

### Drawing linear and smooth curves

All the options for the various tools are set using the Tool Settings panel. For the curve tools, you can select the Curve Degree. A Curve Degree of 1 creates linear (or straight-line) curves, and a Curve Degree of 3 creates a smooth curve.

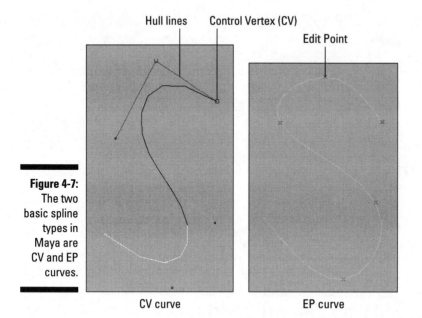

Figure 4-7:
The two
basic spline
types in
Maya are
CV and EP
curves.

The Tool Settings panel is opened to the right of the view panel when the Show/Hide Tool Settings button is clicked. This button is found in the upper-right corner of the interface with the Show/Hide Attribute Editor and the Show/Hide Channel Box buttons, shown in Figure 4-8.

Follow these steps to create the interface layout curves:

1. **Choose File ➪ Open Scene and open the Scene with interface background.mb file.**

   The Scene with interface background file is the file the concluded the last example.

2. **Select the Create ➪ EP Curve Tool menu command from the main menu.**

   The EP Curve Tool lets you create curves by marking the points through which the curve passes.

3. **Click the Show/Hide Tool Settings button, and set the Curve Degree option to 1 Linear.**

   With the Curve Degree set to 1, you can draw straight lines for the outer layout lines and the text areas.

4. **With the EP Curve Tool, click each corner of the layout.**

5. **Set the Curve Degree option to 3 Cubic.**

   With the Curve Degree set to 3, you can draw smooth lines for the curved areas of the interface.

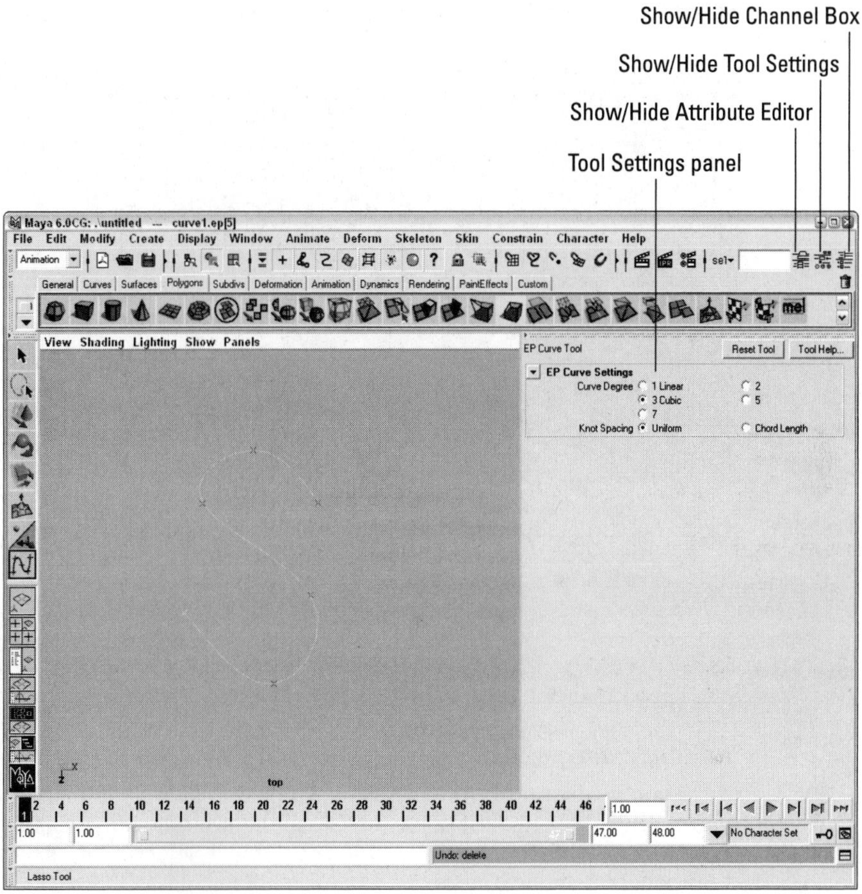

Show/Hide Channel Box

Show/Hide Tool Settings

Show/Hide Attribute Editor

Tool Settings panel

**Figure 4-8:**
The Tool
Settings
panel can
be opened
for any
selected
tool.

6. **Click with the EP Curve Tool to place points to create the curved interface lines.**

   The curved lines don't need to be exact because you'll have a chance to edit the points after they are created.

7. **Select the View ⇨ Image Plane ⇨ Image Plane Attributes ⇨ Image Plane 1 menu command from the panel menu, and then press the Delete key.**

   Selecting and deleting the Image Plane removes the loaded scanned background image, revealing the lines that you've created, as shown in Figure 4-9.

8. **Select the File ⇨ Save Scene As menu command and save the file as Traced interface lines.mb.**

   All the examples in this chapter build from the previous one. By saving the file at the end of each example, you can continue the next example where this one left off.

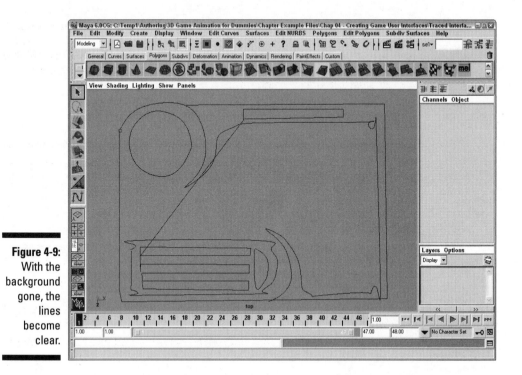

**Figure 4-9:**
With the background gone, the lines become clear.

### Editing curve points

After you've drawn a curve in a view panel, don't worry if it isn't exactly what you want. You can edit it using the Component mode. Maya has two different selection modes that you can work with: Object Selection mode and Component Selection mode.

In Object Selection mode, you can select and move an entire object or curve altogether. In Component Selection mode, you can select and move individual components such as curve points.

To enter Component Selection mode, click the Select by Component Type button found on the Status Line. You can then return to Object Selection mode by clicking the Select by Object Type button also on the Status Line.

You can also enter Component Selection mode by pressing the F9 key and choose Object Selection mode with the F8 key.

After Component Selection mode is enabled, you can select the type of component to work with by right-clicking and holding in the view panel and dragging to select the component type with which you want to work. The available component types depend on the object selected. For CV curves, the components include Hull, Curve Point, Control Vertex, and Edit Points.

Follow these steps to edit the interface layout curves:

1. **Choose File ⇨ Open Scene and open the Traced interface lines.mb file.**

   The Traced interface lines file is the file the concluded the last example.

2. **Click the Select by Component Type button on the Status Line.**

   This enables Component Selection mode, where you can select and move the points.

3. **Right-click in the view panel and, drag to the Edit Points component type.**

   With Edit Points selected from the pop-up menu, all the Edit Points become visible as small X marks on the curves.

4. **Drag the mouse over the Edit Points that you want to move.**

   The points within the dragged area become selected and can be moved using the Move tool.

5. **Select and move the Edit Points to clean up the interface layout.**

   Figure 4-10 shows the interface layout after being cleaned up by moving the Edit Points into place.

6. **Select the File ⇨ Save Scene As menu command and save the file as Edited interface layout.mb.**

   All the examples in this chapter build from the previous one. By saving the file at the end of each example, you can continue the next example where this one left off.

## Snapping curve points

The Status Line also includes several buttons for enabling snapping option. When enabled, these buttons cause a curve point to snap precisely to a grid point, a curve, or a point.

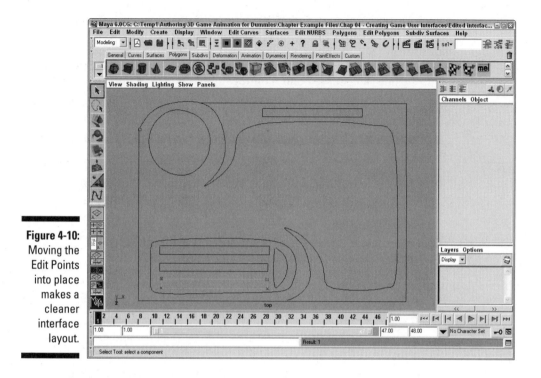

**Figure 4-10:**
Moving the
Edit Points
into place
makes a
cleaner
interface
layout.

# *Adding 3D Effects*

After the layout is complete, you can begin to add 3D effects by extruding or beveling the layout lines. You can also enhance the interface by cleverly adding 3D objects where appropriate.

## *Enhancing with 3D objects*

Adding 3D objects to an interface is a great way to enhance the interface, especially if the object relates to the game, such as a weapon, a logo, or a vehicle.

Default primitive objects such as Boxes, Spheres, Cones, and Cylinders can be used along with custom 3D objects from the game scene. Primitive objects can be found within the Create menu.

Follow these steps to add a primitive object to the interface:

**1. Choose File ⇨ Open Scene and open the Edited interface layout.mb file.**

The Edited interface layout torso file is the file the concluded the last example.

2. **Select the Create ⇨ NURBS Primitives ⇨ Sphere menu command.**

   A sphere primitive appears in the center of the view panel.

3. **With the sphere selected, use the Move tool to move it into position where the Radar is located and use the Scale tool to increase its size.**

   Be sure to check in the Side and Front views to ensure that the sphere's height is correctly positioned.

4. **Select and delete the circular curve that marked the radar's place.**

   The circular curve outline is no longer needed and can be deleted. Figure 4-11 shows the interface with the added sphere.

5. **Select the File ⇨ Save Scene As menu command and save the file as Interface with sphere radar.mb.**

   All the examples in this chapter build from the previous one. By saving the file at the end of each example, you can continue the next example where this one left off.

## Embellishing with 3D text

3D text or embossed text can be used to add 3D effects to the text that is included in the interface.

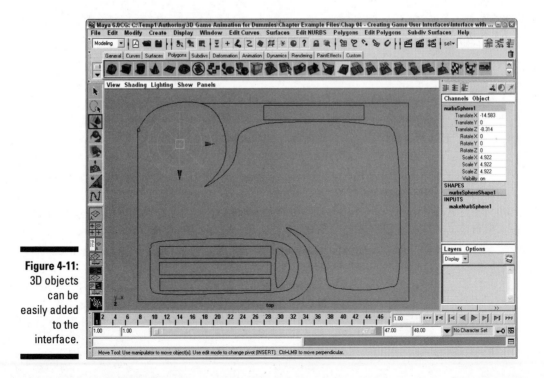

**Figure 4-11:**
3D objects can be easily added to the interface.

Even though you can make 3D text, realize that you don't need to include 3D text. It is more important that the text is legible and readable than visually stunning.

Text is added using the Create ⇨ Text menu command. The Text Curves Options dialog box lets you select the text and the font to use.

Follow these steps to add text to the interface:

1. **Choose File ⇨ Open Scene and open the Interface with sphere radar.mb file.**

   The Interface with sphere radar file is the file the concluded the last example.

2. **Select the Create ⇨ Text ⇨ Options menu command.**

   The Text Curves Options dialog box, shown in Figure 4-12, appears.

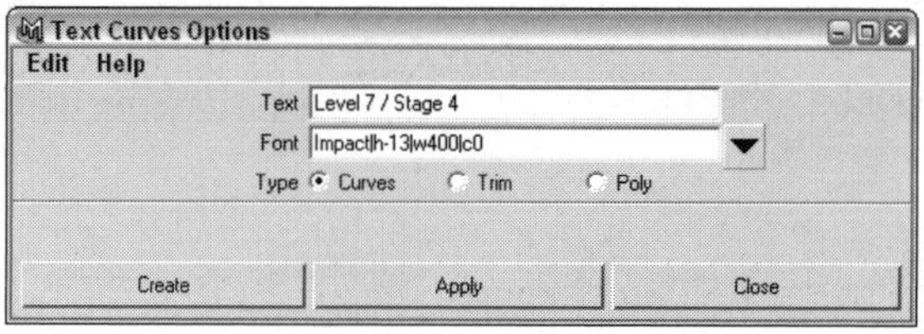

Figure 4-12:
The Text
Curves
Options
dialog box
lets you
specify text
and select
a font.

3. **In this dialog box, type the interface text in the desired font and click the Apply button.**

   The Apply button creates the text without closing the Text Curves Options dialog box.

4. **Select and rotate the text so it is visible in the Top view, and move it into place.**

   Repeat these steps for the other text areas. Figure 4-13 shows the interface with some added text.

5. **Select the File ⇨ Save Scene As menu command and save the file as Interface with text.mb.**

   All the examples in this chapter build from the previous one. By saving the file at the end of each example, you can continue the next example where this one left off.

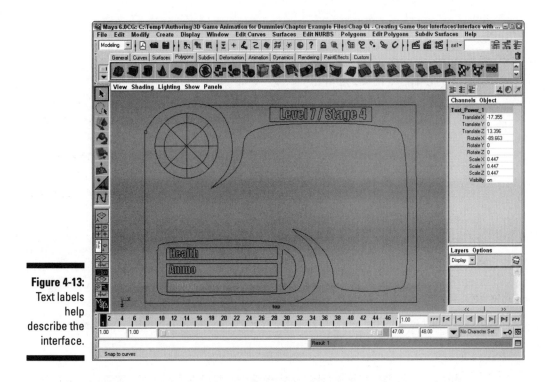

**Figure 4-13:**
Text labels
help
describe the
interface.

# *Beveling the interface border*

Another common way to set the interface off from the game play area is to
bevel the interface border, giving it a 3D look. Before the border can be
beveled, it needs to be combined into a single curve.

Maya includes many features for working with curves that can be used to
extend, trim, and combine curves. These features are located in the Edit
Curves menu.

Follow these steps to extrude the border of the interface:

1. **Choose File ⇨ Open Scene and open the Interface with text.mb file.**

   The Interface with text file is the file the concluded the last example.

2. **Drag over the curves for both the inner and outer border of the interface with the Select tool to select them both.**

   Each of these lines is separate, and they need to be combined in order
   to extrude the area between them.

3. **Select the Edit Curves ⇨ Extend ⇨ Extend Curve menu command.**

   This command extends the ends of each curve so that they intersect
   one another at each end.

**4. Select the Edit Curves ⇨ Cut Curve menu command.**

This cuts each curve at the points where the curves intersect.

**5. Deselect all curves and re-select the two inner and outer interface border curves again.**

By selecting only the two cut border curves, you can work on only the border curves without affecting the other curves that make up the left end of the interface, where the border is a single line.

**6. With the border curves selected, choose the Edit Curves ⇨ Attach Curves menu command.**

This command attaches the two selected curves to one another defining the border area with a single curve that can be extruded.

**7. Select the Surfaces ⇨ Bevel Plus menu command.**

This command bevels the selected curve. If you switch to the Perspective view, then you can see the beveled curve, as shown in Figure 4-14.

**8. Select the File ⇨ Save Scene As menu command and save the file as Beveled interface border.mb.**

This is as far as I'll take the interface: An actual interface would require more work.

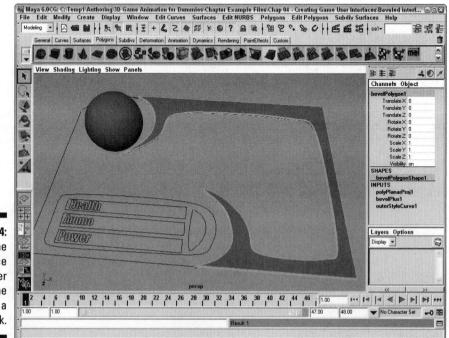

**Figure 4-14:** Beveling the interface border gives the interface a 3D look.

# Chapter 5

# Modeling Scenery and Props

. . . . . . . . . . . . . . . . . . . . . . . . . . . . . . . . . . . . . . . . .

. . . . . . . . . . . . . . . . . . . . . . . . . . . . . . . . . . . . . . . . .

Modeling can take many different forms involving large lumps of clay, plastic kits of small car parts, and runways of beautiful women. However, modeling in 3D for games doesn't involve any of these items.

Before jumping into the task of modeling scenery and prop elements, in this chapter I spend some time discovering exactly what 3D space and coordinates are, and then I take a closer look at the various modeling types and learn how to transform objects. Understanding these background topics gives you a better foundation for working in 3D.

When it comes to the actual modeling features involved in creating 3D game objects, they are as diverse as all the tools in a woodshop, and learning to use these features takes some practice, some experimentation, and lots of discovery. This chapter shows some of the most basic modeling features, but it only scratches the surface of the available features, leaving many that you can learn and study on your own.

One overriding tenet that is unique to 3D games is that the objects not only have to look good, but they need to be optimized for the game engine. To optimize 3D objects for the game engine, you need to build objects using a minimum number of polygons.

# Discovering 3D Space All Around You

It's hard to go anywhere nowadays without running into something 3D. From giant IMAX screens to silly little trinkets included in cereal boxes, 3D images and effects are everywhere. So what exactly is 3D, and how is it different from 2D images?

To answer this question, begin with a simple geometry lesson. A line is 1D. It has only one dimension and is pretty boring. When defining a line, you can talk about its length, which is its only dimension.

A plane is 2D because it has two dimensions known as length and width. Imagine a piece of paper. It is defined by these two dimensions, such as 8½ inches wide by 11 inches high. But, don't imagine 2D images as being limited. Most of the greatest works of art in the history of the world were drawn in 2D.

A box is 3D. The additional dimension is depth. But people aren't being amazed by objects such as boxes that have these dimensions. Instead, images (mostly 2D images) that have the illusion of depth are what get people all excited.

You can create the illusion of depth in many different ways, including stereograms, 3D glasses, and optical illusions, but the method I talk about here involves some pretty amazing software.

# Moving about 3D Coordinates

When drawing in 2D, the task of placing objects is fairly trivial. It is either there or it isn't, but in a 3D software package, placing objects is more like re-arranging the living room furniture. Objects can be placed behind other objects (like putting the magazine rack that your strange uncle made out of grape vines behind the sofa).

To correctly position objects with a 3D software package, you must look at the scene from various points of view. For example, an object hidden behind another object would be clearly visible if you looked at the two objects from a view above them both.

Commonly, 3D software programs show four different scene views at the same time. These views typically include a Front view, a Side view, a Top view, and a Perspective view. The Front, Side, and Top views are called orthogonal views because they show the scene objects in a 2D place using their actual dimensions.

The Perspective view is different. It shows the scene from an angle looking down on the scene objects. From this view, the objects' dimensions are fore-shortened to simulate the effect that occurs naturally. For example, when looking down a long straight road, the telephone poles on either side gradually get smaller the further they are from the viewer. This effect is called perspective, and it is used in the Perspective view to present a realistic look at the scene.

## Selecting scene views

Within a 3D software package, you can typically select the number of view windows that are displayed and which views are displayed in each window. These windowed views define the layout of the software, and typically buttons or commands are available to quickly switch between different layout choices.

Follow these steps to change the layout in Maya:

1. **Choose Window ⇨ View Arrangement ⇨ Four Panes to make four view panes appear.**

   The four default panes are for the Top, Front, Side, and Perspective views, as shown in Figure 5-1. The view name is listed at the bottom of the view pane. Along the top of each view panel is a menu of options.

   You can quickly change the layout to show four view panes by clicking the Four Views button in the menu of Quick Layout buttons, located on the left side of the interface.

2. **From the panel menu for the Top view pane, select the Panels ⇨ Perspective ⇨ Persp menu command.**

   The Top view pane is changed to show the Perspective view.

3. **From the panel menu for the Top view pane, select the Panels ⇨ Orthogonal ⇨ Top menu command.**

   The view pane is switched back to the Top view again.

4. **Select the File ⇨ Save Scene As menu command and save the file as Four view panes.mb.**

   The view pane settings are saved along with the file.

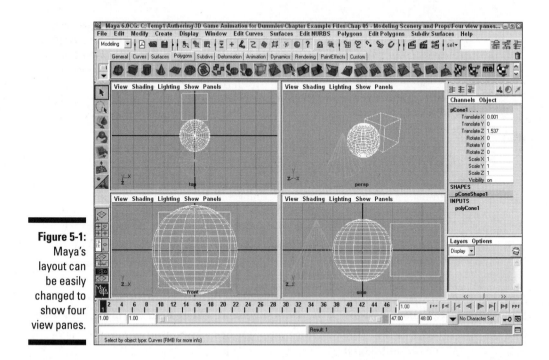

**Figure 5-1:**
Maya's
layout can
be easily
changed to
show four
view panes.

## Navigating scene views

Changing the view's perspective isn't the only way to change the view. A more common method of changing the view is to navigate the view using a number of commands and keyboard shortcuts. These are the most common methods of navigating the view:

- ✔ **Pan** (or track) is to drag the view so the scene objects move to the left, right, top, or bottom of the view window.
- ✔ **Zoom** (or dolly) is to change the size of the scene objects in the view window.
- ✔ **Rotate** (or tumble) is to orbit about the scene object changing the view angle.
- ✔ **Spin** (or roll) is to rotate the scene objects about the center of the view window.

If you ever need a refresher on these navigating commands, try viewing the Learning Movies that appear when you start Maya for the first time. These short and sweet videos aren't long and provide a good, quick review. You can also open these movies using the Help ➪ Learning Movies menu command.

If these navigation terms sound like terms you'd use when controlling a camera, then you're in the right ballpark because each of the views is created from virtual cameras that aren't visible. You can also create and manipulate free-roaming cameras that can be used to view the scene from any location including from the inside of objects. Let's see you try that at your next family reunion.

The Rotate and Spin functions don't work with orthogonal views such as Top, Front, and Side views because the view is locked to maintain a 2D view of the scene.

Follow these steps to navigate a view in Maya:

1. **Right-click the Perspective view to make it the active view.**

   Only one view pane can be active at a time. Right-clicking a view pane makes it active, and all menu commands apply to the active pane.

2. **Choose Window ⇨ View Arrangement ⇨ Single Pane to maximize the Perspective view.**

   The active view pane is maximized in a single pane. The other three panes aren't eliminated; they're just hidden. Maximizing the view often makes working with the scene objects easier.

   Pressing the spacebar switches between a maximized single view pane and four view panes.

3. **From the panel menu, select the View ⇨ Camera Tools ⇨ Tumble Tool menu command and drag in the Perspective view.**

   Dragging with the Tumble Tool causes the scene objects to rotate about the center of the view window. Tumbling a view is one of the best ways to get a feel for the 3D nature of the objects.

   The Tumble Tool can be immediately activated by holding down the Alt key and dragging in the view window with the left mouse button.

4. **From the panel menu, select the View ⇨ Camera Tools ⇨ Track Tool menu command and drag in the Perspective view.**

   Dragging with the Track Tool causes the scene objects to move about the view window.

   The Track Tool can be immediately activated by holding down the Alt key and dragging in the view window with the middle mouse button.

5. **From the panel menu, select the View ⇨ Camera Tools ⇨ Dolly Tool menu command and drag in the Perspective view.**

   Dragging with the Dolly Tool causes the scene objects to get larger or smaller within the view window. Figure 5-2 shows the Perspective view pane after using several of the camera tools.

   The Dolly Tool can be immediately activated by holding down the Alt key and dragging in the view window with the right mouse button.

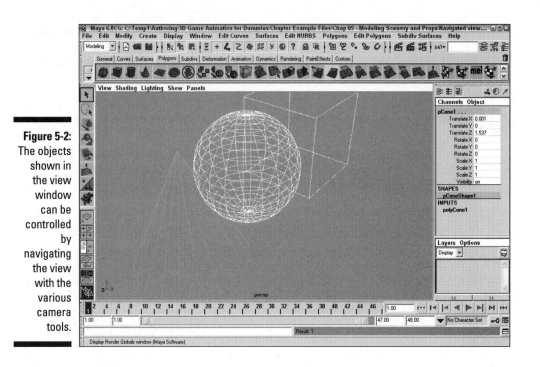

**Figure 5-2:**
The objects shown in the view window can be controlled by navigating the view with the various camera tools.

## Using coordinate values

At the very center of the view is the magic point where all the grids meet. This point is marked by a solid bold line and is called the origin. This is the place where all new objects appear, and it marks the center of the scene.

From this center point, three axes extend in each direction. The X-axis extends left and right, the Y-axis extends up and down, and the Z-axis extends forward and backward. These axes are shown in each view as small color-coded arrows located in the lower left of each view. The X-axis is red, the Y-axis is green, and the Z-axis is blue.

The coordinate values for scene objects are determined by the object's position along each of these three axes. You can view these coordinate values in the Channel Box as the Translate X, Y, and Z values. These values are typically written one after another separated by commas. For example, the coordinate values at the origin are [0,0,0] with all values in one direction getting a positive value and all values in the opposite direction getting a negative value.

For example, a sphere object whose center point is located at [-2,-6,4] would be 2 units to the left of the origin on the X-axis, 6 units below the origin on the Y-axis, and 4 units forward on the Z-axis.

Although the position of 3D objects is defined using only three coordinate values, these values actually define only the location of the object's center, but for a Box object, each corner would have its own position coordinates.

# Exploring the Various Modeling Types

Two famous proverbs apply here. The first is, "variety is the spice of life," and the second is, "there's more than one way to skin a cat." Well, this section won't be doing any cooking needing spices, and all felines can rest easy. The point is that there are many different ways to model 3D objects, and most 3D programs include several unique modeling types.

Some modeling types are good for certain types of objects, and other modeling types are better for others. Learning when to use each type can be tricky, but I'll include some recommendations that will help.

## Polygon modeling for man-made models

The first modeling type is probably the most common and in some ways the easiest method to use. Polygon modeling creates 3D objects by stitching together several simple faces and smoothing over their edges.

The major drawback to polygon modeling is that it can take a large number of polygons to create a realistic model, but this is the most common modeling method used in games. The trick is to make a model that looks good using the fewest number of polygons as possible.

Polygon modeling is useful for creating man-made objects that have sharp edges and specific shapes like machines, gears, and boxes.

Although several different modeling types are available, most game engines can work only with polygon models. So models can be built using any of these modeling methods, but the model must be converted into a polygon model before loading it into a game engine.

## NURBS modeling for natural flowing surfaces

NURBS is an acronym that stands for Non-Uniform Rational B-Spline. This is a long description for a model that is created from mathematically created curves.

NURBS are created by manipulating profile curves that define the model's surface. Because a complex model can be created with only a handful of curves, NURBS models can be much smaller than polygon models.

Another key advantage is that these curves are designed to be smooth, so the objects that they create are also smooth and flow well into each other, making NURBS a good choice for creating natural-looking objects like flowers, muscles, and animals.

## Patch modeling for curved surfaces

Another useful modeling type is patch modeling. Patches are created by stretching polygons over a set of curves. Using patches has two advantages: Their edges are smooth because they are made from curves, and manipulating the surface is as easy as editing a curve.

Maya actually has another modeling type called Subdivision Surfaces that includes the features of both polygons and NURBS.

# Moving, Rotating, and Scaling Objects

One of the first things that you need to learn before you begin modeling is how to select and transform objects. These transformation functions are similar to the camera moves that were used to change the view, except this time the camera is staying put, and the object is moving.

## Transforming objects

3D objects are typically transformed in three different ways:

- **Translation (or moving):** Translating an object changes its position in 3D space.
- **Rotation:** Rotating an object spins it about its center or about a predefined point in space.
- **Scaling:** Scaling changes the size of the object, but it can also be used to change only a single dimension, causing the object to be stretched.

Before an object can be transformed, it must be selected. Selecting 3D objects is usually as simple as clicking them; holding down the Shift key lets you select multiple objects. Another way to select multiple objects is to outline all the objects that you want to select by dragging over them. When multiple objects are selected, they all can be transformed together.

You can always tell when an object is selected because it typically is high-lighted a different color from the rest of the objects.

Because transformation tools are used so often, they can typically be accessed from an easy-to-reach toolbar or by using keyboard shortcuts.

Follow these steps to select and transform an object in Maya:

1. **Choose the Create ⇨ Polygon Primitives ⇨ Sphere menu command.**

   A polygon sphere is placed in the center of the view. The newly created sphere object is selected by default and highlighted in green. Maya high-lights a single selected object in green and multiple selected objects in green and white.

2. **Select the Modify ⇨ Transformation Tools ⇨ Move Tool menu command, and drag the sphere within the view pane.**

   Dragging the sphere in the view pane changes its location shown by the Translate X, Y, and Z values to the right of the view pane.

   The Move, Rotate, and Scale tools can be selected from the toolbox located to the left of the view pane.

3. **Select the Modify ⇨ Transformation Tools ⇨ Rotate Tool menu command, and drag the sphere within the view pane.**

   Dragging the sphere in the view pane changes its location shown by the Rotate X, Y, and Z values to the right of the view pane.

4. **Select the Modify ⇨ Transformation Tools ⇨ Scale Tool menu command, and drag the sphere within the view pane.**

   Dragging the sphere in the view pane changes its location shown by the Scale X, Y, and Z values to the right of the view pane. Figure 5-3 shows the sphere after it's been transformed.

5. **Select the File ⇨ Save Scene As menu command and save the file as Transformed sphere.mb.**

   This is a simple example, but the more you use these commands, the more comfortable you will become with them.

## Snapping objects into place

Suppose your level designer delivers an outline of a level that you need to populate with specific pieces of scenery and that the precise location of every tree is marked. Moving the objects into place will probably be close enough, but there is an exact way to place objects relative to one another.

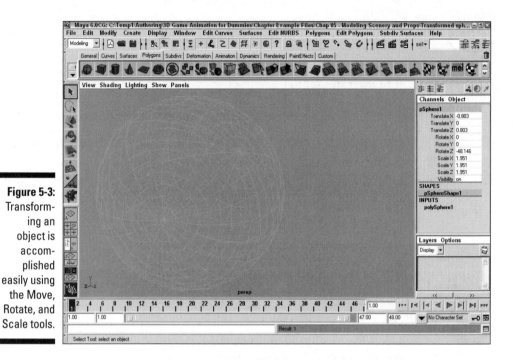

**Figure 5-3:**
Transform-
ing an
object is
accom-
plished
easily using
the Move,
Rotate, and
Scale tools.

Using the various snap modes, you can make objects move and align to an exact grid, point, curve, or plane. This is a helpful feature for placing objects in a level attached to the ground floor. When a snap mode is enabled, you only need to move the object close its position and the object automatically moves (or snaps) to the designated place. Once snapped, you can still move it about as needed.

Grids can be toggled on and off in Maya using the Display ⇨ Grid menu command.

---

# Using manipulators

When one of the transformation tools is selected, a set of guides surrounds the object. This set of guides is called a manipulator, and it lets you constrain the transformation to a single axis.

If you drag over the manipulator with the cursor, the guide that the mouse is positioned over is highlighted. If you click and drag with only a single axis guide selected, then the transformation is limited to that axis only. The guide colors match the axis colors. For example, if you select the Rotate tool, three circular lines surround the object. If you drag the red guide, then the object is rotated about the X-axis only.

Maya include snapping modes in the Status Line, a set of button directly under the menus. These modes are designated by a small magnet icon. The available snapping modes in Maya include:

✔ **Snap to Grids:** This mode snaps the object to specific grid points and is useful when working in one of the Orthogonal views like Top, Front, or Back. Using this mode, you can quickly draw shapes with straight lines.

✔ **Snap to Curves:** This mode snaps an object to a curve and moves it along the length of the curve. It also orients the object perpendicular to the curve.

✔ **Snap to Points:** This mode snaps the object to a point on another object and is useful for connecting objects in a regular pattern.

✔ **Snap to Planes:** This mode snaps and orients an object relative to a polygonal plane which could be on another object. This is a helpful mode for placing scenery about a level so it is attached to the floor.

✔ **Snap to Live Object:** Maya also includes a mode that enables the selected object to become "live." All moved object can then be snapped to the live object.

Follow these steps to draw a shape in Maya using the snap feature:

1. **Choose the Panels ⇨ Orthographic ⇨ Top menu command from the menu at the top of the view panel.**

   The view display changes to show the Top view.

2. **In the Status Line, click to enable the Snap to Grids icon.**

   The icon is displayed as being pressed in when enabled.

3. **Select the Create ⇨ EP Curve Tool menu command, and click at points on the grid to create an arrow shape.**

   With the Snap to Grids mode enabled, clicking near a grid point automatically moves the point to be on the grid.

   If you incorrectly position a curve point, press the Delete key to delete the last placed point.

4. **When the shape is completed, press the Enter key to finish the shape.**

   The perfectly symmetrical arrow shape is shown in Figure 5-4.

5. **Select the File ⇨ Save Scene As menu command and save the file as Snap to grid arrow shape.mb.**

   This is a simple example, but the more you use these commands, the more comfortable you will become with them.

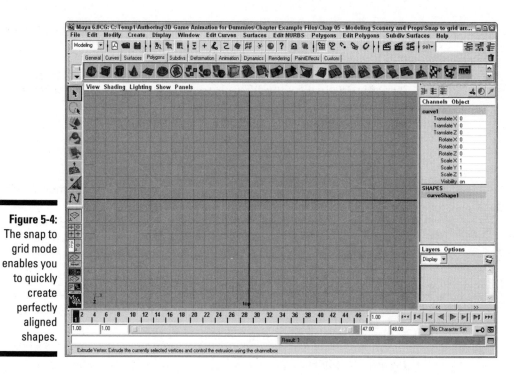

**Figure 5-4:**
The snap to
grid mode
enables you
to quickly
create
perfectly
aligned
shapes.

## Aligning objects

Snapping is great for positioning objects relative to scene elements that are
already set such as game levels or grids, but you'll often want to align two or
more objects relative to each other. Objects can be aligned so their center
points match or the edges are aligned.

Maya includes an Align tool that is used to align objects. It works by interactively placing icons within the scene that you can select to align objects.

Follow these steps to align objects in Maya:

1. **Choose the Create ➪ Polygonal Primitives ➪ Cylinder menu command.**

   A new cylinder object is placed at the center of the view panel.

   You can also quickly create a cylinder object by clicking the cylinder
   icon in the Polygons shelf tab directly above the view panel.

2. **Select and move the cylinder away from the center.**

   Using the Move Tool, drag the cylinder so it is not in the center. The place
   doesn't really matter because I'll use the Align tool later for alignment.

3. **Repeat Steps 1 and 2 until there are three cylinders in the scene.**

   These three cylinders are positioned randomly in the scene.

4. **Drag over two of the cylinders with the Select tool to select them, and then choose the Modify ➪ Snap Align Objects ➪ Align Tool menu command.**

   Several light blue icons appear around the two selected cylinders. These icons are for the various align options.

5. **Locate and click the icon used to horizontally center the cylinders.**

   After clicking the center icon, the two cylinders move to align perfectly around their center locations.

6. **Select one of the aligned cylinders and the third unaligned cylinder. Then, click the end to end align icon in the view so that the objects are aligned as shown in the figure.**

   The unaligned cylinder is placed above the other two aligned cylinders, as shown in Figure 5-5.

7. **Select the File ➪ Save Scene As menu command and save the file as Aligned cylinders.mb.**

   Aligning objects to each other is much easier than moving and positioning objects by hand.

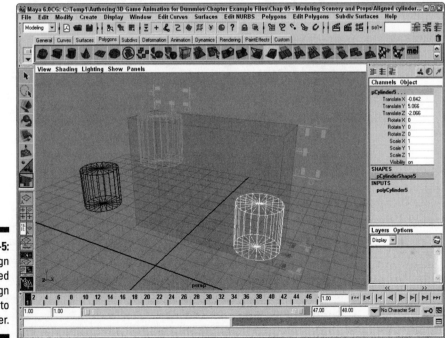

**Figure 5-5:**
The Align Tool is used to align objects to one another.

## Using pivot points

The center point of an object is a special point called the pivot point. This is the location where the manipulator is centered when the Move, Rotate, and Scale tools are selected. It is also the point about which the object is rotated and scaled.

When an object is created, its pivot point is positioned by default in the center of the object, but you can move it to another location if you want. For example, if you are creating a mobile of a planet being circled by some moons, then positioning the moon's pivot point in the center of the planet makes it easy to animate the moon orbiting the planet.

If you press the Insert key, Maya allows you to transform the pivot point. Pressing the Insert key again places the pivot and lets the object be moved again.

You can reposition the pivot point of an object back to the object's center at any time using the Modify ⇨ Center Pivot menu command.

Follow these steps to reposition the pivot point of an object in Maya:

1. **Choose the Create ⇨ Polygonal Primitives ⇨ Sphere menu command.**

   A new sphere object is placed at the center of the view panel.

2. **Repeat Step 1 to create a second sphere object.**

   The second sphere is positioned in the same location as the first.

3. **With the second sphere selected, move it away from the first and scale it down to be smaller than the first.**

   The second sphere will be the moon and will be set to orbit the first.

4. **Press the Insert key to enter pivot point mode.**

   The manipulator for the smaller sphere changes to show that you're in pivot point mode.

5. **With the Move tool, drag the smaller sphere's pivot point to the center of the larger sphere. Then press the Insert key again.**

   By moving the smaller sphere's pivot point to the center of the larger sphere, the smaller sphere can rotate about the larger one.

6. **Select the smaller sphere and rotate it with the Rotate tool.**

   When the smaller sphere is selected, the manipulator appears in the center of the large sphere. Dragging the Rotate tool causes the smaller sphere to orbit about the larger one, as shown in Figure 5-6.

7. **Select the File ⇨ Save Scene As menu command and save the file as Orbiting sphere.mb.**

   The saved file can be compared to the downloaded file of the same name for accuracy.

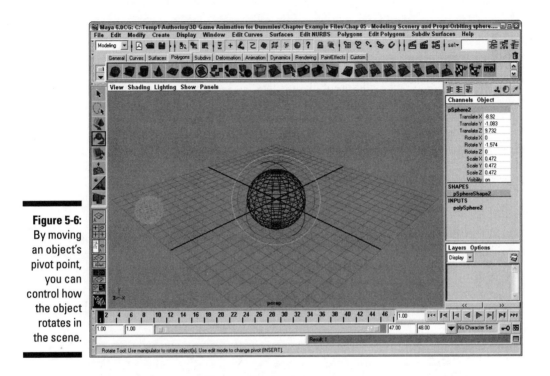

Maya 6.0CG: C:\Temp1\Authoring 3D Game Animation for Dummies\Chapter Example Files\Chap 05 - Modeling Scenery and Props\Orbiting sphere....

**Figure 5-6:**
By moving
an object's
pivot point,
you can
control how
the object
rotates in
the scene.

# *Learning the Art of Modeling*

In addition to knowing the modeling types, you need to know the modeling features. These are the commands used to create the actual models, and these features are even more plentiful than the modeling types.

## *Using the easiest way to model*

The easiest way to model objects is not to build them, but to import the work someone else has done. Each 3D software package includes a way to import pre-created models into the current scene.

Repositories of excellent models exist on the Internet. Some are free, and some are for sale, but remember that you get what you pay for. Often, many of the free models don't turn out to be such a great deal.

One good site for purchasing high-quality models is Digimation. You can find them on the Web at www.digimation.com. Another good content-sharing site is Turbo Squid, located at www.turbosquid.com.

If you download any content off the Internet, be sure that you have permission from the creator to use the item. 3D content is copyrighted and cannot be used without the creator's permission.

There are many different file formats, and every 3D program has its own proprietary format that it alone uses. Luckily, many programs can import and export objects in several different formats. Below is a short list of common 3D formats:

- **Wavefront (OBJ):** This format is common among a variety of 3D programs, including Maya.

- **3D Studio (3DS):** This older format used by 3D Studio is still quite common for importing into other 3D packages.

- **DXF:** This is another older AutoCAD format that is still quite common as an import option.

- **QuickTime (3DMF):** This format is common among many Macintosh 3D programs.

- **LightWave (LWO):** Used to save LightWave objects, this format is common among both Windows and Macintosh systems.

Follow these steps to import an existing 3D model in Maya:

1. **Choose the File ⇨ Import menu command to open the Import dialog box.**

   The Import dialog box is a regular system file dialog box. If you click the File Type list, you can select the file type to import.

2. **Select the OBJ option from the File Type list, locate the Chair.obj file, and click the Import button.**

   The imported object is loaded into the current scene. If the dimensions for the imported object are measured at a different scale than the current scene, then the object may appear very small.

3. **Select the View ⇨ Frame Selection (F) menu command from the panel menu.**

   The view is automatically navigated to display the imported object within the full range of the view, as shown in Figure 5-7.

4. **Select the File ⇨ Save Scene As menu command and save the file as Imported chair.mb.**

   This file can then be imported into other files as needed.

**Figure 5-7:**
Imported objects can give you a jump on creating a complete scene.

## Starting with building blocks

Did you ever play with blocks as a child? Well, if you never got enough of stacking blocks, you can make a really tall 3D virtual tower. Every 3D software package includes some default objects called primitives that are already created and can be added to the scene using a simple command.

Common primitives include the following:

- **Cube (or box):** A simple box with length, height, and depth
- **Sphere (or ball):** Defined by a radius, but can be easily stretched into an ellipsoid
- **Cylinder (or disc):** Defined with a radius and a length
- **Cone:** Same as the cylinder, but includes two radii and a length
- **Torus (or donut):** A ring with a circular cross-section
- **Flat Plane:** A two-sided plane that can be used for a ground plane or a wall

Common primitives by themselves aren't that useful, but you can combine them and edit them by changing their dimensions and stretching them to create many different models or provide a good start. For example, imagine creating a model such as a bicycle. Most of the bicycle parts can be created from these basic primitive objects, such as elongated cubes for the pedals, toruses for the tires, and cylinders for the handlebars.

Follow these steps to add primitive objects to a scene in Maya:

1. **Choose the Create ⇨ Polygon Primitives ⇨ Sphere menu command.**

   A polygon sphere is placed in the center of the view. Unless specified, primitive objects are always placed at the center of the view at a position known as the origin, where the coordinates are 0,0,0.

2. **Choose the Create ⇨ Polygon Primitives menu several more times to create the Cube, Cylinder, Cone, Torus, and Plane primitives.**

   Each new primitive appears at the origin in the center of the view.

3. **Select the Modify ⇨ Transformation Tools ⇨ Move Tool menu command, and drag the primitive objects away from the origin, positioning them about the view.**

   By moving the primitive objects away from the origin, you can see each one clearly, as shown in Figure 5-8.

4. **Select the File ⇨ Save Scene As menu command and save the file as Primitive objects.mb.**

   The assortment of primitive objects can be edited and combined to create a wide variety of models.

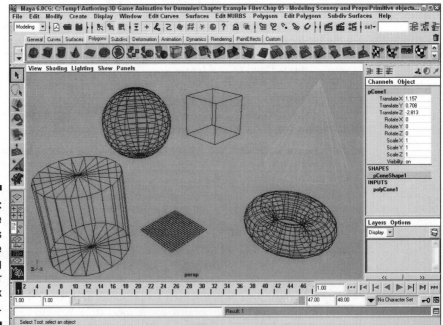

**Figure 5-8:**
Primitive objects provide the building blocks for complex scenes.

# *Editing primitives*

After a primitive object is added to the scene, you're not stuck with the default primitive object. In the editing mode of a 3D program, you can edit the object by moving vertices, edges, and faces using the same transformation tools used to move, rotate, and scale objects.

Before a component can be edited, you first need to select it. To select components, you typically need to be in a special mode that lets you access component elements. This mode can be switched between object and component modes.

Follow these steps to edit the components of a primitive object in Maya:

1. **Choose the Create ⇨ Polygon Primitives ⇨ Sphere menu command.**

   A polygon sphere is placed in the center of the view at the origin, where its coordinates are [0,0,0].

2. **Click the Four Views button in the menu of Quick Layout buttons under the toolbox (or press the spacebar).**

   The workspace is divided into four views showing the Top, Front, Side, and Perspective views.

3. **In the top toolbar, click the Select by Component Type button.**

   All vertices for the sphere object are displayed within the sphere, indicating that you are in component mode.

4. **Click the Select button in the toolbox, and drag over the vertices that make up the top half of the sphere in the Top view.**

   The selected vertices are highlighted in yellow to show that they are selected.

5. **Click the Move button in the toolbox, and drag the selected vertices upward in the Top view.**

   Moving the selected vertices upward in the Top view causes the polygons between the selected and non-selected vertices to be stretched to form a capsule-shaped object.

6. **Click the Scale button in the toolbox, and drag the selected vertices to the left in the Top view.**

   This reduces the size of the selected vertices uniformly while maintaining their relative positions. The resulting object looks like an inverted light bulb, as shown in Figure 5-9.

7. **Select the File ⇨ Save Scene As menu command and save the file as Edited sphere.mb.**

   This is a good example of how a simple primitive can be edited to create an entirely new object.

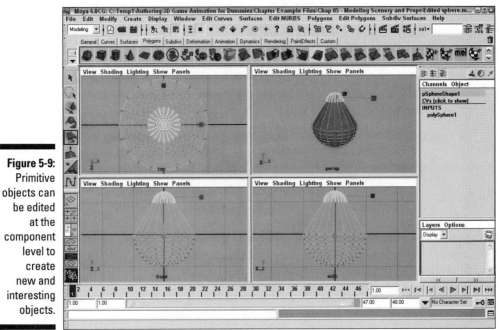

Figure 5-9:
Primitive
objects can
be edited
at the
component
level to
create
new and
interesting
objects.

# Building surfaces from curves and splines

Another common way to model is to start from a simple curve and to use the curve as a guide for creating a 3D object. There are several ways to use curves, including the following: lathing, which revolves the curve about an axis; extruding, which moves the 2D shape perpendicular to itself to create a 3D shape; and lofting, which runs a 2D shape along the path defined by a separate curve.

### Lathing curves

Lathing curves is sometimes called revolving curves. It involves a single curve and a separate straight line that defines the axis of rotation. By selecting the curve and setting how far around you want to rotate the curve, you can create a 3D object. Lathed objects are always symmetrical about their axis.

Lathing objects can be an excellent way to create trees, towers, and lamp post objects to place within a scene. If you don't like the perfectly symmetrical nature of the lathed object, you can always edit it after it is created to add some variation to the object.

Follow these steps to revolve a curve to create a 3D object in Maya:

1. **Click the Four Views button in the menu of Quick Layout buttons under the toolbox (or press the spacebar).**

The workspace is divided into four views showing the Top, Front, Side, and Perspective views.

**2. Choose the Create ⬭ EP Curve Tool menu command, and click in the Front view to place points to create a curve that is a profile of a simple tree.**

The EP Curve tool places points on the curve. Pressing the Enter key when you've completed the curve makes the curve permanent. Also, try to line up the beginning and ending points on the vertical gridlines so the lathed object doesn't have any overlapping portions.

**3. Choose the Surfaces ⬭ Revolve menu command.**

The default settings of the Revolve feature cause the curve to be revolved about its Y-axis. If this isn't what you want, you can change the revolution axis in the Revolve Options dialog box. The revolved profile creates a simple sort of tree object, as shown in Figure 5-10.

Maya has divided its menus into separate categories. The Surfaces menu is part of the Modeling menu set, which can be selected from the drop-down list in the upper-left corner.

**4. Select the File ⬭ Save Scene As menu command and save the file as Simple tree.mb.**

Background objects like trees don't need to be modeled using a high-resolution. This technique can also be used to create other objects such as a vase, a baseball bat, a toy top, and so on.

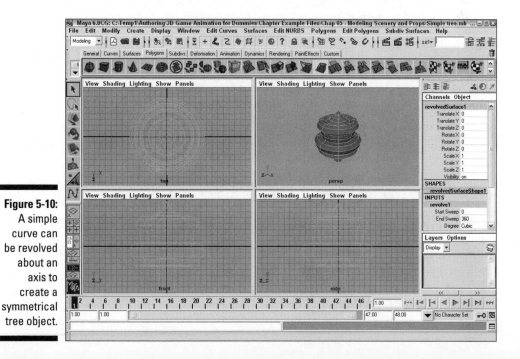

**Figure 5-10:**
A simple curve can be revolved about an axis to create a symmetrical tree object.

## Extruding shapes

Simple shapes can be made into 3D objects by extruding them along the Y-axis a given distance. This causes all edges of the shape to be made into polygon faces. Extruding can typically be done only to a closed curve, which is a curve whose beginning point is positioned the same as its ending point, thereby forming an infinite loop like a circle.

If you look closely among the curve editing commands, you can typically find a command that automatically creates a closed curve from any selected curve by adding an extra edge that joins the two endpoints.

Extruded shapes can be used to make emblems stick out from the side of a wall or to create an entire level from an outline.

Follow these steps to extrude as shape to create a 3D object:

1. **Click the Four Views button in the menu of Quick Layout buttons under the toolbox (or press the spacebar).**

   The workspace is divided into four views showing the Top, Front, Side, and Perspective views.

2. **Choose the Create ⇨ EP Curve Tool menu command, and click in the Front view to create a 2D shape.**

   The EP Curve tool places points on the curve. Pressing the Enter key when you've completed the curve makes the curve permanent. Next, I use a command to make the shape a closed curve so the endpoints don't need to line up.

3. **Choose the Edit Curves ⇨ Open/Close Curves menu command.**

   Another edge is added to the curve to make it a closed curve.

4. **Choose the Surfaces ⇨ Extrude menu command.**

   The closed curve is extruded a distance of 1 along the Z-axis, as shown in Figure 5-11. The Extrude Options dialog box includes options for changing the distance if you need a deeper extrude.

5. **Select the File ⇨ Save Scene As menu command and save the file as Extruded cross.mb.**

   Notice how only the edges of this cross were extruded. If you select a face component, then the entire face would be extruded.

## Lofting along a path

By combining several curves, you can create some really interesting objects. One modeling feature that uses multiple curves is called lofting. Taken from the shipbuilding world where cross-section hulls are pieced together to form a ship, a loft in the 3D world consisting of selecting a shape to follow a curve path.

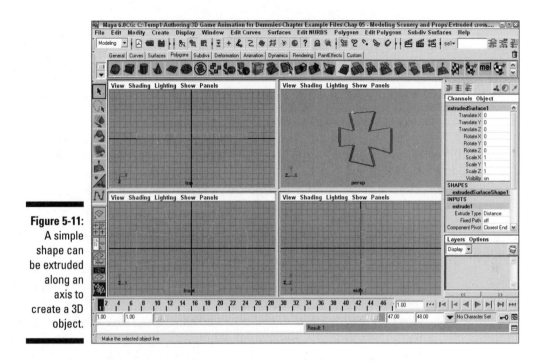

**Figure 5-11:**
A simple
shape can
be extruded
along an
axis to
create a 3D
object.

Lofting works best with closed shapes, so remember to close your shapes in a similar way to the extrude feature.

Lofting is an excellent way to create long sets of walls because you have precise control over the cross section along the length of the wall.

Follow these steps to extrude a shape to create a 3D object in Maya:

1. **Click the Four Views button in the menu of Quick Layout buttons under the toolbox (or press the spacebar).**

   The workspace is divided into four views showing the Top, Front, Side, and Perspective views.

2. **Choose the Create ⇨ EP Curve Tool menu command, and click in the Side view to create a rectangular 2D shape.**

   The EP Curve tool places points on the curve. Pressing the Enter key when you've completed the curve makes the curve permanent. Next, I use a command to make the shape a closed curve so the endpoints don't need to line up.

3. **Choose the Edit Curves ⇨ Open/Close Curves menu command.**

   Another edge is added to the curve to make it a closed curve.

4. **With the closed cross-section curve selected, choose the Edit ⇨ Duplicate menu command.**

   A copy of the closed rectangular shape is created and positioned on top of the original shape.

5. **Select the Move tool in the toolbox, and move the copied shape to the right in the Top view.**

   Position the copied shape at the right end of the Top view separate from the original.

6. **Repeat Steps 4 and 5 to create another copy of the shape, and move it between and below the two existing shapes in the Top view.**

   The three shapes are now positioned to form the path that the wall will follow.

7. **Choose the Select tool in the toolbox, and drag over all three shapes to select them; then choose the Surfaces ⇨ Loft menu command.**

   The three shapes are connected with polygon faces that form a smooth wall running between the created shapes, as shown in Figure 5-12.

8. **Select the File ⇨ Save Scene As menu command and save the file as Simple wall.mb.**

   This example only bends the wall slightly, but you can create many interesting objects by changing each shape dramatically.

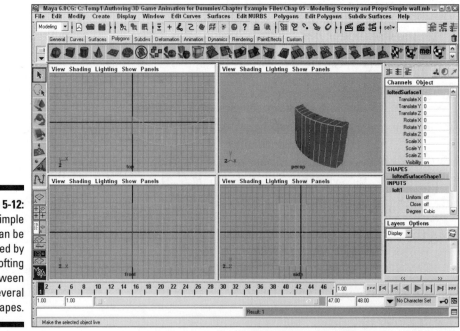

**Figure 5-12:**
A simple wall can be created by lofting between several shapes.

# Creating Lo-Polygon Models That Won't Choke a Game Engine

It is always disheartening to create an awesome model only to have the technical director inform you that the model is 2,000 polygons too heavy and needs to go on a diet. Reworking a detailed model can be tricky, and it's always a struggle to make a model look good while limiting its overall polygon count. But you need to remember that you're making games here, and a character that looks great but moves sluggishly just won't cut it.

The controlling factor is the game engine, and although game engines are getting much better at being able to handle a large number of polygons, the polygon limit needs to be divided among the characters, the enemies, the props and scene elements, and everything else in the game.

Typically, when building models, you have a set number of polygons that you can use for an object. Going over that limit means the polygons need to be taken from some other model. If you've ever played a game and ended up fighting a monster that had no real form, such as a slime monster, then the game team probably ran out of polygons and had to create a simple monster to fill the bad guy list.

The software includes tools that count and keep you informed of the number of polygons included in your current model, but you need to remember to check the statistics occasionally.

Follow these steps to count the number of polygons in a 3D object in Maya:

1. **Choose the Create ⇨ Polygon Primitives ⇨ Sphere menu command.**

   A polygon sphere is placed in the center of the view at the origin, where its coordinates are [0,0,0].

2. **Choose the Display ⇨ Heads Up Display ⇨ Poly Count menu command.**

   The statistics for the current scene are listed in the upper-left corner of the current view and include the number of Vertices, Edges, Faces, Tris, and UVs. Notice that a simple polygon sphere has 400 polygons, as shown in Figure 5-13.

## Tips for reducing polygon count

You can follow several tips as you are beginning to build a model that help you keep your polygon count in check, including the ones described in this section.

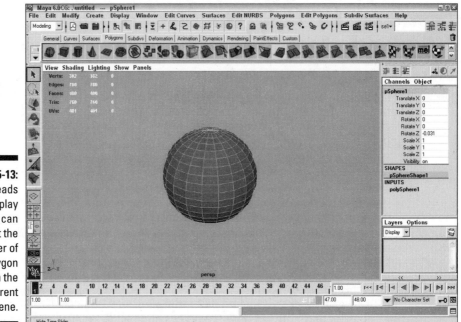

**Figure 5-13:** The Heads Up Display feature can count the number of polygon faces in the current scene.

### Avoid internal hidden polygons

When a simple sphere object is placed on top of a cone object to create an ice cream cone, the polygons on the lower half of the sphere that are within the cone object aren't needed. To reduce the polygons, place only half of the sphere on the cone or combine the two objects into one.

### Avoid default primitive settings

Each primitive object has default settings for the number of segments that it uses for each dimension. For example, setting a box primitive to use 3 segments in each axis creates a box with 54 polygons instead of only 6 for a box with 1 segment per axis. When editing objects, you need the extra faces to create something more than a box, but increase the segments only for the axis you know you need.

When an option parameter is changed within a dialog box, the changed parameter remains for the next time the command is used. Be cautious when increasing the number of segments used to create a primitive object because the change is included in all future primitives unless the options in the dialog box are reset.

Default spheres have 400 polygons that create a smooth-looking sphere, but if the entire sphere isn't needed or if you can get away with a less-than-perfect sphere, you can save a bundle of polygons.

### Hide detailed objects

Take a look at your hand. Even with minimal resolution, modeling a hand can take lots of polygons, but if you surround the fingers with a glove, then the modeling is greatly simplified, and you can save a number of polygons. The same can be said for shoes, hats, helmets, and so on.

### Use simplified curves

When objects are created from curves, every separate curve point is used to create a row of edges. If a curve includes many hundreds of points, which is common when drawing a curve using the Pencil tool, then the resulting polygon object will have thousands of polygons. By using Bézier curves, you can create smooth curves from a minimal number of points.

### Realize that NURBS won't solve your problems

Modeling with NURBS can result in files that are smaller and simplified because keeping track of mathematical curves takes up much less space than remembering the coordinates of all the vertices in an object, but very few game engines can deal with NURBS objects requiring first that the objects get converted to polygons. A well-designed NURBS model will not necessarily be converted efficiently to a polygon model.

## Automating polygon reduction

Most 3D software packages also include commands to reduce the total number of polygons used on the current model. These commands usually include settings for controlling how aggressively the polygons are reduced and options for maintaining any hard edges and material borders.

Be sure to save your model before using a polygon reduction command. Leaving the reduction to the software can result in undesirable results.

Follow these steps to reduce the total number of polygons in a 3D object in Maya:

1. **Choose the Create ⇨ Polygon Primitives ⇨ Sphere menu command.**

   A polygon sphere is placed in the center of the view at the origin, where its coordinates are [0,0,0].

2. **Choose the Display ➪ Heads Up Display ➪ Poly Count menu command.**

   The statistics for the current scene are listed in the upper-left corner of the current view including the number of Vertices, Edges, Faces, Tris, and UVs. Notice how a simple polygon sphere has 400 polygons.

3. **With the sphere object selected, choose the Polygons ➪ Reduce menu command.**

   The default setting for the Reduce command is to reduce the number of polygons by 50 percent. The Faces count for the reduced sphere, shown in Figure 5-14, is 200.

4. **Select the File ➪ Save Scene As menu command and save the file as Reduced sphere.mb.**

   Reducing polygon count can remove details that you don't want to lose. If the reduction results in bad changes, you can always undo the changes with the Edit ➪ Undo menu command.

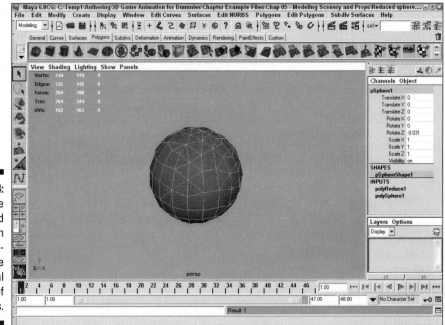

**Figure 5-14:**
The Reduce command can automatically reduce the total number of polygons.

# Chapter 6

# Adding Details with Materials

· · · · · · · · · · · · · · · · · · · · · · · · · · · · · · · · · · · · · · · · · · · · · · ·

· · · · · · · · · · · · · · · · · · · · · · · · · · · · · · · · · · · · · · · · · · · · · · ·

*T*he bad news, delivered in the last chapter, is that all modeled objects need to be constrained to a limited number of polygons in order for them to work well with the game engine. The good news is that you can add lots of detail that is missing from the model using materials and textures. The ability to work with larger and more detailed textures has probably been the single area where game engines have improved the most in recent years.

But textures aren't the only place that details are added back into a model. Textures are only part of the game. Materials are applied along with textures to define the material properties of the surface. These material properties can simulate a wide variety of material properties including color, transparency, specularity, and reflectivity.

This chapter covers the various material properties that you may encounter and shows you how materials can be defined and applied to objects and sub-objects within a scene.

## Defining Materials

If you pick up an object, say, a basketball, and look closely at its surface, how would you describe it? You could use words like orange, leather, smooth, reflective, and non-transparent. These words all describe the surface materials and corresponding properties can be set for a 3D model of a basketball.

Of all the available physical material properties, your experience gives you an understanding of many of the most basic common properties, but several specified within the 3D software are probably new to you. For example, everyone knows what color and transparency are, but how about specularity and luminosity?

## Color

Color is probably the easiest material property to identify, but many different colors can be involved in creating a material. The Object Color (or Diffuse Color) is the property that associated with a material. Materials also have an Ambient Color, which is a general global color applied to all objects in the scene.

## Transparency

Transparency is the ability to see through the surface of an object, such as glass. It is often specified by its opposite term Opacity, which is the inability to see through an object.

## Reflectivity

A reflective surface is one that reflects its surroundings; a mirror is an example of a reflective surface. Reflections are highly dependent on the renderer that is used. The best reflections are produced using a specialized rendering technique known as raytracing.

## Refraction

Refraction is the material property that defines the extent that light bends when it travels through a transparent object. For example, light traveling through oil bends more than light traveling through water. Refraction can typically be computed only when raytracing is used.

## Luminosity

Luminosity (or Incandescence) is a property that defines how much an object emits light on its own. For example, the sun has a high Luminosity value. This property is often used along with a glow effect to radiate in the scene.

## Specularity

Specularity is the ability of a surface to reflect a highlight, which is the surface point where the light is most intense. Specular highlights can come in many different shapes, sizes, and colors.

## *Bump map*

A material bump map creates surface textures, like the rind of an orange peel. In addition to the texture, you can also set the depth of the bump map.

# *Assigning Material Properties to Objects*

Materials are assigned within the 3D software package to different objects or to parts of objects typically using an external interface. Using this interface, you can create a unique material by combining all the various material properties, and this material may then be assigned to the selected object.

## *Changing the view shading*

Even though a material is assigned to an object, that doesn't mean it will be visible. Each view has its own shading option that you can select. By changing the shading option for the view, you can control how quickly the views are updated. These shading options are available for views:

- ✔ **Bounding Box:** Displays all objects as simple boxes. This is the fastest shading method.
- ✔ **Wireframe:** Shows only the edges of all objects.
- ✔ **Hidden Line:** Displays only edges like wireframe, but hides all edges that are on the backside of the object.
- ✔ **Flat Shaded:** Displays all polygon faces as simple flat planes with no smoothing.
- ✔ **Smooth Shaded:** Displays all polygons faces with smoothing between adjacent faces.
- ✔ **Textured:** Displays surfaces with textures.

Materials and textures are typically visible only when the shading option is set to smooth shading or textured. However, even when smooth shading or textured is enabled, some effects such as bump maps and reflectivity are not displayed until the scene image is rendered.

Follow these steps to change the shading option for a view:

1. **Choose File ⇨ Open Scene and open the Scene with interface Ice cream cone.mb file.**

    This file includes a simple model of an ice cream cone with some materials applied to it. It is used to show the shading display method.

2. **Click the Four Views button in the Quick Layout buttons under the toolbox (or press the spacebar).**

   The workspace is divided into four views shown the Top, Front, Side, and Perspective views.

3. **Select the Shading ⇨ Smooth Shade All menu command from the panel menu for the Perspective view (or press the 5 key).**

   The view shading changes to show the material colors for the view.

   Within Maya, you can quickly change the shading option using the number keys with 4 for wireframe, 5 for smooth shading, 6 for textured, and 7 for lights.

4. **Select the Shading ⇨ Smooth Shade All menu command from the panel menu for the Front view (or press the 5 key).**

   All other views show the scene using the wireframe shading method, as shown in Figure 6-1.

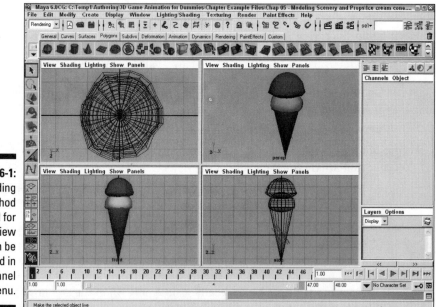

**Figure 6-1:** The shading method used for each view can be changed in the panel menu.

## Using preset materials

If you don't know where to start, you can select from a set of preset materials. Several different categories of common materials are typically included with the software that can be loaded into the scene and applied to objects.

You can use these materials to create new materials by editing their properties, and the new materials can be saved as separate files that can be reused later. By building libraries of materials, you can quickly outfit objects with materials without having to create new materials every time you build a scene.

Follow these steps to access preset materials:

1. **Choose the Create ➪ Polygon Primitives ➪ Sphere menu command.**

   A polygon sphere is placed in the center of the view.

2. **Select the Lighting/Shading ➪ Material Attributes menu command to open the Attribute Editor to the right of the view.**

   The Channel Box to the right of the view pane is replaced with a larger panel of controls called the Attribute Editor. This panel contains all the attributes for every aspect of the selected object including a default material labeled as Lambert1. All the material properties currently assigned to the selected object are displayed in this panel, as shown in Figure 6-2.

   The Lighting/Shading menu command can be found as part of the Rendering menu set. You can select this menu set using the drop-down list at the top left of the interface.

   You can also switch among the Attribute Editor, the Tool Settings, and the Channel Box using the three buttons located at the top right of the interface beneath the Minimize, Maximize, and Close buttons.

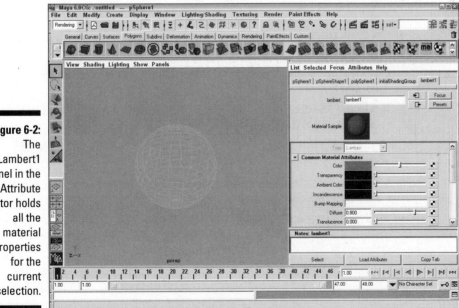

**Figure 6-2:**
The Lambert1 panel in the Attribute Editor holds all the material properties for the current selection.

**3. Click the Texture Map button to the right of the slider for the Color attribute.**

The Texture Map button causes the Create Render Node dialog box, shown in Figure 6-3, to appear. This dialog box includes many preset materials and textures that you can add to the current material.

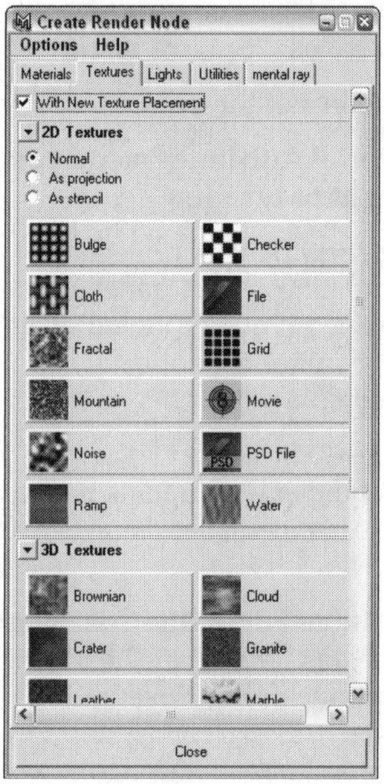

**Figure 6-3:**
The Create Render Node dialog box includes many preset materials and textures.

**4. Click the Cloth texture node in the Create Render Node dialog box.**

The Create Render Node dialog box is closed automatically, and the cloth texture is displayed in the Material Preview shown at the top of the Attribute Editor.

**5. Select the Shading ⇨ Smooth Shade All menu command from the panel menu for the Perspective view (or press the 5 key).**

The material is displayed on the sphere in the Perspective view, as shown in Figure 6-4.

**6. Select the File ⇨ Save Scene As menu command and save the file as Cloth material.mb.**

Materials that are applied to objects are saved along with the object to the file. If a shading view is enabled when saved, then the same shading view will be enabled when the file is re-opened.

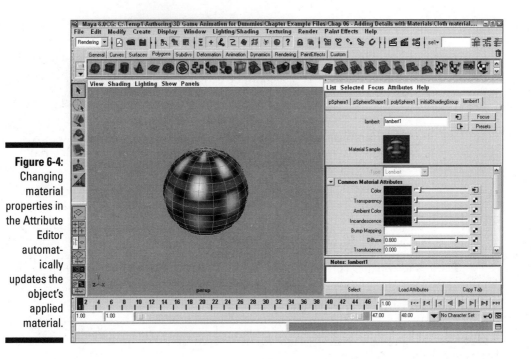

**Figure 6-4:**
Changing
material
properties in
the Attribute
Editor
automat-
ically
updates the
object's
applied
material.

# Creating unique materials

Unique materials are any materials that have a changed property. The first step in creating a new material is to select a shader. A shader is the base algorithm used to render the material. These are the common basic shader types:

- ✔ **Phong:** A good generic shader with sharp specular highlights.

- ✔ **Blinn:** A more advanced version of the Phong shader that offers more control over how the highlights spread across the surface. This shader is good for simulating glass and plastic.

- ✔ **Lambert:** A generic shader without distinct highlights. This shader is good for simulating cloth and other materials that absorb instead of reflect light.

- ✔ **Anisotropic:** An advanced shader that can produce elliptical-shaped highlights. It is good for simulating metals and curved glass.

- ✔ **Sketch (or Cartoon):** Renders objects as if they were drawn by hand.

- ✔ **Metal:** Includes bare properties for simulating metal surfaces such as scattering light.

Follow these steps to select a new shader:

1. **Choose the Create ⇨ Polygon Primitives ⇨ Sphere menu command.**

   A polygon sphere is placed in the center of the view.

2. **With the sphere object selected, choose the Lighting/Shading ⇨ Assign New Material ⇨ Anisotropic menu command.**

   The default Lambert1 node in the Attribute Editor is replaced with a new Anisotropic1 node. This new node has a different set of material properties.

3. **Click the color swatch in the Attribute Editor, and select a new light blue color from the Color Chooser that appears.**

   The Color Chooser, shown in Figure 6-5, includes a palette of colors and color values. The light blue color appears in the Material Preview pane in the Attribute Editor, but the anisotropic highlight isn't visible in the view pane. The scene must be rendered in order to see this highlight.

4. **Select the File ⇨ Save Scene As menu command and save the file as Light blue material.mb.**

   Even though material colors are applied to an object, you can change them at any time using the Attribute Editor.

**Figure 6-5:**
The Color Chooser lets you select the material color.

# Assigning Material Properties to Object Parts

Materials can be assigned to an object component as easily as they can be assigned to an object. The only difference is the initial selection. If an object is selected when the material is assigned, then the material is assigned to the whole object, but if only a portion of the object is selected, then the material is applied to only the selected portion.

Follow these steps to assign a material only to selected polygon faces:

1. **Choose the Create ⇨ Polygon Primitives ⇨ Sphere menu command.**

   A polygon sphere is placed in the center of the view at the origin where its coordinates are [0,0,0].

2. **Select the Lighting/Shading ⇨ Material Attributes menu command to open the Attribute Editor.**

   The Attribute Editor opens to the right of the view pane with the Lambert1 material node selected.

3. **Click the color swatch for the Color attribute in the Attribute Editor, and select a new yellow color from the Color Chooser that appears.**

   The yellow color is applied to the entire sphere object.

4. **In the top toolbar, click the Select by Component Type button. Right-click in the view pane, and select the Face component type.**

   All vertices for the sphere object are displayed, indicating that you are in component mode. But after you select the Face component type, all polygon faces are displayed.

5. **From the panel menu for the Perspective view pane, select the Panels ⇨ Orthogonal ⇨ Side menu command.**

   The view pane is switched to the Side view.

6. **Click the Select button in the toolbox, and hold down the Shift key while you drag over all the polygon faces in every other set of rows.**

   Holding down the Shift key lets you select multiple components together. The selected components are highlighted.

7. **With the face components selected, choose the Lighting/Shading ➪ Assign New Material ➪ Blinn menu command.**

   A new Blinn1 node is added to the Attribute Editor.

8. **Click the color swatch in the Attribute Editor, and select a blue color from the Color Chooser that appears.**

   All the selected polygons are colored blue, but the yellow color remains on those polygons not selected, as shown in Figure 6-6.

9. **Select the File ➪ Save Scene As menu command and save the file as Sphere with stripes.mb.**

   Even though the colors are different on the object, the object still moves together as a single object.

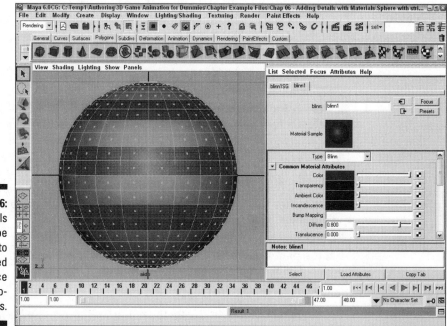

**Figure 6-6:** Materials can be applied to selected face components.

# Chapter 7

# Mapping Textures

• • • • • • • • • • • • • • • • • • • • • • • • • • • • • • • • • • • • • • • • •

• • • • • • • • • • • • • • • • • • • • • • • • • • • • • • • • • • • • • • • • •

*T*extures are images that can be used to enhance materials. Imagine a soup can. The metal part of the can is a shiny and silver with some nice specular highlights, but on top of the material is a printed label. This label is a 2D image that is wrapped around the soup can, so it can be seen from all sides. In this example, the metallic surface is the object's material, and the printed label is the texture.

As textures are wrapped about an object, you can control their placement using UV coordinates and different wrapping methods including planar, cylindrical, and spherical.

3D games use lots of different types of textures. You can apply textures to objects, to scenery, to backgrounds, and so on. Almost every material property can use a texture to define its value. In this chapter, you explore how textures are used to add detail to objects and specifically how they are used within 3D games.

# Wrapping Texture Maps about Objects without Messy Glues

If you add a texture image in place of the Color property, then the image is displayed on the object in place of the color, but how it is wrapped depends on the setting that you use. Some common texture wrapping methods include:

- **Planar:** A copy of the complete texture is placed on every co-planar object face, such as every side of a box object.

- **Cylindrical:** The texture image is wrapped about a cylindrical object so that opposite side edges meet on the backside of the cylinder object.

- **Spherical:** The texture image is distorted to wrap seamlessly about a spherical object.

- **Projected:** The image is projected, using its actual resolution, onto the object. If the object is smaller, then only a portion of the texture covers the object.

- **Faceted:** The entire texture image is placed on every face of the object.

Most 3D software packages include an interactive tool that can be used to help you place textures on the surface of an object's face.

Follow these steps to wrap a texture about an object:

1. **Choose the Create ⇨ Polygon Primitives ⇨ Cylinder menu command.**

   A polygon cylinder is placed in the center of the view.

2. **Select the Lighting/Shading ⇨ Assign New Material ⇨ Lambert menu command to create a new material for the cylinder object.**

   The Lambert2 node in the Attribute Editor is opened with the material properties for the assigned material displayed.

3. **Click the Texture Map button to the right of the slider for the Color attribute.**

   The Texture Map button causes the Create Render Node dialog box to appear. This dialog box includes many preset materials and textures that you can add to the current material.

4. **Enable the As Projection option and click the Checker texture node in the Create Render Node dialog box.**

   The As Projection option, located at the top of the 2D Textures category in the Create Render Node dialog box, adds a utility node to the material that lets you change the wrapping method. The current wrapping method listed in the Projection Type drop-down list is Planar, as shown in Figure 7-1.

5. **In the Attribute Editor, set the Projection Type to Cylindrical.**

   By setting the Projection Type to Cylindrical, the checker texture is evenly wrapped about the cylinder object, as shown in Figure 7-2.

6. **Select the File ⇨ Save Scene As menu command and save the file as Wrapping methods.mb.**

   By revisiting the Attribute Editor, you can change the wrapping method later if you want.

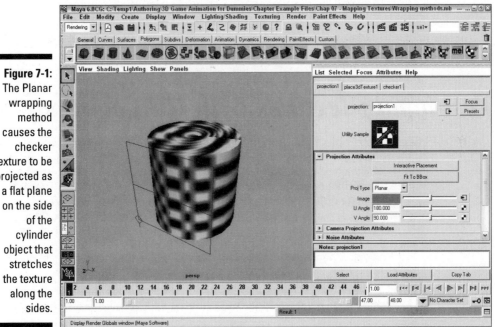

**Figure 7-1:** The Planar wrapping method causes the checker texture to be projected as a flat plane on the side of the cylinder object that stretches the texture along the sides.

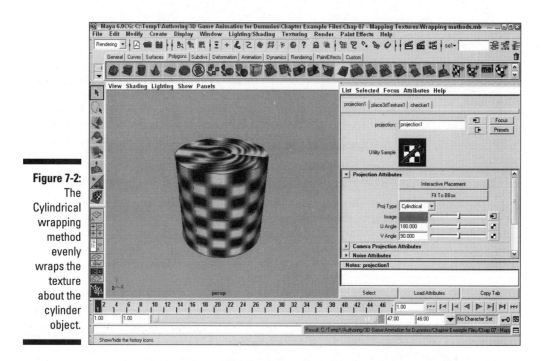

**Figure 7-2:**
The Cylindrical wrapping method evenly wraps the texture about the cylinder object.

# *Positioning Textures with UV Coordinates*

Imagine a box object that is modeled to be the center of a picture frame. The 2D coordinates of one face of the box object can be described using UV coordinates where the U coordinate is the horizontal distance from the left edge and the V coordinate is the vertical distance from the bottom edge. Therefore, a UV coordinate of [0,0] would position the lower-left corner of the texture in the lower-left corner of the box object, and if the box were 200×200×200 units, then offsetting the UV coordinates to [100,100] would place the lower-left corner of the texture right in the middle of the box object.

## *Offsetting a texture*

Texture images by default are positioned so the lower-left pixel of the image is matched to the lower-left corner of the polygon face to which it is applied. This correctly places the texture for most cases, but if you want to offset the position of the lower-left image corner, you can use the UV Offset values to position the texture relative to the lower-left object corner.

## Scaling a texture

Another default texture behavior is to scale the texture image so that it perfectly fits the polygon face to which it is applied, but this distorts the texture, which could cause real problems if the texture includes any text.

By scaling a texture in the UV directions, you can precisely control whether the image is scaled to fit the polygon face or whether it retains its original dimensions.

Scaling values are sometimes controlled by a Coverage value that sets how much of the image covers the polygon face. A setting of 1.0 would stretch the texture to cover the entire polygon face, and a setting of 0.5 would cause the polygon face to be covered by half of the texture.

## Rotating a texture

A texture can also be rotated about its corner position or about the center of the polygon face using rotate commands. A rotation value of 180 would turn the texture upside down, and a rotation value of 360 would rotate the texture a full rotation.

## Tiling a texture

If the texture settings are such that the texture doesn't fill the entire polygon face, then you can enable a Tile option for both the U and V directions that causes the texture to be repeated end to end until the entire polygon face is covered. This is particularly handy when using small textures mapped onto rocks or walls.

Follow these steps to position a texture on an object face:

1. **Choose the Create ⇨ Polygon Primitives ⇨ Cube menu command.**

   A polygon cube is placed in the center of the view. For this example, I'm using a box object positioned within a picture frame.

2. **Select the Lighting/Shading ⇨ Assign New Material ⇨ Lambert menu command to create a new material for the cube object.**

   The Lambert2 node in the Attribute Editor is opened with the material properties for the assigned material displayed.

3. **Click the Texture Map button to the right of the slider for the Color attribute.**

   The Texture Map button causes the Create Render Node dialog box to appear. This dialog box includes many preset materials and textures that you can add to the current material.

4. **Enable the Normal option and click the File texture node in the Create Render Node dialog box.**

   The File1 node in the Attribute Editor opens.

5. **In the Attribute Editor, click the Browse button to the right of the Image Name field, and then locate and load the texture image.**

   Clicking the Browse button opens a file dialog box where you can select the texture image to load. For this example, I loaded an image of the Alamo saved as a JPEG file. The loaded file is positioned to fill the entire polygon face, as shown in Figure 7-3.

6. **Click the place2dTexture1 tab at the top of the Attribute Editor, and set the Repeat UV values each to 2.0.**

   The place2DTexture1 node includes all the properties for positioning the texture on the polygon face. By increasing the Repeat UV values to 2.0, you set the image to repeat twice in both directions, thereby creating four texture images to cover the polygon face, as shown in Figure 7-4.

   If you select a view window and press the 6 key, the Texture View is enabled, and the applied texture will be visible on the applied object.

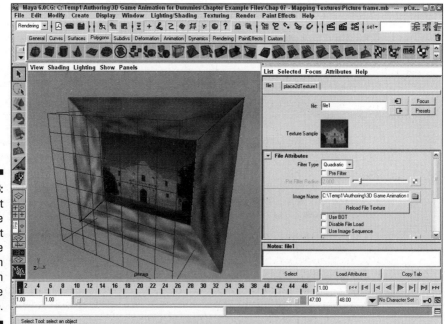

**Figure 7-3:** The default texture placement fills the polygon face with the texture image.

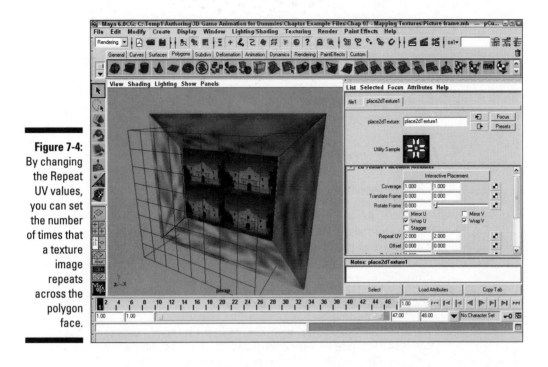

**Figure 7-4:**
By changing
the Repeat
UV values,
you can set
the number
of times that
a texture
image
repeats
across the
polygon
face.

7. **Select the File ⇨ Save Scene As menu command and save the file as Picture frame.mb.**

By repeating some textures over a large area you can create grass, carpet, and dirt textures.

# Creating Seamless Textures That Tile Together: Look Ma, No Seams

If the texture image isn't large enough to fill the entire polygon face of an object, then you can set it to be tiled vertically and/or horizontally so the entire object is covered. If you're using a texture to tile a floor, then this makes perfect sense, but tiled textures can also be used to add a skin texture to an animal or a repeating bark texture to a tree. The key to having these textures work is to make them blend together so that it appears the entire object is covered.

But imagine a texture image that is bright yellow on one side and red on the other side. The seams of the texture would be painfully obvious as the texture is tiled. To fix these apparent seams, you need to create a texture image whose opposite side matches seamlessly. Wrapping an object with a seamless texture makes the object appear fully covered.

## Creating noisy tiles

One way to create seamless tiles is to avoid having discernible edges. By adding a noise pattern to a texture that is to be used as a tile, the edges aren't distinguishable due to the randomness of the noise pattern, so the textures tile together with no seams.

## Filling a solid tile

Another common technique for creating a seamless tile is to create a background with a solid color and add the texture details within the solid background. For example, creating a white background with a pattern in its middle that doesn't touch any of the edges would tile perfectly without seams. This works just like tiling a floor with ceramic tiles.

## Matching opposite edges

Probably the trickiest method involves matching opposite edges, so that a line that leaves the left side of the texture continues on the right side. Creating tiles in the manner ensures that the texture can be placed without seams because the opposite edges match up when tiled.

Some 2D image-editing packages, such as Adobe's Image Ready and Corel's Painter include tools, let you automatically create seamless textures by repeating lines that are drawn off the edge of the texture on the opposite edge.

Follow these steps to position a texture on an object face:

1. **Choose the Create ➪ Polygon Primitives ➪ Sphere menu command.**

   A polygon sphere is placed in the center of the view.

2. **Select the Lighting/Shading ➪ Assign New Material ➪ Phong menu command to create a new material for the sphere object.**

   The Phong1 node in the Attribute Editor is opened with the material properties for the assigned material displayed.

3. **Click the Texture Map button to the right of the slider for the Color attribute.**

The Texture Map button causes the Create Render Node dialog box to appear. This dialog box includes many preset materials and textures that you can add to the current material.

4. **Enable the Normal option and click the Noise texture node in the Create Render Node dialog box.**

   The Noise1 node in the Attribute Editor opens.

5. **Click the place2dTexture1 tab at the top of the Attribute Editor, and set the Repeat U value to 5.0 and the Repeat V value to 10.0.**

   By increasing the Repeat U and Repeat V values to 5.0 and 10.0, you're setting the noise image to be repeated horizontally 5 times and vertically 10 times, as shown in Figure 7-5. Notice that the texture appears seamless across the sphere's surface.

6. **Select the File ⇨ Save Scene As menu command and save the file as Seamless noise.mb.**

   The trick to creating an efficient seamless texture is to avoid regular patterns.

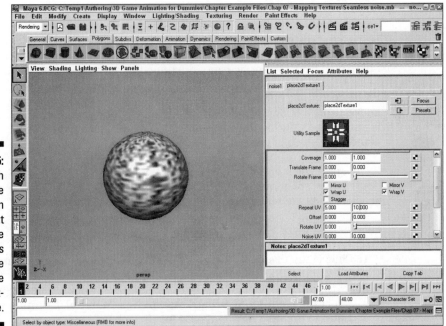

**Figure 7-5:** Even though the texture has been set to repeat across the sphere's surface, the seams are undetectable.

# Creating Raised Texture with Bump and Displacement Maps

In the previous examples, the textures were all applied to the Color attribute, but many other values can also use textures. For these attributes, the texture image is used to determine the value for the selected property. These values are determined by the brightness of the texture at each pixel.

For example, if you change the Transparency value from 0 to 100, then the entire selected material becomes completely transparent, but if you apply a checker texture to the Transparency attribute, then all places where the checker texture is dark, the transparency value is 0, and all places on the checker texture that are white have a transparency value of 100. If the texture has a mid-gray color, then the transparency value is set to 50.

## Using bump maps

Textures applied as bump maps can actually be used to raise and indent the surface to create the illusion of a texture like an orange rind or a rough surface like sandpaper. Bump maps work by raising the bright pixels of the bump map from the surface and indenting the darker pixels of the bump map.

When describing bump maps, the word illusion is used because the texture added using a bump map doesn't really change the geometry of the object. It is applied only during the rendering process. Displacement maps, however, actually change the geometry.

If you apply the bump map correctly but don't see it within the active view, don't be too concerned. Bump maps can typically be seen only when the scene objects are rendered.

Follow these steps to use a bump map:

1. **Choose the Create ⇨ Polygon Primitives ⇨ Sphere menu command.**

   A polygon sphere is placed in the center of the view.

2. **Select the Lighting/Shading ⇨ Assign New Material ⇨ Blinn menu command to create a new material for the sphere object.**

   The Blinn1 node in the Attribute Editor is opened with the material properties for the assigned material displayed.

3. **Click the Texture Map button to the right of the Bump Map attribute.**

   The Texture Map button causes the Create Render Node dialog box to appear.

4. **Click the Grid texture node in the Create Render Node dialog box.**

   The Grid1 node in the Attribute Editor opens. Using the attributes in this node, you can change the Bump Depth value to make the bumps deeper. Figure 7-6 shows the sphere after being rendered. You can learn more about rendering in Chapter 16.

5. **Select the File ⇨ Save Scene As menu command and save the file as Bump map sphere.mb.**

   To make a bump map match a color texture, you can apply the same texture to both the Color and Bump attributes.

**Figure 7-6:**
The lines of the grid texture extend from the surface of the sphere.

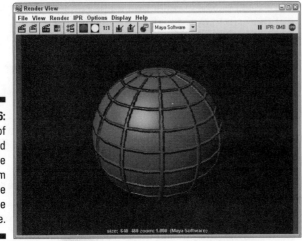

## Using displacement maps

Displacement maps are similar to bump maps in that a texture file can be used to raise and indent the surface of an object, but the key difference is that a displacement map actually causes a change in the geometry of the object, which can affect shadows within the scene.

# Creating Realistic Environments with Textures

Textures are also commonly used to create a realistic environment. Two places that textures are used to create a realistic environment are as a reflection map that casts a reflection onto shiny objects and as a background image that appears behind the 3D objects.

## Using reflection maps

A reflection map, often called an environmental map, is a map that surrounds the entire scene that is used to reflect the surroundings off the objects.

Imagine a shiny racing car traveling down a busy street. If the material of the car is a shiny candy apple red, then realistically the car should reflect its surroundings, but if the scene doesn't include any modeled objects behind the camera, then there is nothing to reflect. A reflection map is the answer.

Reflection maps enclose the object using several different shaped objects including a sphere or a cube. These reflection maps can be applied to the Color attribute, but that would only invert the texture. A better attribute to use for the reflection map is the Ambient Color attribute.

 Reflection maps, like bump maps, are typically seen only when the object is rendered.

Follow these steps to add a reflection map:

1. **Choose the Create ⇨ Polygon Primitives ⇨ Sphere menu command.**

   A polygon sphere is placed in the center of the view.

2. **Select the Lighting/Shading ⇨ Assign New Material ⇨ Blinn menu command to create a new material for the sphere object.**

   The Blinn1 node in the Attribute Editor is opened with the material properties for the assigned material displayed.

3. **Click the Texture Map button to the right of the Ambient Color attribute.**

   The Texture Map button causes the Create Render Node dialog box to appear.

4. **Enable the Normal option and click the File texture node in the Create Render Node dialog box.**

   The File1 node in the Attribute Editor opens.

    Even though a reflection map is applied, it will not be visible in the view window. Reflection maps are visible when the scene is rendered.

5. **In the Attribute Editor, click the Browse button to the right of the Image Name field, and then locate and load the texture image.**

   Clicking the Browse button opens a file dialog box where you can select the texture image to load. For this example, I loaded an image of the Alamo saved as a JPEG file. Figure 7-7 shows the sphere after being rendered with a reflection map. You can learn more about rendering in Chapter 16.

6. **Select the File ⇨ Save Scene As menu command and save the file as Reflection map.mb.**

   Remember that the reflection map is only clearly visible when reflected off a shiny object.

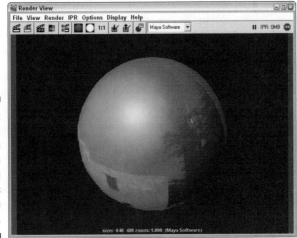

**Figure 7-7:**
Only a portion of the reflection map is visible on the sphere.

# Adding a background image

Cleverly using background images can save you lots of time by reducing the number of scenery and prop objects you need to model, but if you're not careful with background images, they can destroy an otherwise effective scene.

Background images are 2D images tacked on behind all the scene objects. As you move through the scene, the scene objects maintain their 3D nature, changing perspective as you move through them, but the background image does not. This effect can be masked by making a simple movie of the background with slowly moving clouds or such.

Another gotcha with background images is that they don't cast or receive shadows.

Background images are typically tied to the camera that is used to view the scene. Background images can also be loaded into the current view as a reference to help you as you model.

TIP

In addition to texture image, different 3D software packages allow a variety of cloud textures, materials, and procedural textures to be used as backgrounds.

Follow these steps to add a reflection map:

1. **Choose the Create ⇨ Polygon Primitives ⇨ Cube menu command.**

   A polygon cube is placed in the center of the view. This object helps to show where the foreground objects are located relative to the background image.

2. **Select the View ⇨ Image Plane ⇨ Import Image menu command from the panel menu located at the top of the current view.**

   This menu command opens a file dialog box where you can select the texture image to load as a background image. For this example, I again loaded the Alamo.jpg image. Figure 7-8 shows the cube object rendered with the background image.

3. **Select the File ⇨ Save Scene As menu command and save the file as Background image.mb.**

   Background images are rendered with the scene, but they can also be used to load templates, as demonstrated in Chapter 4.

**Figure 7-8:**
Background images can be used effectively to create an environment.

## Creating a skybox for backdrops

One problem that occurs when working with background images is that the texture needs to altered every time the camera changes position. A common technique that fixes this problem is to create a skybox.

A skybox is a dome-shaped object that has a seamless 360-degree background texture mapped to it. All scene objects are then placed inside this skybox object. Using the skybox ensures that a background image is visible, regardless of where the camera is positioned.

The skybox also eliminates the need for individual reflection maps.

# Painting on Textures to Add Dirt and Grime

Although most textures are created externally and wrapped onto objects, most 3D software programs also include a separate set of tools for painting directly on the objects themselves.

Using these painting tools, you can add details, such as dirt and grime, to the texture applied to the object after the texture image has already been applied.

One helpful way to use these paint tools is to add realistic dirt and grime to objects. Adding these layers of dirt to the texture map can be tricky because you're not always sure where the map will match the folds of the skin or the edges and corners of an object where dirt is likely to accumulate.

Painting tools are also helpful for defacing nice textures with spray paint to resemble graffiti.

3D painting tools typically let you select from a selection of brushes that offer different styles. You can also adjust the brushes' size, pressure, and color.

In some software, the painting tools work only if the surface has a texture file applied to it.

Follow these steps to use the painting tools:

1. **Choose the Create ⇨ Polygon Primitives ⇨ Cube menu command.**

   A polygon cube is placed in the center of the view.

2. **Select the Lighting/Shading ⇨ Assign New Material ⇨ Lambert menu command to create a new material for the cube object.**

   The Lambert2 node in the Attribute Editor is opened with the material properties for the assigned material displayed.

3. **Press the 6 key to enable a Texture view.**

   In Texture view, you'll be able to see the brush strokes as you paint.

4. **Select the Texturing ⇨ 3D Paint Tool menu command to access the painting tool, and then select the Window ⇨ Settings/Preferences ⇨ Tool Settings menu command to open the Tool Settings panel to the right of the view pane.**

All the settings for the 3D Paint Tool are displayed within the Tool Settings panel. Initially, there isn't a surface to paint on, so you'll need to create one.

You can also switch among the Attribute Editor, the Tool Settings, and the Channel Box using the three buttons located at the top right of the interface beneath the Minimize, Maximize, and Close buttons.

5. **In the File Textures section of the Tool Settings panel, click the Assign/Edit Textures button. In the Assign/Edit File Textures dialog box that appears, set the SizeX and SizeY values to 256 and click the Assign/Edit Textures button.**

   This creates a texture that you can paint on top of that is saved with the scene file.

6. **Set the Brush Scale value to 1.0 and the color to light blue, and drag over the top of the image in the view pane.**

   The color is added to the texture image on all the cube faces, as shown in Figure 7-9.

7. **Select the File ⇨ Save Scene As menu command and save the file as Painting tool.mb.**

   The ability to paint directly on an object's surface is very helpful as you add materials to objects.

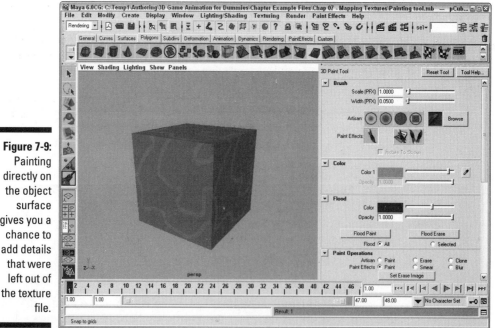

**Figure 7-9:** Painting directly on the object surface gives you a chance to add details that were left out of the texture file.

# Efficiently Coloring Objects with Vertex Colors

Texture maps can take up memory, and multiple layers of texture maps can take up lots of memory, so game programmers are always looking for ways to efficiently add object details without consuming large blocks of memory.

One way to efficiently add color details is to use a vertex color map. These maps keep track of a certain color value for each vertex, which is much more memory efficient than holding another entire texture map in memory.

Colors at adjacent vertices can be interpolated across the polygon face to create some interesting effects.

# Baking Textures for Quick Model Loading

Most 3D game objects include multiple texture maps that are loaded into channels that can be turned on and off as needed. For example, one channel can include a texture of a car when it is first taken off the showroom floor, another channel can hold a texture showing the car after traveling through the mud a couple of times, and a third channel can hold the texture used to display the car after some fender-benders.

Baking textures is a process that combines several textures on different channels into a single file. These baked textures can include precomputed reflection, light, and bump effects.

By baking textures, you can free up the game engine for other tasks such as AI, because it doesn't need to spend its cycles computing how a texture should look under the given lighting conditions. This can be a huge resource savings.

# Chapter 8

# Creating Effective Lighting

. . . . . . . . . . . . . . . . . . . . . . . . . . . . . . . . . . . . . . . . . . . . .

*In This Chapter*

▶ Starting with basic lighting

▶ Exploring the different light types

▶ Creating lights

▶ Changing light properties

▶ Using light special effects

▶ Creating realistically lighted scenes

▶ Creating a prelighted map

. . . . . . . . . . . . . . . . . . . . . . . . . . . . . . . . . . . . . . . . . . . . .

If 3D games didn't have any lights, then they would be pretty boring (although some games have had levels that were all in the dark that relied on sound to present information to the game player, but bear with me). Lights are important and can make a huge impact on the success of a game.

Lighting is more than just randomly placing some light objects about the scene. They can be used to draw the players' attention to a particular door that they should enter or a key that they should find. Sometimes, lights are used to reveal a secret passage, but lights are always used to set the ambiance of the scene.

Good lighting isn't always about making sure everything is seen. Too much light can be just as big a problem as too little light. Throughout this chapter, I'll take a closer look at lighting, offer some techniques and tips, and discuss the various lighting options available to you.

# Starting with a Basic Three-Point Lighting Configuration

Actual scene environments include many lights, but at a minimum, you should make sure that characters in the scene are lighted using a basic three-point lighting configuration. This basic lighting configuration includes a main light that shines down on the character from a position above and to the side of the character. This main light is also used to cast shadows.

The second light is positioned in front of the character a little above ground level to highlight the character's details from underneath. This secondary light should be about one-third the brightness of the main light and should not be set to cast shadows.

The third light is a backfill light positioned behind the character. It is used to outline the character and to separate it from the background. The backfill light should also be about one-third the brightness of the main light and also shouldn't be set to cast shadows.

Changing the colors of the secondary and backfill lights to a darker hue also adds some needed color variation to the character, but keep the saturation low.

## Avoiding too many or too few lights

Over-lighting a scene happens when too many lights are added to a scene; under-lighting is when too few lights are used in the scene. Why bother modeling or texturing the details of an object if the lighting is just going to wash out the details or if the scene is too dark to see them?

I can't tell you a magic number for the number of lights that a scene needs. Light placement really is an art that you get a feel for the more you do it. A good place to learn is to examine the lights used in other games. Ask yourself these questions: Where are the light sources? Where are they positioned relative to the main character? Which lights cast shadows? Does the scene have any ambient light? Is the lighting geared for indoor or outdoor? What details are washed out or not visible?

Scene lights aren't renderable and can be placed anywhere within the scene as needed. This means that you can do more than place lights within a torch or a lamp post. Light objects can be positioned within a dark corner to add more light to the surrounding area.

If you plan on using any photographic textures in the scene, then you need to be aware of the scene lighting. Photographic textures already have a dose of light, and exposing them to additional scene lights over-exposes the images. To handle this problem, dim the scene lights or reduce the brightness of the image.

# Exploring the Different Light Types

Just as real life has different types of lights, each with its own properties and characteristics, several different 3D software lights can be selected. The main difference in these lights is how they cast light rays into the scene.

## Point light

Point lights are perhaps the simplest type of light. They cast light rays in all directions from a single point and are useful for recreating the light from a candle, a light bulb, or a lamp post.

## Area light

Area lights are like a bank of point lights that cover an area. They are significantly more intense than simple point lights and are useful for representing banks of fluorescent lights.

## Direct light

Intense lights from a distant location, such as the sun, strike the scene with parallel light rays. Direct lights can be pointed at objects for lighting that simulates the sun. Direct lights also don't have any falloff.

## Ambient light

Ambient light is a general light setting that globally lights everything in the scene, including shadows. Ambient light can be used to lighten a dark scene without adding any light sources.

## Spot light

Spot lights, like direct lights, are also directional and can be pointed at objects, but spot lights have a well-defined cone of influence with falloff.

# Creating Lights

Creating lights adds an icon to the scene that can be positioned and oriented as needed. These icons can also be animated and moved to create dynamic lights, but the light icon is not rendered with the rest of the scene.

The menu command to create a light lets you select the light type to place in the scene, but most software packages let you change the light type in the properties panel when the light is selected.

Most software packages include a set of default lights that light the scene in the absence of any placed lights. If you create and render a scene without any lights added to the scene, these default lights are used to light the scene. After a light is added to the scene, the default lights are disabled.

Follow these steps to create a new light in Maya:

1. **Choose the Create ⇨ Polygon Primitives ⇨ Sphere menu command.**

   A polygon sphere is placed in the center of the view.

2. **Select the Create ⇨ Lights ⇨ Spot Light menu command.**

   A new spot light object is added to the scene in the center of the view inside the sphere.

3. **Select the Modify ⇨ Transformation Tools ⇨ Move Tool menu command, and drag the light object outside the sphere.**

   With the spot light outside of the sphere, its influence lights the sphere object.

4. **Select the Lighting ⇨ Use All Lights menu command from the panel menu (or press the 7 key).**

   This menu command enables all lights, as shown in Figure 8-1. Notice how the light shines off the sphere object closest to the light object.

5. **Select the Window ⇨ Attribute Editor menu command to open the Attribute Editor.**

   The Attribute Editor opens to the right of the view pane showing the properties for the currently selected light.

6. **Select the Area Light option from the Type drop-down list in the Attribute Editor.**

   By changing the light type, the light object changes along with the light effects on the sphere object in the view pane, as shown in Figure 8-2.

7. **Select the File ⇨ Save Scene As menu command and save the file as Area light.mb.**

   Lights are treated like other objects and can be transformed and deleted just like other objects.

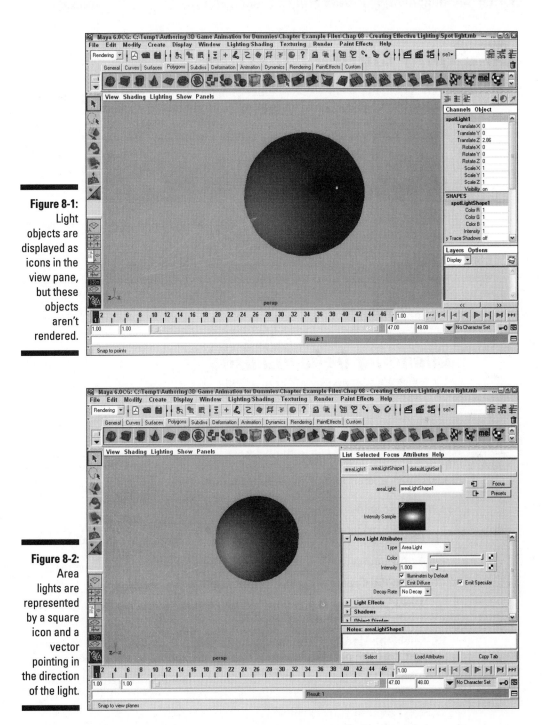

**Figure 8-1:**
Light objects are displayed as icons in the view pane, but these objects aren't rendered.

**Figure 8-2:**
Area lights are represented by a square icon and a vector pointing in the direction of the light.

# Changing Light Properties

Each light in the scene has a number of different properties that you can set, and each light should have its own set of properties. For example, a spot light includes properties for setting its cone of influence that aren't needed for the point light. Very rarely does every light in a scene have the same settings.

## Using light color

Light color bathes your scenes in a designated color, but this can also change the surface colors of objects in the scene.

Light color can also dramatically change the scene's mood. White and bright yellow lights can be used for outdoor noonday lighting conditions; pastel blues, pinks, and oranges can be used for pasty indoor lighting; and dark blue can be used for night scenes.

## Changing light intensity

Light intensity is the setting that determines how bright a light shines in the scene. Be careful to not include too many bright lights, or you may risk over-exposure.

Light intensity values can actually be set to a negative value that pulls light from the scene, but using negative lights often causes more problems than it helps solve and should be used with caution.

Follow these steps to change light properties in Maya:

1. **Choose the Create ⇨ Polygon Primitives ⇨ Sphere menu command.**

   A polygon sphere is placed in the center of the view.

2. **Select the Create ⇨ Lights ⇨ Point Light menu command.**

   A new point light object is added to the scene in the center of the view inside the sphere.

3. **Select the Modify ⇨ Transformation Tools ⇨ Move Tool menu command, and drag the point light object outside the sphere to the left side.**

   With the spot light outside of the sphere, its influence lights the sphere object.

4. **Select the Lighting ⇨ Use All Lights menu command from the panel menu (or press the 7 key).**

   This menu command enables all lights.

5. **Select the Window ⇨ Attribute Editor menu command to open the Attribute Editor.**

   The Attribute Editor opens to the right of the view pane showing the properties for the currently selected light.

6. **Click the color swatch for the Color attribute in the Attribute Editor, change the color to light blue, and set the Intensity to 10.**

   The high Intensity value causes the entire left side of the sphere to turn blue.

7. **Repeat Steps 2 through 6 to create another point light, but position this light outside of the sphere to the right and change its color to yellow.**

   This additional light colors the entire right side of the sphere yellow, as shown in Figure 8-3.

8. **Select the File ⇨ Save Scene As menu command and save the file as Strong point lights.mb.**

   If light from two different point lights strike the same surface of an object, then the light is doubled.

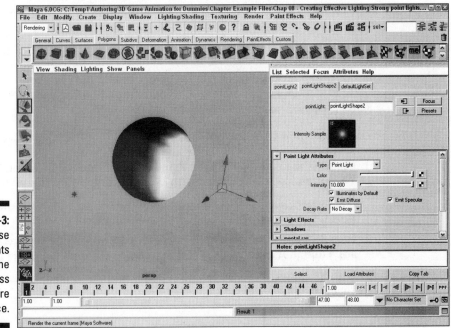

Figure 8-3:
Intense
point lights
spread the
light across
the entire
sphere face.

## Enabling shadows

Shadows are helpful in defining the depth and position of an object in the scene, but shadows should be enabled only for the main light source. Enabling shadows for multiple light sources multiplies the shadows. Shadow color is also controlled by the ambient color property for the scene.

Most 3D programs deal with two different types of shadows — Shadow Maps and Raytraced Shadows.

### Using shadow maps

Shadow maps are image maps that hold the shadow information. The details of the shadow, including the hardness of the shadow edges, are determined by the size of the shadow map. Larger shadow maps have more precise shadows, but require more memory.

### Using raytraced shadows

Another alternative to shadow maps is to create the shadows using raytracing. Raytracing is a rendering algorithm that calculates lighting effects by casting light rays into the scene from all light sources and following these light rays as they bounce about the scene.

Creating shadows using raytracing creates extremely accurate shadows with hard precise edges, but raytracing can add lots of extra time to the rendering phase.

### Blurring shadows

One common shadow property that you can set for both Shadow Maps and raytraced shadows is the amount of shadow blur. Blurring a shadow creates a softer image and is more realistic for outdoor light.

Follow these steps to enable shadows in Maya:

1. **Choose the Create ⇨ Polygon Primitives ⇨ Plane menu command. Then scale the plane object with the Scale Tool to fill the view pane.**

   A 2D square plane is placed in the center of the view. Shadows can be seen only if an object is behind or below the object to catch the shadows.

2. **Choose the Create ⇨ Polygon Primitives ⇨ Torus menu command. Then scale and move the torus object to position it above the plane object.**

   With the torus object positioned above the plane object, it can cast shadows onto the plane object.

3. **Select the Create ➪ Lights ➪ Point Light menu command. Move the light object above and slightly in front of the torus object.**

   A new point light object is added to the scene in the center of the view inside the sphere and positioned so it can cast shadows onto the plane below it.

4. **Select the Lighting ➪ Use All Lights menu command from the panel menu (or press the 7 key).**

   This menu command enables all lights.

5. **Select the Window ➪ Attribute Editor menu command to open the Attribute Editor.**

   The Attribute Editor opens to the right of the view pane showing the properties for the currently selected light.

6. **Set the Intensity for the point light to 3.0. Then expand the Shadows section in the Attribute Editor, and enable the Use Depth Map Shadows option.**

   Selecting the Use Depth Map Shadows option enables shadows for the current light, but these shadows aren't visible in the view pane and can be seen only when the scene is rendered. Figure 8-4 shows a rendered image of the scene.

7. **Select the File ➪ Save Scene As menu command and save the file as Shadows.mb.**

   Shadows can also be colored differently depending on the Ambient light color.

**Figure 8-4:**
Shadow
map
shadows
offer a quick
way to add
shadows to
a scene.

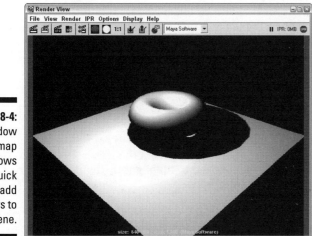

## Setting falloff

The sun is bright and shines with the same relative intensity all over the Earth, but most lights aren't like the sun. A candle, for instance, shines fairly bright if you are right next to the flame, but as you move away from the flame, the light becomes gradually less intense. The property of how light decays with distance is known as *falloff*.

Several different mathematical algorithms are used for computing falloff, including the following:

- **Linear:** This method makes the light decay by equal amounts as the distance increases.
- **Cubic:** This method decays the light at a much faster rate than linear falloff.
- **Quadratic:** This method decays light at an even faster rate than cubic falloff.

# Using Light Special Effects

Light is a wonderful phenomenon that provides all kinds of effects, such as glows, flares, fog, and so on. These effects can make an ordinary weapon such as a fighting stick into a futuristic weapon like a light saber that every kid wants to carry around on Halloween, or light can make a simple grenade into a light implosion weapon.

Lighting effects such as these are attached to a light object, which may or may not be used as a light source. An interesting effect is to apply a glow to a light source that includes a Light Intensity value of 0.

## Adding lens flares

If you point an actual camera at a bright light source, you may see a series of bright circles, streaks, and glows shining from the light source. This effect is called a lens flare, and it can be used to highlight the light source or a shiny object to make it appear extra bright.

The lens flares interface typically includes several different properties for enabling streaks, rings, glows, and halos. Each of these flare types can have a unique color, intensity, and thickness.

Follow these steps to enable a lens flare in Maya:

1. **Choose the Create ⇨ Polygon Primitives ⇨ Sphere menu command.**

   A polygon sphere is placed in the center of the view.

2. **Select the Create ⇨ Lights ⇨ Point Light menu command; move the light object to the front-top edge of the sphere object.**

   A new point light object is moved to the position where the lens flare will be located.

3. **Select the Lighting ⇨ Use All Lights menu command from the panel menu (or press the 7 key).**

   This menu command enables all lights.

4. **In the Attribute Editor, expand the Light Effects section and click the Texture Map button to the right of the Light Glow attribute.**

   Clicking the Texture Map button adds an Optical FX node to the light and opens it in the Attribute Editor. This node includes all the properties for defining how the lens flare looks.

5. **In the Attribute Editor, enable the Lens Flare option, set the Glow and Halo Types to Lens Flare, and set the Star Points to 5.0.**

   The lens flare effect is displayed only when the scene is rendered and is shown in Figure 8-5.

6. **Select the File ⇨ Save Scene As menu command and save the file as Lens flare.mb.**

   Lens flares can add a lot to a scene, but they can also hide details in the scene.

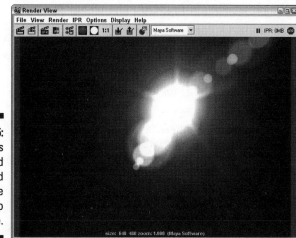

**Figure 8-5:**
Lens flares can be used to add intense highlights to a scene.

## Adding fog

Fog by itself isn't particularly interesting because it works only to obscure objects in the scene. However, when fog is combined with light beams such as spot lights, the result is a beam of light that is visible as it travels through the scene.

Light fog (or volume fog) includes settings for its color and density. More dense fog makes more of the light beam visible, while less dense fog makes less of the light beam visible.

Follow these steps to enable a light fog in Maya:

1. **Select the Create ⇨ Lights ⇨ Spot Light menu command; move the light object to the lower-left corner of the scene.**

   A new spot light object is added to the scene and positioned so it casts a beam of light across the scene.

   Not all light effects are available for all light types. For example, light fog and lens flares aren't available for Ambient or Directional lights.

2. **In the Attribute Editor, set the light color to yellow, its Intensity to 3.0, and its Cone Angle to 10.**

   By narrowing the spot light cone, the beam of light becomes more focused, like a laser.

3. **In the Attribute Editor, expand the Light Effects section and click the Texture Map button to the right of the Light Fog attribute.**

   Clicking the Texture Map button adds a Light Fog node to the light and opens it in the Attribute Editor. This node includes all the properties for defining how the light fog appears in the scene.

4. **In the Light Fog node in the Attribute Editor, set the Density to 0.5.**

   The light fog effect is displayed only when the scene is rendered and is shown in Figure 8-6.

5. **Select the File ⇨ Save Scene As menu command and save the file as Light fog.mb.**

   Fog can be used to make a beam of light visible in the scene.

## Making glowing lights

Another common lighting effect is to make lights glow. This is useful for objects like the sun, treasure, or simply objects that you want to highlight — for example, the door to escape a level.

**Figure 8-6:**
Light fog
makes the
light visible
in the
scene.

There are several different ways to make an object glow. One way is to increase the object's luminance value. This causes the object to appear as if it were emitting light.

Within Maya, a glow effect can be added to an object or to a light using the Attribute Editor. For each, you can set the glow color and intensity by mapping it to a texture node.

Follow these steps to make a glowing light in Maya:

1. **Select the Create ➪ Lights ➪ Point Light menu command.**

   A new point light object is placed in the center of the view panel.

2. **In the Attribute Editor, expand the Light Effects section and click the Texture Map button to the right of the Light Glow attribute.**

   Clicking the Texture Map button adds an Optical FX node to the light and opens it in the Attribute Editor. This node includes all the properties for defining how the glow looks.

3. **In the Attribute Editor, open the Glow Attributes section, set the Glow Intensity value to 8.0, the Glow Spread values to 6.0, the Glow Noise and Glow Radial Noise values to 0.5, and the Glow Star Level to 5.0.**

   The glowing light effect is displayed only when the scene is rendered and is shown in Figure 8-7.

4. **Select the File ➪ Save Scene As menu command and save the file as Glowing light.mb.**

   The glowing light with noise produces an interesting effect from a single light.

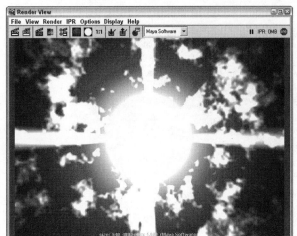

**Figure 8-7:**
A glowing
light can
add a rich
light effect
to a scene.

# Creating Realistically Lighted Scenes with Raytracing, Radiosity, and Global Illumination

When a scene is rendered, you can render the lighting in several different ways. The most common approach is to render scenes using a scanline process, which renders the image one row of pixels at a time.

The scanline rendering method computes light effects one pixel at a time, which doesn't take into account the entire scene. Most game engines use this method, but other methods exist that are much more realistic in their results. Three such methods are raytracing, radiosity, and global illumination.

## Raytracing

Raytracing was briefly described earlier in this chapter in the section that covered shadow topics. It is a method that shoots a light ray into the scene for every pixel in the final image. Not only are the results of where the light ray hits computed, but the light ray is followed as it is bounced, reflected, and refracted about the scene.

Raytracing can take a long time to render a single image making it inappropriate for games, but as computers get faster, maybe raytracing will be an option someday. Even if raytracing is still too slow to be used for a real-time game, some raytracing aspects can still be used; for example, you can use it to calculate shadows.

The real benefit of raytracing becomes apparent when the scene includes lots of reflective and refracting surfaces such as glass and water.

## Radiosity

In real life, as light bounces around a room, some of its energy is absorbed by the object it strikes and some of its energy is reflected off the object onto other objects in the scene. Think for a second of how you can look down a darkened hallway and tell whether a light is on in a room with an open door even if you can't see the light source directly. The hallway is lighted by the bouncing light rays.

Radiosity is a method for calculating lighting that keeps track of the light energy of each light ray and cumulatively adds all the light energy together to light the scene. The net result is to create very realistic lighting solutions for indoor environments.

Radiosity, like raytracing, can take a long time to render, but an approximate radiosity solution can be quickly estimated using several different techniques. Some game engines are beginning to use these estimation techniques to light indoor scenes.

## Global illumination

Global illumination is a lighting method that employs some of the same techniques as raytracing and radiosity, but it's applied to an outdoor lighting scene. Because outdoor scenes don't have enclosed spaces that allow the light to bounce back and forth, light energy is computed for global illumination using light scattering calculations.

Estimating global illumination is starting to appear within the newer game engines to create a more realistic outdoor lighting solution.

# Creating a Prelighted Map for Quick Scene Loading

Calculating lighting solutions traditionally is one of the aspects of the rendering process that takes longer than all the other rendering calculations, so game programmers have developed a way to capture the lighting for all the static scene lights before the scene is ever loaded into a game engine. By pre-rendering lighting effects, the game engine can scream as it computes the remaining tasks.

Pre-rendering lighting effects is accomplished by creating a lighting map for all the static objects in the scene. These lighting maps take up additional memory, but after they're loaded, they can display the lighting effects without having to recompute them for the static objects. Dynamic objects and lights still need to be computed and added to the existing lighting effects, but the overall workload is greatly reduced.

# Part III
# Designing, Modeling, and Animating Game Characters

The 5th Wave          By Rich Tennant

I told Russell he should data model before we go any further.

Miss Claudia Schiffer, please.

# In this part . . .

As a player, when you're first dropped into a game environment you may be impressed with the look of the level. But a week later, you'll be telling your friends about the huge monster you had to fight in the first level, and you won't even mention the environment. Game characters are often the most detailed and biggest animation challenge.

This part takes you through modeling and animating characters. It also introduces the basics of animation and then delves into the specific animation tasks of facial animation, and dynamics.

# Chapter 9

# Techniques for Modeling Characters

**Y**our game could have the coolest objects, weapons, vehicles, and scenery, but chances are that none of them make it on the cover of the game box. That spot is reserved for the game's main character.

Game characters are infused with personality, and it is this personality that helps players identify with the game characters just as they would with a movie hero or a famous literary character from a novel. The paddles in Pong didn't have much personality, and neither did the ship in Asteroids, but even as early as Pacman, game characters began to develop their own personalities and relate to other personalities. (Pacman even got a wife in Ms. Pacman — a bow was all it took.)

As games have grown up, many game characters have become very important culture icons identified pervasively. I'll bet that you can identify most of the following characters: Mario, Luigi, Donkey Kong, and Laura Croft.

Keep in mind as you begin to model a character that it needs to be infused with personality that distinguishes it from all other characters and makes it unique.

# Modeling Methods

As you begin the huge task of defining the game characters, keep the following ideas in mind.

## Knowing when to buy instead of build

In an earlier chapter, I mentioned the benefit of buying models, but to really distinguish your character from other games, these pre-created models won't be of much help. However, these pre-built models can always be edited and can provide a jump start to creating your unique character.

## Creating low-polygon models

In the back of your mind, always remember that your model must be controlled by the game engine, and that heavy models can make that difficult. As you begin creating a character, you should have a very good idea of how many polygons your character can be.

As you model smaller details such as fingertips and ears, remember to use modeling techniques that keep your polygon count in check.

## Using symmetry

If your character is human or human-based, then you have many chances to use symmetry to your advantage. You can model a single arm and mirror it to the other side of the character.

The drawback to symmetry is that it can make your character too perfect. All humans have a degree of imperfection that makes us unique. These imperfections are the features that give a character personality.

## Using a default stance

When modeling a character, don't worry initially about posing the character or placing it in a unique stance. The most useful character stance for starting out has the character standing facing forward with its arms out stretched and its legs separated about shoulder width. This standard stance makes it easier to place bones within the character later on.

## Using mesh smooth features

As you initially model the character, don't worry so much about the smoothness of each individual section. The goal initially is to merely rough out the general volume of the character. After the character is roughed out, a Mesh Smooth command can be used to apply a general smoothing to the entire character. By applying a general smoothing algorithm only once for the entire character, you can ensure that connected body parts flow well together.

# Modeling the Torso

The first place to start when modeling a character is with the torso, which includes the chest, abdomen, hips, and pelvis. The torso can start as a simple box object separated into polygon rows for the shoulders, the breasts, four or four rows of stomach muscles, and the pelvis.

If you create separate body parts in a hierarchy, then you may think that the chest would be a good root parent object, but actually the pelvis is the best parent object for a human character. The reason behind this choice is that the body can bend at the hips, and with the pelvis as the root parent, both the abdomen and legs can bend about their parent.

After you create the box object, move the box vertices to set the width for the shoulders, the stomach, and the hips, and gradually meet at a point at the bottom of the pelvis.

Follow these steps to create a torso object in Maya:

1. **Choose the Create ⇨ Polygon Primitives ⇨ Cube ⇨ Options menu command to open the Polygon Cube Options dialog box.**

   The Options menu is a small dialog box icon to the right of the menu. The Polygon Cube Options dialog box opens and includes settings for the cube dimensions and the number of subdivisions along each axis.

2. **Select the Edit ⇨ Reset Settings menu command in the Polygon Cube Options dialog box.**

   This menu command resets all the option settings to their default values, which is a simple cube with one segment per axis.

3. **Set the Height value to 3, the Segments along Height to 4, and click the Create button.**

   Because I'm modeling only half the torso, the width and depth values can be equal and the four segments can be used to create profiles for the shoulders, ribs, stomach, and pelvis.

**4. Press the spacebar to switch to a four view workspace.**

To move the components, you want to see the torso object from the side and top views.

**5. In the toolbar at the top of the interface, choose the Select by Component Type button.**

In component mode, you can select and move all the vertices that are shown.

**6. Drag over the top-right two sets of vertices, and move them to the right in the Front view. Then drag the bottom-right set of vertices in the Front view to the left.**

Moving the top-right set of vertices makes a nice shoulder where the left arm can be connected. Dragging the bottom-right vertices to the left makes a pelvis where the left leg can be connected. The middle two sections represent the rib cage and the stomach, as shown in Figure 9-1.

Note that only the vertices on the right side of the object are moved, because I'll later mirror the torso about its center.

**7. Select the File ⇨ Save Scene As menu command, and save the file as Box torso.mb. Close the file when you are finished.**

All the examples in this chapter build from the preceding one. By saving the file at the end of each example, you can continue the next example where this one left off.

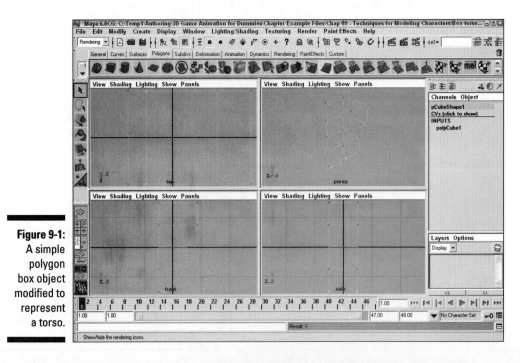

**Figure 9-1:**
A simple polygon box object modified to represent a torso.

# Chamfering edges

Unless you want a boxy character, you can smooth the torso box along the vertical edges of the box using the Bevel command. Chamfering the box edges replaces the edges with a face that is a rounder shape. The goal isn't to make the surface perfectly smooth at this point, only to rough out the general shape.

Follow these steps to chamfer the edges of a torso object in Maya:

1. **Choose File ⇨ Open Scene and open the Box torso.mb file.**

   The Box torso file is the one from the preceding example.

2. **In the toolbar at the top of the interface, choose the Select by Component Type button. Then right-click in the view, and select the Edge component mode.**

   By selecting the edge component mode, you can select edges to apply commands to.

3. **With the Select tool, drag over the entire right side of the torso object to select all the exterior edges in the Front view. Then hold down the Ctrl key and deselect the interior edges.**

   The Ctrl key allows you to remove items from the current selection, and the Shift key lets you add items to the current selection. Now all edges around the outside of the torso should be selected except for those on the left side, which represents the mid-line of the torso.

4. **Select the Edit Polygons ⇨ Bevel ⇨ Options menu command. In the Polygon Bevel Options dialog box, set the Offset Distance value to 2.0, the Segments to 2, and click the Bevel button.**

   The Bevel command replaces all selected edges with two face segments that start at a distance of 1.0 from the original edge. The result is a smoother torso around the exterior of the object, as shown in Figure 9-2. All the modeling commands are found in the Modeling menu set.

5. **Select the File ⇨ Save Scene As menu command and save the file as Beveled torso.mb. Close the file when you are finished.**

   All the examples in this chapter build from the preceding one. By saving the file at the end of each example, you can continue the next example where this one left off.

# Sculpting muscles

Many 3D software packages include a mode where you can raise or lower a surface using a Sculpt tool, but before you can use this tool, you need to add sufficient polygons to make the surface smooth. Polygons can be added to an area using a subdivide feature.

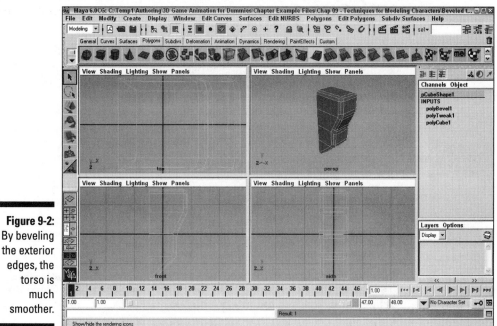

Figure 9-2:
By beveling
the exterior
edges, the
torso is
much
smoother.

### Subdividing polygons

When subdividing a polygon, you may need to apply the Subdivide command several times in order to get a sufficient number of polygons to show the sculpted area.

Most Subdivide commands subdivide the entire object instead of just the face, which adds unneeded polygons to the model. For example, to create smooth pectoral muscles in the chest area, you need to subdivide the polygons in front of the box. But if the Subdivide command is applied to the entire object, then the back is also subdivided, adding polygons to an otherwise flat area.

Follow these steps to subdivide the chest area polygons:

1. **Choose File ⇨ Open Scene and open the Beveled torso.mb file.**

   The Beveled torso file is the one from the preceding example.

2. **In the toolbar at the top of the interface, choose the Select by Component Type button. Then right-click in the view on the object and select the Face component mode.**

   Using the face component mode, you can select polygon faces to apply commands to.

3. **With the Select tool, drag over the two polygon faces in the Front view in the chest region. Then press and hold the Ctrl key, and deselect the selected polygons at the top of the Top view.**

   When the two faces are selected in the Front view, four polygons are actually selected — two in the front of the object and two in the back. By deselecting the top two polygons in the Top view, you're removing the selected polygons on the back side of the torso.

4. **Select the Edit Polygons ⇨ Subdivide menu command. Select the same command a second time to subdivide the selected polygons a second time.**

   When the Subdivide command is applied the first time, each of the selected polygon faces is divided into several additional faces, but it isn't quite enough, so the command needs to be applied a second time, as shown in Figure 9-3.

5. **Select the File ⇨ Save Scene As menu command and save the file as Subdivided chest.mb. Close this file when you are finished.**

   All the examples in this chapter build from the preceding one. By saving the file at the end of each example, you can continue the next example where this one left off.

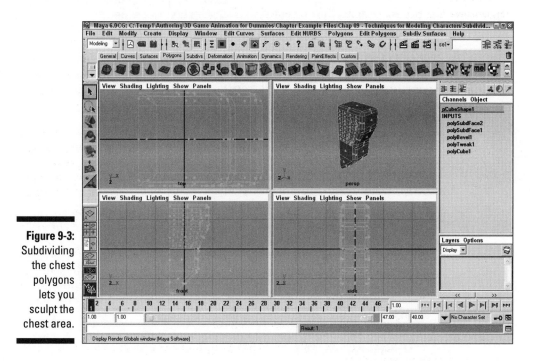

**Figure 9-3:**
Subdividing the chest polygons lets you sculpt the chest area.

### *Using the Sculpt tool*

Sculpt tools typically use brushes that you can define, but the critical setting is the size of the brush. It is best to set the brush much smaller than the actual area you want to increase and use the falloff setting to let the adjacent polygons flow to the raised ones. This results in a smoother overall surface rather than an abrupt one.

The general areas where you need to concentrate on sculpting in the torso region include the pectoral muscles, the shoulders, and the stomach muscles.

Follow these steps to sculpt the chest muscles in Maya:

1. **Choose File ➪ Open Scene, and open the Subdivided chest.mb file.**

   The Subdivided chest file is the file one from the preceding example.

2. **In the toolbar at the top of the interface, choose the Select by Object Type button.**

   The Sculpt tool requires you to be in Object mode and not in component mode.

3. **Right-click the Perspective view to make it the active view, and then press the spacebar to switch to a single view workspace.**

   It is easier to sculpt in the Perspective view if it is larger.

4. **Select the Edit Polygons ➪ Sculpt Polygons Tool menu command. Select the Window ➪ Settings/Preferences ➪ Tool Settings menu command to open the Tool Settings panel.**

   The Tool Settings panel opens to the right of the view pane and displays all the settings for the Sculpt Polygons tool.

5. **In the Tool Settings panel, set the Radius (U) to 0.5, select the Gaussian Brush and the Pull Operation option, and set the Maximum Displacement value to 0.1. Then drag over the chest area to raise the muscles from the surface.**

   The Radius value lets you set the size of the brush. As you change the brush size, a circular icon appears in the view as you move the cursor over the object. The circular icon gives you an idea of how large the sculpt tool is. The Gaussian Brush moves the center of the sculpted area the designated displacement value and all adjacent polygons to a lesser extent. The Pull operation is used to raise the polygons from the surface, as shown in Figure 9-4. An arrow on the Sculpt tool icon shows the direction in which the polygons will move.

6. **Select the File ➪ Save Scene As menu command and save the file as Chest muscle.mb. Close this file when you are finished.**

   All the examples in this chapter build from the preceding one. By saving the file at the end of each example, you can continue the next example where this one left off.

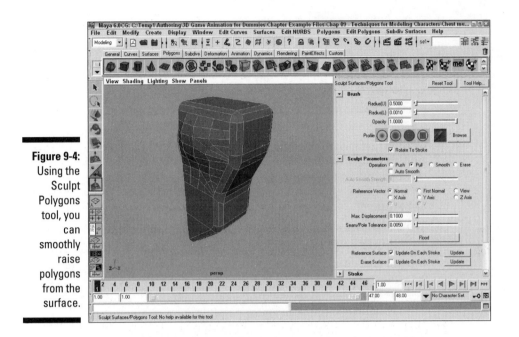

**Figure 9-4:**
Using the
Sculpt
Polygons
tool, you
can
smoothly
raise
polygons
from the
surface.

## Cutting limb holes

In order to attach the limbs to the torso in a manner that is seamless, you need to create some holes in the areas where the limbs will be attached, including holes in the pelvis for the legs and holes in the shoulders for the arms. These holes should go right up to the edge of the box so a lip left on the box doesn't cause the limb to be indented.

You also need to create a hole where you can attach the neck, but this can be done after the body is mirrored, later in this chapter.

Follow these steps to cut limb holes in Maya:

1. **Choose File ➪ Open Scene and open the Chest muscle.mb file.**

   The Chest muscle file is the one from the preceding example.

2. **In the toolbar at the top of the interface, choose the Select by Component Type button. Then right-click in the view, and select the Face component mode.**

   By selecting the face component mode, you can select polygon faces to apply commands to.

3. **Press the spacebar to switch to a four-view workspace.**

   To move the components, you want to see the torso object from the side and top views.

4. **In the Side view, select the top large polygon with the Select tool where the shoulder is located.**

   The polygon is highlighted in the view pane.

5. **Select the Edit Polygons ⇨ Cut Faces Tool menu command. Then click in the upper-left corner near the corner of the selected polygon a small distance from the corner, and drag to rotate the Cut tool until it's positioned to cut off the corner of the polygon.**

   By selecting the polygon face before using the Cut Faces tool, the cuts are limited to the selected polygon face. The Cut Faces tool works when you click where the center of the cut plane is located, drag to rotate the cut plane, and click again to make the cut. This divides the polygon into two polygons.

6. **Repeat Steps 4 and 5 until a cut is made near each corner of the shoulder's polygon face.**

   With all four cuts made, the rectangular face should now include an octagon-shaped polygon face. The goal is to make a cut near each corner of the polygon face to create an octagon shape that is closer to a circular limb than the current rectangle.

7. **Repeat Steps 4 through 6 for the rectangular polygon at the bottom of the Side view where the pelvis is located.**

   You need to cut holes for the arm limbs and the leg limbs.

8. **Select the Edit Polygons ⇨ Make Hole Tool menu command. Then click the center of the octagonal polygon face twice for the shoulder polygon to select both sides, and press the Delete key to create the hole. Then repeat for the leg hole.**

   By removing the cut polygon faces, you have a place where the limbs can be attached. If you rotate the object in the Perspective view with the Smooth Shading enabled, the holes become apparent, as shown in Figure 9-5.

9. **Select the File ⇨ Save Scene As menu command and save the file as Limb holes.mb. Close this file when you are finished.**

   All the examples in this chapter build from the preceding one. By saving the file at the end of each example, you can continue the next example where this one left off.

# Creating and Attaching Limbs

Arms and legs can be created using simple cylinder objects separated into six segments. These segments can be used to deform the arms into thigh, bicep, lower leg, and lower arm sections with an extra row of polygons for elbows and knees.

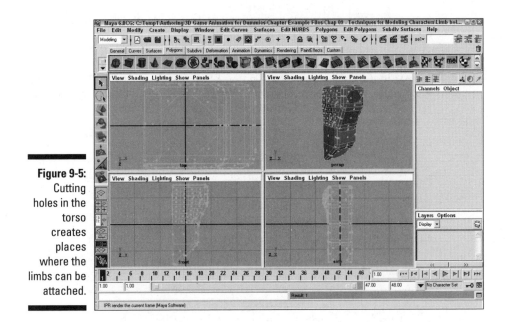

**Figure 9-5:**
Cutting
holes in the
torso
creates
places
where the
limbs can be
attached.

The length of the arms should stretch from the shoulder to about the hip, or a little less than the torso's length; the legs should be a little more than the length of the torso with a greater radius value. Be sure to leave a little room for a row of polygons used to connect the limbs to the hands and feet.

Follow these steps to create limb objects in Maya:

1. **Choose File ➪ Open Scene, and open the Limb holes.mb file.**

   The Limb holes file is the on from the preceding example.

2. **Choose the Create ➪ Polygon Primitives ➪ Cylinder ➪ Options menu command to open the Polygon Cylinder Options dialog box.**

   The Polygon Cylinder Options dialog box opens and includes settings for the cylinder dimensions and the number of subdivisions along each axis.

3. **Select the Edit ➪ Reset Settings menu command in the Options dialog box.**

   This menu command resets all the option settings to their default values, which is a simple cylinder.

4. **Set the Radius value to 0.25, the Height value to 2.5, the Subdivisions Around Axis to 8, and the Subdivisions Along Height to 3. Select the X-axis and click the Create button.**

   This creates a simple cylinder that is as long as the torso with an equal number of polygon divisions to match the torso hole. Creating the cylinder along the X-axis positions the arm to extend straight out from the body.

5. **Select the Move tool, and move the cylinder in the Front view until it is positioned to the right of the torso.**

   The cylinder is in position and ready to be attached to the torso.

6. **Repeat Steps 2 through 5 to create a second cylinder for the leg. In the Polygon Cylinder Options dialog box, set the Radius value to 0.35, the Height to 3.5, and enable the Y-axis option.**

   After moving the leg cylinder into place, you need to use the Rotate tool to slightly align the leg with its hole, as shown in Figure 9-6.

7. **Select the File ⇨ Save Scene As menu command and save the file as Limb cylinders.mb. Close this file when you are finished.**

   This file includes the torso, the arm limb, and the leg limb.

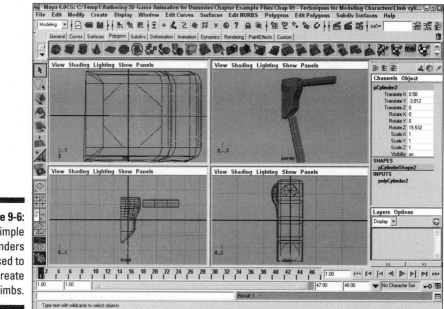

**Figure 9-6:**
Simple cylinders are used to create limbs.

## Tapering limbs

Before moving vertices to create actual limb muscles, you can taper the entire limb to gradually reduce the cross section of the limb.

Follow these steps to taper the limb objects in Maya:

1. **Choose File ⇨ Open Scene and open the Limb cylinders.mb file.**

   The Limb cylinders file is the one from the preceding example.

2. **Select the arm cylinder. In the toolbar at the top of the interface, choose the Select by Component Type button. Then right-click in the view, and select the vertex component mode.**

   By selecting the Vertex component mode, you can select vertices to apply commands to.

3. **With the Select tool, drag over the left middle row of vertices in the Front view, and move them to where the center of the bicep is located. Then repeat for the right middle row and position it for the elbow.**

   By positioning the two middle rows of vertices, you can define the portions of the cylinder that are to be used for the upper and lower arm segments.

4. **Select the right two rows of vertices, and scale them down using the Scale tool. Select the rightmost row of vertices, and scale it down even further. Then select the row of vertices in the center of the bicep, and scale it upward.**

   These scale transforms give the arm limb some shape.

5. **Repeat Steps 3 and 4 for the leg object.**

   The leg needs to be tapered just like the arm, but the calf is a better place to show a bulge than the thigh, as shown in Figure 9-7.

6. **Select the File ⇨ Save Scene As menu command and save the file as Tapered limbs.mb. Close this file when you are finished.**

   This file includes tapered limbs.

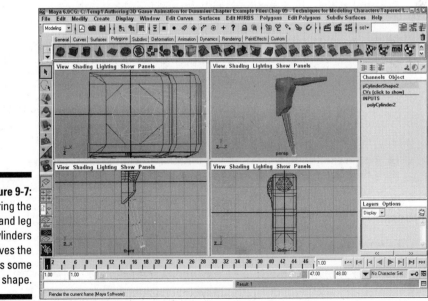

**Figure 9-7:** Tapering the arm and leg cylinders gives the limbs some shape.

## Lofting limbs

Another way to construct limbs is to create and position the cross-section shapes for each limb change and then loft between these cross sections to create the limb.

When creating the loft cross sections, keep the number of points that make the cross section to a minimum. If the cross section shapes include 24 points, then each section of the loft includes at least 24 polygons.

## Connecting limbs

After the limb is created, you need to position it into place. You can connect the limbs to the torso by welding vertices between the limb and the torso. Welding vertices ensures that the connected polygons are joined and smoothed across the polygon faces.

Follow these steps to connect the limbs to the torso in Maya:

1. **Choose File ⇨ Open Scene and open the Tapered limbs.mb file.**

   The Tapered limbs file is the one from the preceding example.

2. **In Object mode, select the arm, leg, and torso objects, and then choose the Polygons ⇨ Combine menu command.**

   Before vertices can be welded, the objects need to be part of the same object. The Combine command can combine separate objects into a single object.

3. **In the toolbar at the top of the interface, choose the Select by Component Type button. Right-click in the view, and select the Face component mode. Then select and delete the face polygons that make up the end of each limb.**

   In order to attach the limbs without trapping some polygons within the joint, you need to create another hole at the end of each limb. This can be done by simply selecting the faces and pressing the Delete key.

4. **In the toolbar at the top of the interface, choose the Select by Component Type button if necessary. Then right-click in the view, and select the Vertex component mode.**

   By selecting the Vertex component mode, you can select vertices to apply commands to.

5. **Near the joint between the arm and the shoulder, select two matching vertices that are near each other on the arm and the torso. Use the Ctrl key to remove any vertices other than the two to be welded together, and select the Edit Polygons ⇨ Merge Vertices menu command.**

   The two selected vertices are combined into one.

6. **Repeat selecting pairs of vertices and combine them with the Edit Polygons ⇨ Merge Vertices menu command for both the arm and leg.**

   After combining all the vertices to connect the arm and the leg to the torso, the arm and leg are no longer separate objects, but permanently attached to the torso, as shown in Figure 9-8.

   In some cases, the vertices may be too far apart to be combined. If this happens, simply select one of the vertices and move it closer before trying the Weld command. If a different number of vertices exists on the limb and the torso, then simply connect two vertices to one.

7. **Select the File ⇨ Save Scene As menu command and save the file as Attached limbs.mb. Close the file when you are finished.**

   This file includes the attached limbs.

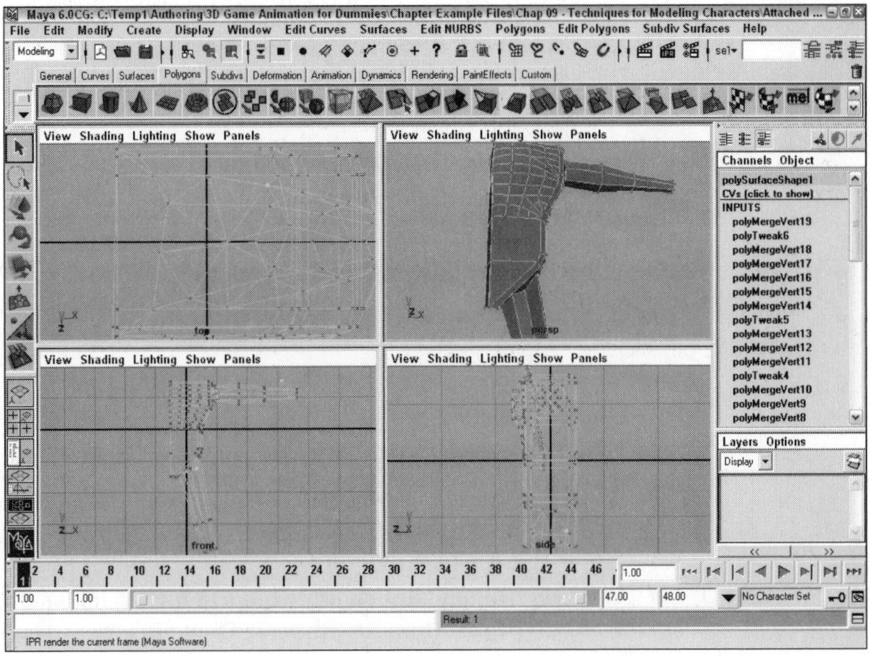

**Figure 9-8:** Attaching the arm and leg cylinders is accomplished by welding vertices together.

## Bridging limbs

Another way to connect limbs to the torso is with the Bridge command. This feature builds connecting polygons between two facing polygon holes. This same method of attaching limbs can be applied to connect hands, feet, and the head.

# Modeling Hands and Feet

No single part of the character has more polygons (except maybe the head) than the hands if you choose to model them. If you can get away with body armor that doesn't show the fingers, or create an alien character with only three fingers, then you can limit the number of polygons and avoid a headache.

## Extruding fingers

A simple hand can be created by dividing a rectangular box widthwise into seven separate segments. By selecting and extruding every other widthwise segment, you can create individual fingers. The length of each finger can then be changed by dragging the vertices at the end each finger.

Follow these steps to create the fingers of a hand object in Maya:

1. **Choose File ⇨ Open Scene and open the Attached limbs.mb file.**

   The Attached limbs file is the one from the preceding example.

2. **Choose the Create ⇨ Polygon Primitives ⇨ Cube ⇨ Options menu command to open the Polygon Cube Options dialog box.**

   The Polygon Cube Options dialog box opens and includes settings for the cube dimensions and the number of subdivisions along each axis.

3. **Select the Edit ⇨ Reset Settings menu command in the Options dialog box.**

   This menu command resets all the option settings to their default values, which is a simple cube with one segment per axis.

4. **Set the Width, Height, and Depth values to 0.25, 0.05, and 0.25, and set the Subdivisions Along Depth to 7. Then click the Create button.**

   The new box object is placed in the middle of the scene.

5. **Select and move the new object to the right end of the arm object.**

   Position the hand object near the end of the object and pan the view to see the hand object up close.

6. **In the toolbar at the top of the interface, choose the Select by Component Type button. Right-click in the view pane, and select the Face option.**

   In component mode, you can select and move all the polygon face components that are shown.

7. **Select every other polygon face in the Side view, and then hold down the Ctrl key and remove the opposite end polygons in the Top view. Then select the Edit Polygons ⇨ Extrude Face menu command.**

   The Extrude Face command makes an interactive icon appear in the view pane. Drag the interactive icon in the Top view to extend the fingers.

8. **While still in Face component mode, select the polygon face at the end of each finger and drag each to the left in the Top view to shorten the fingers appropriately, as shown in Figure 9-9.**

   Shortening the fingers is a simple detail that adds to the realism of the hand without adding any new polygons. Note also that each finger has been shorted a different length.

9. **Select the File ⇨ Save Scene As menu command and save the file as Simple fingers.mb. Close the file when you are finished.**

   This file includes some fingers extended from the end of a hand object.

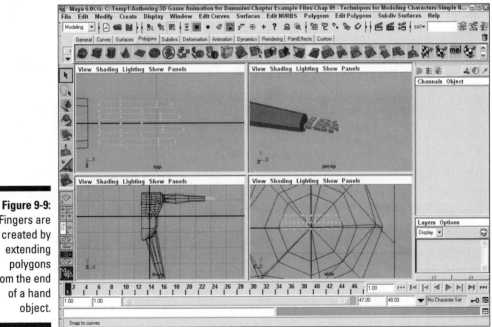

**Figure 9-9:**
Fingers are created by extending polygons from the end of a hand object.

## Adding a thumb

After you've created a hand with fingers, you can add the thumb using another box object. Cut a hole in the side of the hand object and weld the vertices. Be sure to divide the thumb box into two segments to create a thumb joint. The thumb should also be angled downward, away from the fingers. Attach the thumb so it is pointing forward, away from the body.

Follow these steps to create the fingers of a hand object in Maya:

1. **Choose File ⇨ Open Scene and open the Simple fingers.mb file.**

   The Simple fingers file is the one from the preceding example.

2. **Choose the Create ⇨ Polygon Primitives ⇨ Cube ⇨ Options menu command to open the Polygon Cube Options dialog box.**

   The Polygon Cube Options dialog box opens and includes settings for the cube dimensions and the number of subdivisions along each axis.

3. **Select the Edit ⇨ Reset Settings menu command in the Options dialog box.**

   This menu command resets all the option settings to their default values, which is a simple cube with one segment per axis.

4. **Set the Width, Height, and Depth values to 0.25, 0.05, and 0.1, and click the Create button.**

   The new box object is placed in the middle of the scene.

5. **Select and move the object to be near the hand object. Then rotate the thumb so it is pointing at an angle away from the hand.**

6. **In the toolbar at the top of the interface, choose the Select by Component Type button. Right-click in the view pane, and select the Face option. Cut the polygon on the side of the hand with the Edit Polygons ⇨ Cut Faces Tool menu command. Then delete the cut face and the end of the thumb object.**

   In component mode, you can select the polygon that you want to cut with the Cut Faces tool to limit the cuts to that polygon. Then select and delete the cut polygon and the end of the thumb object.

7. **In Object mode, select the thumb object and the hand object and use the Polygons ⇨ Combine menu command to combine the two objects into one.**

   In order to weld vertices together, the vertices must be part of the same object.

8. **Enable component mode again and select the Vertex mode. Then select and weld pairs of vertices to attach the thumb to the hand with the Edit Polygons ⇨ Merge Vertices menu command.**

   By welding vertices together, the thumb becomes a permanent part of the hand object and moves with the hand object.

9. **While still in Vertex component mode, select the vertices at the end of the thumb object and move them to size the thumb appropriately.**

   After reordering the thumb vertices, the thumb looks correct, as shown in Figure 9-10.

10. **Select the File ⇨ Save Scene As menu command and save the file as Hand with thumb.mb. Close the file when you are finished.**

    This file includes a hand with a thumb.

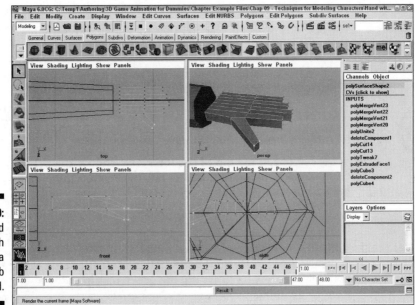

**Figure 9-10:**
The hand looks much better with a thumb attached.

## Modeling shoes

Most of the time, you'll model shoes rather than feet. Naked feet seem to be the exception rather than the norm. Shoes with buckles are also easier to model than laces, but shoelaces can be added to a texture map.

Follow these steps to create character shoes in Maya:

1. **Choose File ⇨ Open Scene, and open the Hand with thumb.mb file.**

   The Hand with thumb file is the one from the preceding example.

2. **Choose the Create ⇨ Polygon Primitives ⇨ Cube ⇨ Options menu command to open the Polygon Cube Options dialog box.**

   The Polygon Cube Options dialog box opens and includes settings for the cube dimensions and the number of subdivisions along each axis.

3. **Select the Edit ⇨ Reset Settings menu command in the Options dialog box.**

   This menu command resets all the option settings to their default values, which is a simple cube with one segment per axis.

4. **Set the Width, Height, and Depth values to 0.25, 0.25, and 0.75, and set the Subdivisions Along Depth to 3. Then click the Create button.**

   The new box object is placed in the middle of the scene.

5. **Select and move the new object to the end of the leg object.**

   Position the foot object near the end of the leg object, and pan the view to see the foot object up close.

   The foot can be out of proportion with the rest of the body at this point. The important thing is to make the foot about the same size as the end of the leg in order to easily connect the two parts.

6. **In the toolbar at the top of the interface, choose the Select by Component Type button. Right-click in the view pane, and select the Vertex option.**

   In component mode, you can select and move all the vertex components that are shown.

7. **Select the four bottom vertices in the Top view, and scale them to make the front of the foot wider. Then scale the same vertices down in the Front view by dragging the green manipulator to flatten the front of the foot.**

   Widening and flattening the foot gives it a wider base for holding up the character.

8. **With the Move tool, drag the scaled vertices downward in the Side view until all foot vertices for the bottom of the foot are level, as shown in Figure 9-11.**

   Shortening the fingers is a simple detail that adds to the realism of the hand without adding any new polygons.

9. **Select the File ⇨ Save Scene As menu command and save the file as One foot.mb. Close the file when you are finished.**

   This file includes a single foot object created from a polygon cube.

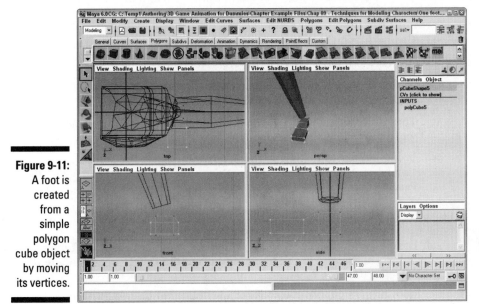

**Figure 9-11:**
A foot is created from a simple polygon cube object by moving its vertices.

## Creating toes

Toes are rarely created as part of a character thanks to shoes and boots, but if you need to create them, they can be created in the same manner as fingers, only smaller and without any joints. Also, make sure the large toe is much larger in size than the other toes.

## Adding nails

If you're adding fingernails and toenails to your character, then you're working with a high-resolution model. Fingernails are typically added using a texture map, but they can also be modeled by indenting the last finger polygon.

In some cases, you'll want to model just the hands (such as the first person view of a hand holding a weapon such as the Quake games), so the details of the hands including fingernails may be necessary.

## Connecting hands and feet

Hands and feet can be added to the end of the limbs using the same technique to attach the limbs to the body, but you may be dealing with a different number of vertices between the two ends, so you may need to create some triangular polygons to match two vertices to one.

Follow these steps to connect the hand to the arm and the foot to the leg in Maya:

1. **Choose File ⇨ Open Scene and open the One foot.mb file.**

   The One foot file is the one from the preceding example.

2. **Switch to Object mode, and combine the hand object with the body object using the Polygons ⇨ Combine menu command.**

   The two separate objects are combined so that the vertices can be welded.

3. **In the toolbar at the top of the interface, choose the Select by Component Type button. Right-click in the view pane, and select the Face option.**

   In component mode, you can select and move all the face components that are shown.

4. **Drag over all the face objects at the end of the arm and the face objects at the end of the hand. and press the Delete key to delete the selected polygon faces.**

   By deleting these polygons faces, you create holes in each of the objects. By creating these holes, the end polygons don't get trapped within the arm when the vertices are welded.

5. **In Component mode, select the row of vertices at the end of the arm and scale them in the Y-axis direction to flatten them in the Side view.**

   When you flatten the height of the arm cylinder at the end near the hand, the vertices better align with the hand vertices.

6. **In the toolbar at the top of the interface, choose the Select by Component Type button. Then right-click in the view and select the Vertex component mode.**

   By selecting the Vertex component mode, you can select vertices to apply commands to.

7. **Near the joint between the arm and the hand, select two matching vertices that are near each other on the arm and the hand. Use the Ctrl key to remove any vertices other than the two to be welded together and select the Edit Polygons ⇨ Merge Vertices menu command.**

   The two selected vertices are combined into one. You may often need to combine two or move vertices on the hand object with one vertex on the arm object.

8. **Repeat selecting pairs of vertices and combining them with the Edit Polygons ⇨ Merge Vertices menu command.**

   After combining all the vertices connect the arm and hand, as shown in Figure 9-12.

TIP

After welding all the vertices together, you can rotate about the attached body parts in the Perspective view to check for gaps. In the shaded view, gaps show up clearly.

9. **Repeat these steps for the foot object, remembering to first create holes by deleting polygons at the end of the leg and at the top of the foot.**

10. **Select the File ⇨ Save Scene As menu command and save the file as Attached hand and foot.mb. Close the file when you are finished.**

   This file includes an attached hand and foot.

**Figure 9-12:** Attaching the hand and foot is accomplished by welding vertices together.

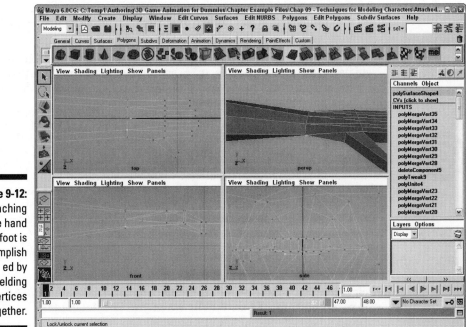

# Mirroring the Body

If you've modeled half the body with attached limbs, hand, and foot, you can create the opposite half of the body using the mirror feature. This creates a perfectly symmetrical body. Be sure to weld the vertices that line up along the center line of the body.

Even though the head is also symmetrical, I recommend that you mirror the body independent of the head. You'll also find that keeping a copy of the body separate from its head makes it easy to create another character quickly by simply changing the character's head.

After mirroring the body, you need to cut a hole in the top of the torso where the neck and head can be connected.

Follow these steps to mirror the body in Maya:

1. **Choose File ⇨ Open Scene and open the Attached hand and foot.mb file.**

   The Attached hand and foot file is the one from the preceding example.

2. **In the toolbar at the top of the interface, choose the Select by Component Type button. Then right-click in the view and select the Vertex component mode. Select and move all vertices that cross the midline to the left of the midline in the Top view.**

   When mirroring the body, the leftmost point is used as the point about which the mirror takes place. If a point is beyond the midline, then a gap exists along the midline. When I sculpted the chest muscles, some of the vertices got pushed past the midline.

   If any vertices weren't positioned on the midline during the Mirror command, a gap is created, but you can eliminate these gaps using the Edit Polygons ⇨ Weld Vertices command to weld together vertices on either side of the gap.

3. **Switch to Object mode, and choose the Polygons ⇨ Mirror Geometry ⇨ Options menu command. In the Mirror Options dialog box, select the –X option, the Merge With the Original option, and the Merge Vertices option. Then click the Mirror button.**

   A new half of the body is created and attached to the existing half, as shown in Figure 9-13.

4. **Select the File ⇨ Save Scene As menu command, and save the file as Mirrored body.mb. Close the file when you are finished.**

   This file includes a mirrored body.

# Making the Body Proportional

When you build the body piece by piece, chances are good that the various body parts are disproportional to one another, such as a huge torso with large hands and tiny feet. After the entire body is together, you may need to select and scale certain parts.

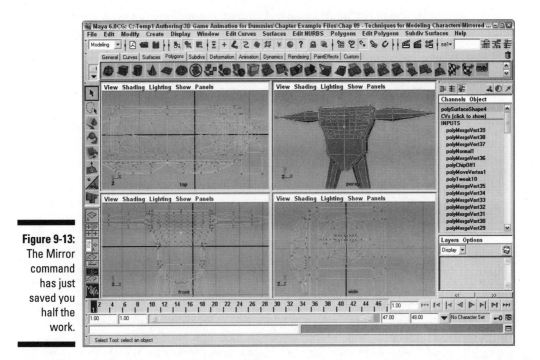

**Figure 9-13:**
The Mirror command has just saved you half the work.

Scaling body parts provides a great opportunity to endow your character with personality. You can make the character tall or broad, with big feet or small hands.

The easiest way to scale individual parts is to select together all the vertices that make up a body part and then move the body part back into place.

Follow these steps to scale the various body parts in Maya:

1. **Choose File ⇨ Open Scene and open the Mirrored body.mb file.**

   The Mirrored body file is the one from the preceding example.

2. **In the toolbar at the top of the interface, choose the Select by Component Type button. Then right-click in the view, and select the Vertex component mode.**

   In Vertex component mode, you can drag over all the vertices that make up a particular body part.

3. **Press and hold the Shift key, select all the vertices that make up one of the hands, and scale them up to better match the body size. Move the scaled hand closer to the body. Then repeat this step for the opposite hand.**

Scaling each hand independently can result in hands that are different sizes, but you can do this so that the hands aren't moved farther from the body center.

4. **Repeat Steps 1 through 3 to scale the feet.**

Scaling the feet gives the character a bigger base to stand on, as shown in Figure 9-14.

5. **Select the File ⇨ Save Scene As menu command, and save the file as Scaled hands and feet.mb. Close the file when you are finished.**

This file includes a complete body with larger hands and feet.

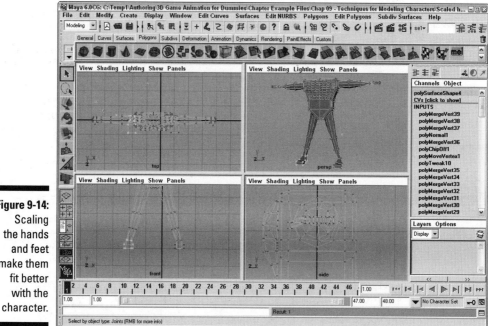

**Figure 9-14:** Scaling the hands and feet make them fit better with the character.

# Getting "Ahead": Creating a Head

The head is the key element of the character and is viewed more than any other body part, so it needs some attention to make it look right.

Heads can be started from a sphere or a cylinder, and although heads are symmetrical, it is best to model head objects as a whole to add some imperfections that give it character.

Follow these steps to create a head shape in Maya:

1. **Choose File ⇨ Open Scene and open the Scaled hands and feet.mb file.**

   The Scaled hands and feet file is the one from the preceding example.

2. **Choose the Create ⇨ Polygon Primitives ⇨ Cube ⇨ Options menu command to open the Polygon Cube Options dialog box.**

   The Polygon Cube Options dialog box opens and includes settings for the cube dimensions and the number of subdivisions along each axis.

3. **Select the Edit ⇨ Reset Settings menu command in the Options dialog box.**

   This menu command resets all the option settings to their default values, which is a simple cube with one segment per axis.

4. **Set the Width, Height and Depth values to 1.0, 1.5, and 1.0, and set the Subdivisions Along Width, Height, and Depth to 9, 9, and 3. Then click the Create button.**

   The new box object is placed in the middle of the scene. The head is scaled to fit the body. The subdivisions provide some resolution for creating the different head features.

5. **Select and move the new box object to the top of the body.**

   Position the head object centered at the top of the body.

6. **With the head selected, choose Display ⇨ Hide ⇨ Hide Unselected.**

   All objects are hidden except for the head object. Hiding objects keeps them in the current file, but doesn't display them. This lets you focus on the object at hand, which is essential for working with the head in the rest of this section.

7. **Select the File ⇨ Save Scene As menu command, and save the file as Box head.mb. Close the file when you are finished.**

   This file includes a hidden body and a box to use for the head.

## Extruding a neck

A neck can be created at the bottom of the head object by extruding the polygons at the bottom of the head object. Remember that the head needs to be attached to the rest of the body by welding vertices or by using a Bridge command.

## Using Booleans

Another way to add a neck to a head object is with a Boolean command. Boolean commands work on two overlapping objects and can be used to combine the two objects (called a Boolean Union command), subtract one object from another, or find just the intersecting portions of the two objects.

The resulting operation eliminates the original two objects and all internal polygons.

Booleans can also work in certain cases for attaching limbs, and limbs combined as Booleans don't need to be attached by welding vertices.

A Boolean works well for creating a neck object because the neck is round and can be made from a cylinder primitive object.

Follow these steps to create a neck using a Boolean Union operation in Maya:

1. **Choose File ⇨ Open Scene and open the Box head.mb file.**

    The Box head file is the one from the preceding example.

2. **Choose the Create ⇨ Polygon Primitives ⇨ Cylinder ⇨ Options menu command to open the Polygon Cylinder Options dialog box.**

    The Polygon Cylinder Options dialog box opens and includes settings for the cube dimensions and the number of subdivisions along each axis.

3. **Select the Edit ⇨ Reset Settings menu command in the Options dialog box.**

    This menu command resets all the option settings to their default values, which is a simple cube with one segment per axis.

4. **Set the Radius and Height values to 0.4, 0.5, and 0.75, the Subdivisions Around Axis to 12, and select the Y Axis option. Then click the Create button.**

    The new cylinder object is placed in the middle of the scene.

5. **Select and move the new cylinder object so it is positioned below but overlapping the bottom of the head object. Then move the cylinder up in the top view until the edge of the cylinder is aligned with the edge of the box.**

    This alignment causes the back of the neck to be aligned with the back of the head. It also creates a chin that sticks out at the front of the head.

6. **Drag over both objects with the Select tool, and choose the Polygons ⇨ Boolean ⇨ Union menu command.**

    The Boolean Union command combines the two objects into one and eliminates all the internal polygons, as shown in Figure 9-15.

7. **Select the File ⇨ Save Scene As menu command, and save the file as Added neck.mb. Close the file when you are finished.**

   This file includes a head object with an attached neck.

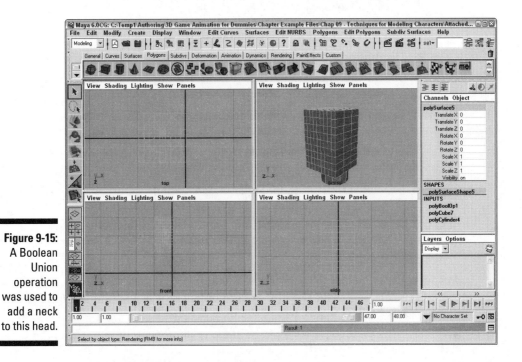

**Figure 9-15:**
A Boolean Union operation was used to add a neck to this head.

# Modeling the windows to the soul: Creating eyes

Of all the face features, the eyes seem to be the one element that gives the character life. If the eyes are missing or modeled incorrectly, the whole character seems lifeless. Keep this in mind if you ever need to model a zombie character.

There are two common approaches to modeling eyes. The first is to cut a slit in the front of the face and pull the connected polygons forward to form eyelids. The easiest way to cut a slit is to use the Break Vertices command, which places a separate vertex for each polygon that meets at the corner. These vertices can then be moved to reveal the slit underneath. The eyeball spheres can then be placed within the head. This technique is good if you need a character that does lots of blinking, but it is difficult to align the eyelids exactly without lots of polygons.

Another approach is to indent some polygons within the head to create shallow eye sockets within which the eyeball spheres can be placed. This look is good for cartoon-like characters that have bulging eyes.

Follow these steps to create eyes in Maya:

1. **Choose File ⇨ Open Scene, and open the Added neck.mb file.**

   The Added neck file is the one from the preceding example.

2. **Choose the Create ⇨ Polygon Primitives ⇨ Sphere ⇨ Options menu command to open the Sphere Options dialog box.**

   The Sphere Options dialog box opens and includes settings for the sphere dimensions and the number of subdivisions along each axis.

3. **Select the Edit ⇨ Reset Settings menu command in the Options dialog box.**

   This menu command resets all the option settings to their default values.

4. **Set the Radius value to 0.1, the Subdivisions Along Axis and the Height to 12, and select the Z Axis option. Then click the Create button.**

   The new sphere object is placed in the middle of the scene.

5. **Select and move the new sphere object so it is positioned within the head object where one of the eyes is located.**

   This eye alignment should be sticking out a small distance from the inside of the head.

   Orient the sphere so that the end where all the polygons meet is pointing outward. This orientation makes it easier to color pupils using vertex colors.

6. **Select the box object. In component mode, right-click in the Top view and select the Vertex option. Select two vertices positioned close to where the corners of the eyes are located, and choose the Edit Polygons ⇨ Split Vertex menu command.**

   Each selected vertex is split into four different vertices, each attached to a different polygon.

7. **Select and move the split vertices forward to cover the eyeball sphere on the top and bottom.**

   Move each vertex into position. You may also want to weld back together some vertices that are positioned on top of each other, to maintain continuity.

Moving the split vertices can be tricky because you don't know which vertex is attached to which polygon. Try moving each vertex into the center of a nearby polygon, making the edges visible. You can then align each vertex where it should go.

8. **In Object mode, select the eyeball sphere and choose the Lighting/ Shading ⇨ Assign New Material ⇨ Blinn menu command from the Rendering menu set. In the Attribute Editor that appears, drag the Color slider to the right to make the eyeball sphere white.**

   Materials and textures typically aren't applied during the modeling process, but making this quick color change makes the eyeballs easier to recognize and position.

9. **With the eyeball sphere selected, choose the Edit ⇨ Duplicate menu command to create a copy of the eyeball. Then move the copy to the left in the Front view, and repeat Steps 6 through 8 to create this eyeball's eyelids.**

   Although these steps could be created and mirrored, working without symmetry on the head gives you move control over the individual head parts. With both eyes, the head looks like Figure 9-16.

10. **Select the File ⇨ Save Scene As menu command, and save the file as Added eyes.mb. Close the file when you are finished.**

    This file includes a head object with two added eyes.

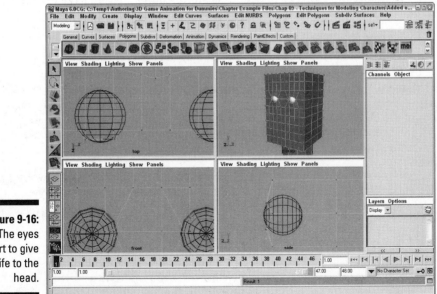

**Figure 9-16:** The eyes start to give life to the head.

### Linking eyes to the head

Eyeballs can be modeled easily using two primitive spheres, but it is important to make them independent of the rest of the body so that they can be moved and rotated independently. Remember to link them to the rest of the character with the head as the parent so they move along with the rest of the body, but they should be a separate object.

The eye's pupil, iris, and blood veins can be mapped onto the eye using a texture.

Follow these steps to link the eyes to the head in Maya:

1. **Choose File ⇨ Open Scene and open the Added eyes.mb file.**

   The Added eyes file is the one from the preceding example.

2. **Select one of the eyeball spheres, hold down the Shift key, and select the head object. Then choose the Edit ⇨ Parent menu command.**

   This makes each eyeball a child to the parent head object. Moving a parent object moves all the children objects with the parent.

   Be sure to select the objects in the correct order. If the head object is selected first, then the head is parented to the eyeball object. You can test the parenting by moving one of the objects. Child objects can move independently without affecting their parents.

3. **Select the File ⇨ Save Scene As menu command and save the file as Linked eyes.mb. Close the file when you are finished.**

   This file includes a head object with two eyes linked to the head.

### Working with pivot points

Each object can have a pivot point, which is the point about which the object is rotated and scaled. Although most pivot points are located in the center of the object when an object is created, they can be located anywhere within the scene. For example, placing the pivot point for the moon at the center of the Earth causes the moon to rotate about the Earth.

Eye pivot points should be located at the center of the eye so the eye remains in position as it is rotated back and forth to represent the eye's movement.

## Creating a nose

Noses, like breasts and chest muscles, can be created with a Sculpt tool or by simply dragging some vertices away from the head object. If you plan on creating nostrils, then either map a pair of black dots onto the nose surface texture or use an Inverted Bevel command to indent the polygons.

Follow these steps to link the eyes to the head in Maya:

1. **Choose File ⇨ Open Scene, and open the Linked eyes.mb file.**

   The Linked eyes file is the one from the preceding example.

2. **In Component mode, right-click in the Front view and select the Vertex option. Then select two adjacent vertices that are beneath and in between the eyes, and move them away from the head.**

   Selecting a single point creates a single point, but two vertices make a broader nose with more character that is easier to sculpt and select.

3. **Select and move the two vertices directly above the ones moved in Step 2, and move them away from the face about half the distance as the first two you moved. Then select the two vertices directly below the first two vertices, and move them outward and upward in the Side view.**

   Moving the top vertices creates a nose bridge in between the eyes; moving the two below makes the nose stick out more, as shown in Figure 9-17.

4. **Select the File ⇨ Save Scene As menu command and save the file as Added nose.mb. Close the file when you are finished.**

   This file includes a head object with two eyes and a nose.

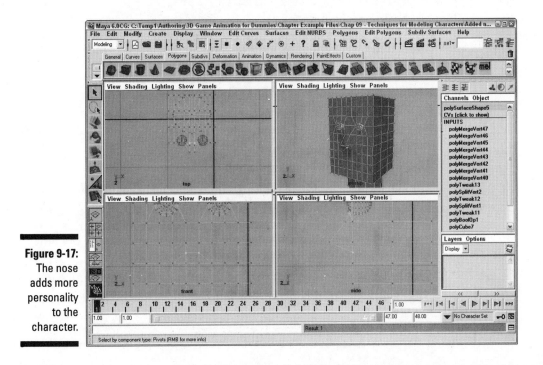

**Figure 9-17:** The nose adds more personality to the character.

# Creating ears

Creating ears with all the polygons it takes to make them look good is often not worth the trouble. Instead, ears can be painted onto the head texture or covered with a hat or hair.

To create ears easily, extrude and flair some polygons on the side of the head and indent the center of the ears. The details are then included as part of the texture map.

# Creating a mouth

The mouth and lips should be modeled initially with the lips closed and without any expression. This is the default expression. Other expressions can be added later, as discussed in Chapter 12.

Although it may seem convenient to create a mouth by simply cutting a hole in the face and placing a black object behind, this can cause problems with any smoothing algorithms that are applied to the object. It is best to indent a portion of the face object to create the mouth interior. A texture map can be used to make the mouth interior dark.

### Adding lips

Lips can be created by beveling and smoothing a row of polygons around the mouth. The lips are one place where extra polygons should be used. By selecting a thin row of polygons to move away from the rest of the mouth, the lips become distinguished from the rest of the face.

Applying a different color (even if it is subtle) to the lips also distinguishes the lips and highlights the mouth.

Follow these steps to create lips in Maya:

1. **Choose File ⇨ Open Scene and open the Added nose.mb file.**

   The Added nose file is the one from the preceding example.

2. **In component mode, right-click in the Front view of the object and select the Face option. Then select a symmetrical row of interior polygons that are below the nose but not to the chin, and choose the Edit Polygons ⇨ Subdivide menu command twice.**

   Each polygon is divided into several additional polygons, and applying the same command a second time creates even more polygons.

3. **Choose the Vertex component mode, and select about seven columns of vertices on one side of the mouth. Scale in the Y-axis downward to pull the vertices closer together. Deselect the inner most column, and scale the remaining vertices a bit further. Continue until the outermost column meets at a point to form the corner of the mouth.**

I'm not trying for a smile or any type of expression, just a plain expressionless face for the default.

4. **Choose the Edge component mode, and select the top and bottom interior rows of edges in the Front view. Pull the edges away from the head in the Side view. Then move the center row of edges inward.**

By moving these edges, you create lips, as shown in Figure 9-18.

5. **Select the File ⇨ Save Scene As menu command and save the file as Added lips.mb. Close the file when you are finished.**

This file includes a head object with a pair of lips.

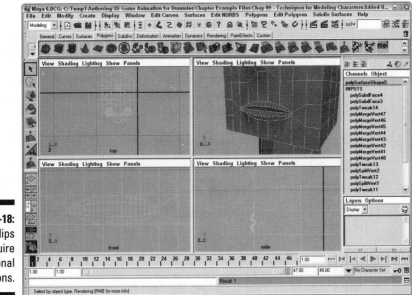

**Figure 9-18:**
The lips require additional polygons.

## Creating teeth

Teeth can consist of simply a row of box objects that are smoothed. The teeth should be separate, like the eyes, from the rest of the character, but linked to the face object. Initially, the teeth aren't visible because the mouth is closed, but as you begin to create phonemes for when the character talks, you need the teeth to be visible.

### Creating a tongue

The tongue, like the teeth, needs to be a separate object and is included with certain expressions as the character talks.

# Adding facial hair

Hair styles are covered later in the chapter, but facial hair is unique. Some 3D programs include hair modeling features that let you grow hair on any selected group of polygons, but using these features requires lots of memory and rendering time.

A better solution is to simply paint the facial hair on the character using a texture map.

# Sculpting the head

At any time during the head modeling task, you can use the Sculpt tools to smooth the rough parts of the head. Be careful how these tools are used, because they can alter the head features that you've worked hard to create.

Follow these steps to sculpt the head in Maya:

1. **Choose File ➪ Open Scene and open the Added lips.mb file.**

   The Added lips file is the one from the preceding example.

2. **Right-click the Perspective view to make it the active view panel and then press the spacebar to switch to a single view.**

   The Perspective view is maximized within the interface, so sculpting the head in this view is easier.

3. **With the head selected, choose the Edit Polygons ➪ Sculpt Polygons Tool menu command. Then choose the Window ➪ Settings/Preferences ➪ Tool Settings menu command to open the Tool Settings panel to the right of the interface.**

   With the Sculpt Polygons tool selected, the Tool Settings panel includes all the controls for the Sculpt tool.

4. **In the Tool Settings panel, set the Brush Radius (U) and (L) to 0.1 and select the Smooth option for the Operation. Then drag over the hard edges in the Perspective view to smooth the head shape.**

   The Smooth option is a good place to start because it can quickly remove the box edges. The best way to use the Sculpt tool is to rotate the view so you're looking directly at an edge and then drag the Sculpt Polygon Tool over the edges.

5. **Continue to rotate the Perspective view, and smooth all the hard edges for the entire head.**

   After some rough sculpting with the Sculpt Polygons tool, the edges are roughly smoothed, as shown in Figure 9-19.

6. **Select the File ⇨ Save Scene As menu command and save the file as Final head.mb. Close the file when you are finished.**

   This file includes a smoothed head object.

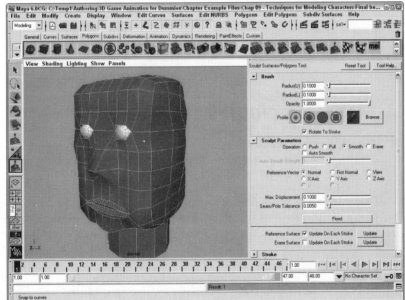

Figure 9-19:
Smoothing
the hard
edges helps
the head to
look more
like a head
and less
like a box.

If you're a little disappointed in the results of the character, keep in mind that these tutorials left out lots of tweaking to keep the number of steps reasonable. You also modeled the character using a minimal number of polygons, and lastly, the character is missing materials and texture maps that add lots of detail.

# Creating Hair

Several 3D software packages include tools for creating beautiful, flowing, dynamic hair one strand at a time. The results are amazing, but the time it takes to compute this type of hair is out of the question for the current set of game engines, not to mention the incredibly high polygon count.

Game character hair instead consists of a simple model that can include pig-tails such as Laura Croft's hairstyle or a limited number of hair strands that are dynamic to show the character's motion.

Another alternative is to create painted hair that gives the artist more control over the hair style, but this lacks the 3D look.

# Adding Accessory Props

After a model is complete, you'll want to add several accessories. These can help further distinguish the character by defining its personality. Good examples of character-related accessories are Mario's lucky red cap, Laura Croft's dual sidearms, and James Bond's black tie.

## Modeling clothes

A well-placed set of clothes can save you from having to model lots of body details like a six-pack set of abdominal muscles, but it can also add polygons for things like shoelaces.

Clothing can be classified as any item that mostly stays permanent with the character throughout the game. The shield that Link (in the Legend of Zelda games) carries doesn't count as clothing because it can be removed and dropped.

Loose-fitting clothes can cause animation problems because it takes some work to make the cloth flow realistically, but tight-fitting clothes require that muscle details be animated.

For permanent clothes, the clothes should be the actual model and not just a covering for the character. By extruding the mesh around the clothing edges, you can simulate clothes that are sufficiently tight on the body so as not to worry about animating cloth, but separated enough from the body to be displayed as clothes.

Texture maps and materials can add lots to the details of the clothes.

# Dressing a head

Using a hat, a helmet, or a head-dress allows you to remove all concerns over hair completely, but keep in mind that these items may be removed during game play, and hair may still need to be displayed.

# Adding jewelry

Jewelry from watches, rings, earrings, and necklaces are useful in certain places and are yet another way to distinguish your characters.

# Embedding weapons and props

Weapons and props are any items that the character can pick up, hold, and use. They need to be designed so that the character looks realistic when holding the object.

One way to match items is to create dummy objects for the hand and for the prop object. *Dummy objects* are non-rendered objects that specify a position in 3D space. These dummy objects can then be positioned so they are aligned when the object matches the character.

For example, you can create a dummy object near the hand of a character that is linked to the character's hand, and a dummy object near the grip of a weapon that is linked to the weapon.

To make the character hold the weapon, simply align the two dummy objects to one another's position and link the weapon's root to the hand's dummy object. This aligns and orients the weapon or prop exactly where it needs to be to make the character carry the weapon. To make the character drop the weapon, break the link between the weapon and the hand.

# Chapter 10

# Discovering the Basics of 3D Animation

· · · · · · · · · · · · · · · · · · · · · · · · · · · · · · · · · · · · · · · · · · · · · · · · ·

## In This Chapter

▶ Setting an animation's pacing and frame rate

▶ Creating keyframe animations

▶ Enabling automatic keyframing

▶ Animating an object moving along a path

▶ Following an object's motion with trajectories

· · · · · · · · · · · · · · · · · · · · · · · · · · · · · · · · · · · · · · · · · · · · · · · · ·

*N*ow that you've finally made to it a chapter on 3D animations, I feel inclined to divulge a tightly held secret. The secret is that 3D animation isn't difficult at all.

What makes 3D animation so easy is that the software knows the exact position of all the objects in the scene. With this information, it can calculate how to move between locations. So, as an animator, you need only to set the beginning and ending points: Let the software worry about all the stuff in between.

The beginning and ending points of an animated object are called keyframes. Keyframe animation is just one type of animation made possible with 3D software. Another type of 3D animation is called path animation, where the object simply follows a curve from beginning to end. Both of these animation types are extremely easy to use and provide a good starting point for your journey.

This chapter explains how to set up an animation sequence, how to animate an object using keyframes, and how to animate an object by making it follow a path. Using these basic animation techniques will enable you to create animations of a character's special jump-flip escape move, an enemy's two-fisted lightning blast attack, or props such as fiery arrows flying from a distant location. Maya is used to show these techniques.

# Pacing an Animation with Frame Rates: What's the Going Rate?

Animation is an illusion created by rapidly flipping through a series of similar images that change slightly between successive images to create the illusion of motion. Each of these independent images is called a frame.

Before diving into creating an actual animation, you need to do some setup work first, such as setting the frame rate and the total number of frames. This determines how long the animation sequence is and how fast it plays. Both of these are critical to game play, and both can be controlled precisely.

Frame rates are common in animation as a way to describe how quickly the frames of an animation sequence are displayed. It is common in gaming to measure the frames per second (*fps*) in order to get a feel for how smoothly the animation sequences are playing.

A *rate* is something that changes over time, so *frame rate* refers to frames of animation that change over time. Frame rate can also refer to the number of frames that are displayed per given second.

Common frame rates are 12 and 24 fps, but you can set the frame rate to be 22.3 if you feel like it. Keep the following points in mind when you're deciding on the proper frame rate for your game animation:

- **12 fps** is considered *half speed*, and it represents the lowest frame rate that is still discernable as motion. You may want to use a half-speed frame rate for animation sequences that will appear on the Web or to simulate a television broadcast or film that is playing. Anything slower than 12 fps looks choppy and uneven.

- **24 fps** is common because it is the frame rate used by the film industry. You'll want to use this frame rate for all your game animations and for all cut scenes.

- **30 fps** is the frame rate used by television. This frame rate is typically overkill for games and shouldn't be used.

- **Rates over 30 fps** are used with high speed film, but they will choke most game engines. You really shouldn't use them.

When you're working with 3D animation for games, you typically want to stick with 24 fps or less, depending on the specifications of the game engine you're using.

## Changing the frame rate

Depending on where you intend your animation to be displayed, you may need to change the frame rate. For most games, you want the fps set to 24.

Follow these steps to change the frame rate in Maya:

1. **Choose Window ⇨ Settings/Preferences ⇨ Preferences to open the Preferences dialog box.**

   The Preferences dialog box, shown in Figure 10-1, includes all the preference settings for the entire interface conveniently divided into panels that are accessed from the list on the left. The Frame Rate setting is found in the Timeline panel (not in the Animation panel).

**Figure 10-1:**
Maya's
Preferences
dialog box
includes
several
settings for
controlling
the length
and speed
of an
animation.

| Preferences | | | □◨⊠ |
|---|---|---|---|
| Edit  Help | | | |

Categories
Interface
  UI Elements
  Help
Display
  Kinematics
  Animation
  Manipulators
  NURBS
  Polygons
Settings
  Cameras
  Dynamics
  Files/Projects
  Keys
  Modeling
  Rendering
  Selection
  Snapping
  Sound
  **Timeline**
  Undo
  Web Browser
Modules

**Timeline: Animation Timeline and Playback Preferences**

**Timeline**

| Playback Start/End | 1.00 | 48.00 |
| Animation Start/End | 1.00 | 48.00 |

Height    ⦿ 1x    ○ 2x    ○ 4x
Key Ticks    ○ None    ⦿ Active    ○ Channel Box
Options    ☐ Timecode    ☑ Snapping
Timecode Offset    00:00:00:00

**Playback**

Update View    ⦿ Active    ○ All
Looping    ○ Once    ⦿ Oscillate    ○ Continuous
Playback Speed    Real-time [24 fps] ▾    Other 12.00
Playback by    1.000

| Save | | Cancel | |

You can also open the Timeline panel of the Preferences dialog box by clicking the Animation Preferences button in the lower-right corner of the interface.

2. **Select a frame rate from the Playback Speed drop-down list.**

   The Frame Rate setting in Maya is called Playback Speed. The options include Play Every Frame, Real Time (24 fps), Half (12 fps), Twice (48 fps), and Other. Selecting the Other option lets you set the Playback Speed to whatever you'd like.

3. **Click the Save button.**

   The Playback Speed value is updated and saved with the scene.

## Setting the total number of frames

The Timeline panel in the Preferences dialog box also includes settings for controlling the total number of frames that make up the animation sequence. The length of the animation is determined by the total number of frames divided by the frame rate. For example, an animation sequence with 48 frames running at 24 fps would be 2 seconds long.

You don't need to open the Preferences dialog box to change the total number of frames in an animation. Below the Time Slider is a bar called the Range Slider; to either side of the Range Slider are text fields that display the total number of frames and the frames in the current range. Entering a number in the rightmost text field increases the total number of frames.

## Moving the Time Slider to select a frame

The last little bit of setup that you need to know is how to work with the Time Slider, shown in Figure 10-2. The ingenious device lets you move (or slide) back and forth through the available frames. The current frame is highlighted by a black rectangular marker, and its number is displayed to the right of the Time Slider.

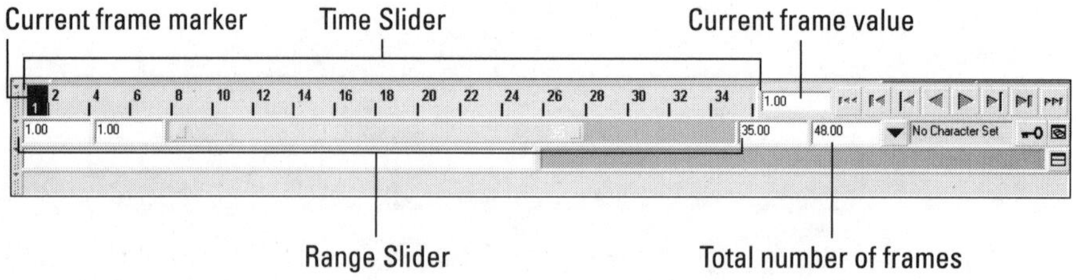

**Figure 10-2:**
The Time Slider and the Range Slider both appear at the bottom of the Maya interface.

Current frame marker     Time Slider          Current frame value

Range Slider          Total number of frames

If you look closely at the current frame number, you'll notice that it is expressed with a decimal. Maya actually lets you specify frame rate as a fraction of time.

# Creating Simple Animations with Keyframes

The simplest animation sequences involve moving a single object in one direction. A spider moves across the floor, or an asteroid speeds through space toward an unsuspecting space station.

Creating such a sequence using traditional animation techniques would require that you draw every frame of the animation, but in 3D, you simply mark the beginning and ending points of the moving object and let the software compute all the frames between these two points.

If you know the setting of an object at one point in time and another setting at a different time, then the software can easily calculate (or interpolate) the settings that exist at any point between those two points that are marked with keyframes. For example, if a sphere is at X=0 at frame 1 and X=100 at frame 20, then at frame 10 the sphere is at X=50, if it moves in a straight line.

These beginning and ending points are recorded and called *keyframes*. An animation sequence can include many keyframes that record all the intermediate positions of the object as it moves about the scene.

A keyframe keeps track of the settings of an object at a given moment in time. This setting could be any object attribute, such as the position of a sphere, its radius, or its color.

For a quick example, suppose you create a model of an arrow that needs to pierce an apple on the head of a character across the room. The first keyframe for the arrow is in the bow that is firing it, and the last keyframe is through the apple. After setting these two keyframes, the software can compute the position of the arrow for every in-between frame.

Using keyframes allows animators to make their objects move in complex ways by defining only the beginning and end positions.

## Animating an object by creating position keyframes

After an animation is set up, the process of animating objects can be accomplished in several ways. The first and most basic method uses keyframes. Keyframes set the beginning and ending positions of an object and the software interpolates all positions between these two keyframes to locate the intermediate location of the object for each frame. This simple example shows how keyframes can be used to animate an object that is changing positions.

Follow these steps to create two position keyframes in Maya:

1. **Select the object that you want to animate.**

   Click the Select tool in the toolbox, and click the object to animate.

2. **Drag the Time Slider to the frame where the motion begins.**

   Keyframes can be set for any frame, depending on when you want the motion to start.

3. **Choose Animate ⇨ Set Key (or press the S key).**

   The Set Key menu command records the position information for the selected object and stores it in a keyframe. It then makes a mark on the Time Slider for the created keyframe. This marker is a thin red line positioned at the current frame.

   If the Animate menu isn't available, then you need to switch to the Animation menu set using the drop-down list in the upper-left corner of the interface.

4. **Drag the Time Slider to the frame where the motion ends.**

   The ending keyframe, like the beginning one, can be positioned at any frame, depending on how many frames you want the motion to cover.

5. **Move the object to the ending position.**

   Moving objects is accomplished with the Move tool, which may be selected from the toolbox.

6. **Choose Animate ⇨ Set Key (or press the S key).**

   This keyframe marks the end of the object's motion. It is also marked with a thin red line on the Time Slider, as shown in Figure 10-3.

7. **Drag the Time Slider to see the object's motion.**

   You can also press the Play Forward button to see the object move.

8. **Select the File ⇨ Save Scene As menu command and save the file as Keyframed sphere.mb.**

   Any keyframes that are created are attached to the object and saved with the file.

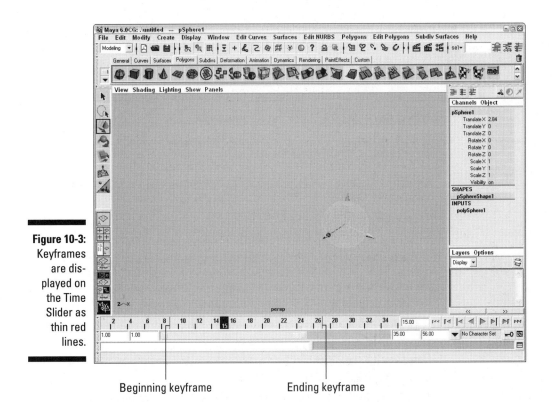

**Figure 10-3:** Keyframes are displayed on the Time Slider as thin red lines.

Beginning keyframe          Ending keyframe

## Animating an object with rotation and scale keyframes

In addition to the Move tool, you can also use the Rotate and Scale tools to set keyframes for the rotation and scaling of an object. To set these keyframes, simply use the Rotate or Scale tools in place of the Move tool. Rotation and scaling keyframes appear on the Time Slider just like position keyframes.

Using the Rotate and Scale tools, shown in Figure 10-4, you can make objects spin or change their size. For example, you can makes the tires of a vehicle rotate as the vehicle moves down the road, or you can increase the size of a monster after it has drunk a magic potion.

Select tool

**Figure 10-4:**
**Toolbox**
**Select and**
**Transform**
**tools.**

— Lasso Select tool

— Move tool

— Rotate tool

Scale tool

A single frame can include multiple keyframes controlling its position, rotation, and scaling.

Follow these steps to create keyframes for translation and rotation in Maya:

1. **Select the Create ⇨ Polygon Primitives ⇨ Sphere and the Create ⇨ Polygon Primitives ⇨ Plane menu commands.**

   A sphere and a plane object are placed in the center of the view panel.

2. **Drag the center manipulator for the plane object with the Scale tool to increase its size. Then select and position the sphere at one end of the plane object.**

   This position is the start position of the sphere, which I'll animate rolling across the plane surface.

3. **Choose Animate ⇨ Set Key (or press the S key).**

   The Set Key menu command records the position and rotation information for the selected object and stores it in a keyframe. It then makes a mark on the Time Slider for the created keyframe. This marker is a thin red line positioned at the current frame, which is frame 1.

4. **Drag the Time Slider to frame 30.**

   The ending keyframe, like the beginning one, can be positioned at any frame, depending on how many frames you want the motion to cover.

5. **Move the sphere to the opposite end of the plane object.**

   Moving objects is accomplished with the Move tool, which you can select from the toolbox.

6. **Select the Rotate tool and spin the ball about its center for an entire revolution.**

   Rotating objects is accomplished with the Rotate tool. Any rotations applied to the sphere are also recorded when a key is set.

7. **Choose Animate ⇨ Set Key (or press the S key).**

   This keyframe marks the end of the object's motion and rotation. It is also marked with a thin red line on the Time Slider.

8. **Drag the Time Slider to see the object's motion.**

   Notice how the sphere is rotating as it moves, as shown in Figure 10-5.

9. **Select the File ⇨ Save Scene As menu command and save the file as Rolling sphere.mb.**

   Keyframes for the translation and the rotation are kept separate, but both are saved along with the file.

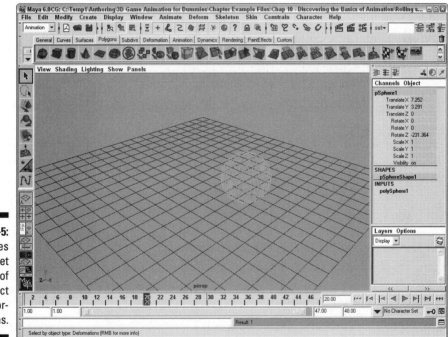

**Figure 10-5:**
Keyframes can be set for any of the object transformations.

# Creating an attribute keyframe

An object's position and rotation isn't the only thing that can be set as a keyframe. Actually, any attribute or setting may be marked as a keyframe.

When an object's attribute has a keyframe applied to it, its attribute in the Channel Box is shaded brown.

Follow these steps to create keyframes for the Color and Transparency attributes in Maya:

1. **Select the Create ➪ Polygon Primitives ➪ Cone menu command.**

   A cone object is placed in the center of the view panel.

2. **Open the Attribute Editor and click the Lambert1 tab. Drag the Color attribute slider to the left to make the cone fully black.**

   The Lambert1 node is opened and all the material attributes for this object are displayed.

3. **Right-click the Color attribute and select the Set Key option from the pop-up menu. Then repeat this step for the Transparency attribute.**

   Selecting the Set Key menu option from the right click pop-up menu sets a key for the selected attribute.

4. **Drag the Time Slider to frame 30.**

   The ending keyframe, like the beginning one, can be positioned at any frame, depending on how many frames you want to cover.

5. **Drag the Color slider to the right to change the cone's color to white. Then drag the Transparency slider to the right to make the cone fully transparent.**

   Changing an attribute doesn't automatically set a key unless the Auto Key mode is enabled.

6. **Right-click both the Color and Transparency attributes and select the Set Key menu option from the pop-up menu.**

   Rotating objects is accomplished with the Rotate tool. Any rotations applied to the sphere are also recorded when a key is set.

   Keys for attribute changes are not displayed on the Time Slider.

7. **Press the 5 key to see the material applied to the cone object in the view panel.**

   The color changes can only be seen in the view panel when the shader display mode is enabled.

8. **Drag the Time Slider to see the resulting animation.**

   The cone slowly changes from black to white as it also disappears, as shown in Figure 10-6.

9. **Select the File ➪ Save Scene As menu command and save the file as Disappearing cone.mb.**

   With the cone selected, you can see the selected edges on the back side of the cone as the object slowly becomes transparent.

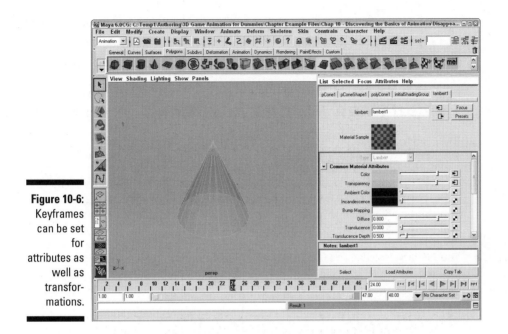

**Figure 10-6:**
Keyframes can be set for attributes as well as transformations.

## Locating keyframes with the Animation Controls

The lower-right corner of the Maya interface includes a set of Animation Controls, shown in Figure 10-7, that look like they were pulled from a television remote. Using these controls, you can quickly jump to the start or end of the current frame set, jump to the previous or next frame, or play the animation sequence forward or backward.

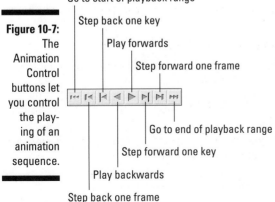

**Figure 10-7:**
The Animation Control buttons let you control the playing of an animation sequence.

Go to start of playback range

Step back one key

Play forwards

Step forward one frame

Go to end of playback range

Step forward one key

Play backwards

Step back one frame

The Animation Controls also include buttons that let you move to the previous key or the next key. Using these buttons, you can quickly move between keyframes for the selected object.

## Copying and pasting keyframes

If the keyframe you've created is in the correct position, but you want to shorten the number of frames it runs over, you can cut, copy, and paste keyframes between frames using the Time Slider.

All keyframes for the selected object are displayed on the Time Slider. When you right-click the Time Slider, a menu appears that includes options to cut, copy, and paste the keyframe for the selected frame.

You can also access the Cut, Copy, and Paste commands for keys by choosing Edit ➪ Keys.

## Automating the creation of keyframes with Auto Keyframing

As if keyframing isn't easy enough, you also have an option to make it automatic. Just like auto pilot for a plane, by enabling Auto Keyframing, you don't need to think about setting keyframes: They are created automatically anytime you make a change.

You should always be aware of when Auto Keyframing is enabled, because sometimes you don't want keyframes created for every action.

The Auto Keyframe button in Maya is located in the lower-right corner of the interface, and it looks like a key. The key turns bright red when enabled to remind you that it is turned on.

## Moving an Object Along a Path

Keyframing isn't the only easy way to animate objects. Another cool trick is having an object follow a path. To use this technique, you need an object to animate and a path for the object to follow. This technique is especially useful for games where you want vehicles, projectiles, and enemies following a set path.

Another common way to animate objects is to define a path and have an object move from the beginning to the end of the path over a given number of frames. Path animations are useful for making certain objects move through a game scene following a predefined path.

*REMEMBER*

A path that has an object attached to it is called a Motion Path in Maya.

## Animating an object moving along a path

Maya includes multiple tools for creating paths, including drawing them with the mouse and setting control points. Also be aware that the order in which you select the object and the path makes a difference.

Follow these steps to animate an object following a path in Maya:

1. **Create a path.**

   Maya includes several different ways to create paths or curves. You can create a smooth curve with the Create ⇨ EP Curve tool or the Create ⇨ CV Curve tool. You can draw a curve using the Pencil Curve tool, which is also found in the Create menu.

2. **Select the object that you want to animate and the path that it will follow.**

   Click the Select tool in the toolbox, and click the object to animate. Then hold down the Shift key, and click the path.

3. **Choose the Animate ⇨ Motion Paths ⇨ Attach to Motion Path menu command.**

   The object snaps to the path.

4. **Drag the Time Slider to see the object's motion.**

   You can also click the Play Forward button to see the object move. The object is automatically set to begin at the start of the path at the first frame and reach the end of the path at the final frame.

5. **Select the File ⇨ Save Scene As menu command and save the file as Sphere following path.mb.**

   Motion paths are hidden during the rendering process, but the object still follows the path.

## Tracking an object's motion with trajectories

Trajectories are used to visualize the movement of objects through a scene and provide a useful way to see an object's motion. You can also use trajectories to edit objects' motion.

For any object that is animated, you can take a look at the trajectory path that it follows and edit the trajectory path to modify the motion of the object. To see an object's trajectory, choose Animate ➪ Create Motion Trail.

Using the Options dialog box, you can set how the trajectory is drawn and whether frame numbers appear. Figure 10-8 shows a simple animated sphere with its trajectory enabled. Notice that the frame numbers on the trajectory match the keyframes on the Time Slider.

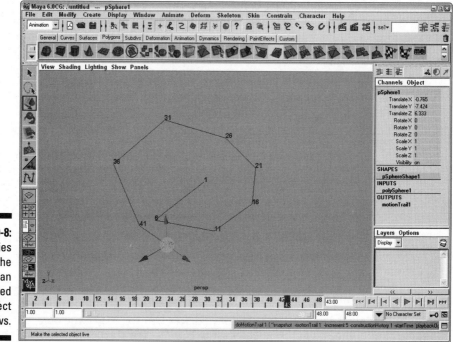

**Figure 10-8:** Trajectories show the trail that an animated object follows.

## Ghosting objects to get a sense of their motion

Ghosting is a feature that lets you see an object's position before or after the current frame. This is helpful in providing you some insight into the object's speed and direction.

To enable ghosting in Maya, choose Animate ➪ Ghost Selected. The Options dialog box lets you choose the number of ghosted objects that appear. Figure 10-9 shows the same sphere as in Figure 10-6, this time with ghosting enabled.

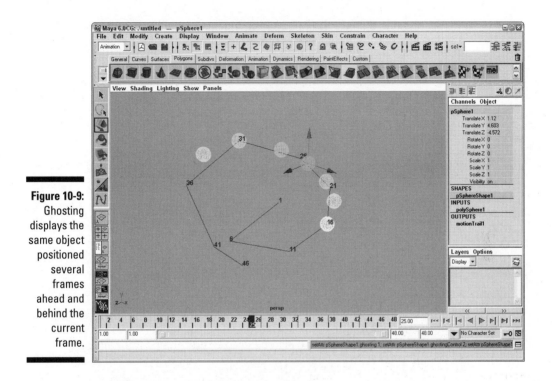

Figure 10-9:
Ghosting
displays the
same object
positioned
several
frames
ahead and
behind the
current
frame.

# Using Animation Editors

After keyframes are created, you can access several different animation tools to further refine the animation. Two common animation editors include the Graph Editor, which displays all animation values as graphs; and the Dope Sheet, which is used to position keys relative to one another and to a sound track.

## Viewing animation graphs

If you animate an object moving between two keyframes and graph its position for each frame, the graph shows a straight line between the two keyframes, but the motion doesn't need to be a straight line. Consider a weapon that launches a grenade onto an opposing army. If the bomb could only travel in straight lines, it wouldn't look as good as having it move in a gentle arc.

Most 3D packages include an interface that lets you view the animation graphs of objects. You can also edit these graphs to create all kinds of different motions.

In Maya, animation graphs can be seen in the Graph Editor, which is opened using the Window ➪ Animation Editors ➪ Graph Editor menu command. Figure 10-10 shows the Graph Editor with several animation curves.

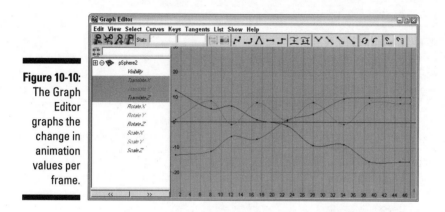

**Figure 10-10:** The Graph Editor graphs the change in animation values per frame.

In addition to displaying the animation curves, the Graph Editor also includes controls for controlling the shape of the curve, including linear to smooth curves. The Graph Editor can also be used to edit the position of existing keys and to create new keys.

## Synchronizing animation keys

Another useful tool when working with animations is the Dope Sheet, shown in Figure 10-11. This editor displays all keys as cells in a spreadsheet. This format makes it easy to line up certain keys so that, for example, a bullet can be animated to turn red as it approaches maximum velocity. The Dope Sheet also makes possible aligning certain keys with an audio track.

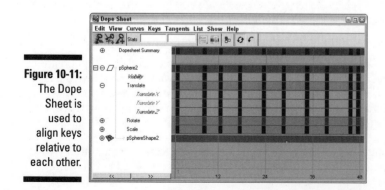

**Figure 10-11:** The Dope Sheet is used to align keys relative to each other.

The Dope Sheet in Maya is accessed by selecting the Window ⇨ Animation Editors ⇨ Dope Sheet menu command. Sound files can be imported into Maya using the File ⇨ Import menu command.

Follow these steps to align a bouncing ball to a sound file in Maya:

1. **Select the Create ⇨ Polygon Primitives ⇨ Sphere and the Create ⇨ Polygon Primitives ⇨ Plane menu commands.**

   A sphere and a plane object are placed in the center of the view panel.

2. **Drag the center manipulator for the plane object with the Scale tool to increase its size. Then select and position the sphere above the plane object at one end.**

   This position is the start position of the sphere, which you'll animate bouncing across the plane surface.

3. **Choose Animate ⇨ Set Key (or press the S key).**

   The Set Key menu command records the position of the sphere at frame 1.

4. **Drag the Time Slider to frame 10. Move the sphere forward slightly and down until it touches the plane object. Then press the S key to create another keyframe.**

   This key marks the first bounce of the sphere.

5. **Drag the Time Slider to frame 20. Move the sphere forward again and up until it is above the plane object, but not as high as the starting position. Then press the s key to create another keyframe.**

   This key marks the rebound of the sphere.

6. **Drag the Time Slider to frame 30. Move the sphere forward even more and down until it touches the plane object. Then press the S key to create another keyframe.**

   This key marks the second bounce of the sphere.

7. **Drag the Time Slider to frame 40. Move the sphere forward to the end of the plane. Then rotate the sphere a full revolution and press the S key to create another keyframe.**

   This final key causes the sphere to roll to the end of the plane following its second bounce.

8. **With the sphere selected, choose the Window ⇨ Animation Editors ⇨ Graph Editor menu command.**

   The Graph Editor appears with the keyframed motions graphed, as shown in Figure 10-12.

**Figure 10-12:**
The
animation
curves
for the
bouncing
sphere are
displayed in
the Graph
Editor.

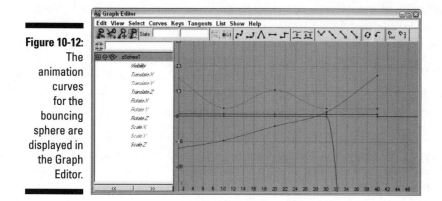

9. **Select the File ⇨ Import menu command and select and load the boing.wav sound file.**

   The loaded sound file is added to the file, but needs to be enabled before it appears in the Dope Sheet.

10. **To enable the sound file, right-click the Time Slider and select the Sound ⇨ Boing option from the pop-up menu.**

    The sound file's wave pattern is added to the Time Slider, as shown in Figure 10-13.

**Figure 10-13:**
When a
sound file
is added
to a scene,
its wave
pattern is
displayed in
the Time
Slider.

Sound wave pattern

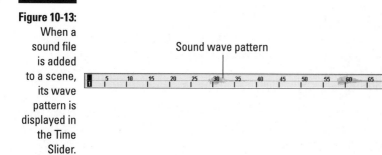

11. **Enter a value of 100 in the text field to the right of the Range Slider. Then drag the right end of the Range Slider so that the entire sound wave is visible.**

    This increases the total number of frames to 100, allowing you to see the entire sound wave.

12. **With the sphere selected, choose the Window ⇨ Animation Editors ⇨ Dope Sheet menu command. In the Dope Sheet menu, select View ⇨ Frame Playback Range.**

    The Dope Sheet opens with the sound wave and the sphere object keys visible. The Frame Playback Range command causes all frames to be visible in the Dope Sheet. All keys are displayed as black rectangles.

13. **Click the rightmost key to select it, and drag it with the middle mouse button to the right end of the Dope Sheet. Select and drag the second-to-the-last key and align it with the second sound wave form. Then select and drag the second key to align it with the first wave form, and drag the third key between the second and fourth.**

    The keys should then be aligned to correspond with the bounce sounds that are part of the sound file. The resulting Dope Sheet is shown in Figure 10-14.

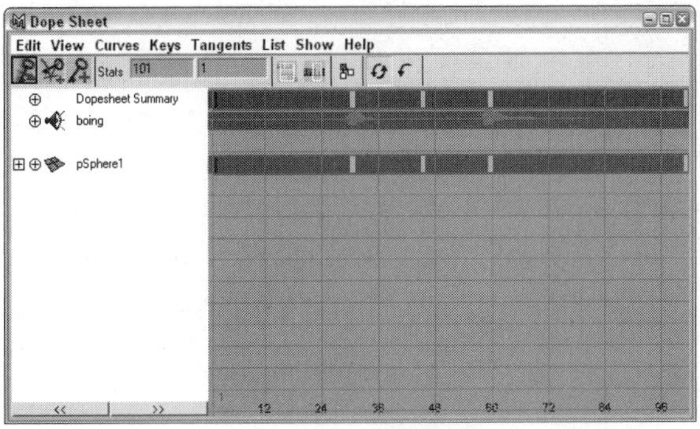

**Figure 10-14:**
The keys on the Dope Sheet are aligned to the waveforms of the sound file.

14. **Drag the Time Slider (or click the Play Animation button) to see and hear the resulting animation.**

    The ball falls and is animated bouncing off the floor with sound played as it hits each time, as shown in Figure 10-15.

15. **Select the File ⇨ Save Scene As menu command and save the file as Bouncing ball.mb.**

    The sound file is saved independently of the scene file. If the scene file cannot find the sound file, then it will simply play the animation without sound.

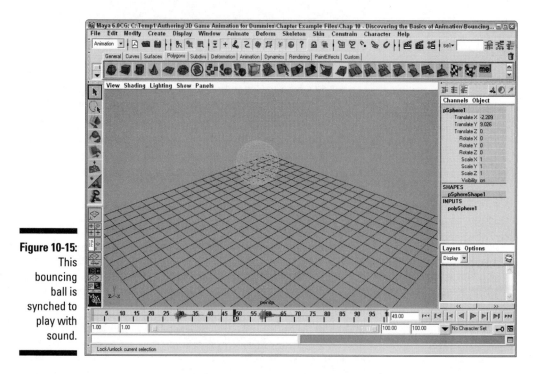

**Figure 10-15:**
This
bouncing
ball is
synched to
play with
sound.

# Chapter 11

# Animating Characters

● ● ● ● ● ● ● ● ● ● ● ● ● ● ● ● ● ● ● ● ● ● ● ● ● ● ● ● ● ● ● ● ● ● ● ● ● ● ● ● ● ● ● ● ● ● ●

## In This Chapter

▶ Rigging characters

▶ Creating realistic skin

▶ Attaching skin to a skeleton

▶ Creating muscle bulges

▶ Integrating motion capture

● ● ● ● ● ● ● ● ● ● ● ● ● ● ● ● ● ● ● ● ● ● ● ● ● ● ● ● ● ● ● ● ● ● ● ● ● ● ● ● ● ● ● ● ● ● ●

*C*haracter animation is the golden chalice of the game industry. It is the capability that all games need, that all game companies seek, and that is elusive to find. Many 3D software companies are taking this quest and endowing their software with some amazing new features that make character animation much easier.

These new features come in both software and hardware forms. Software solutions include features such as the Biped feature found in 3ds max that enables you to animate complex walk cycles by simply placing footsteps in the scene, and Alias' Motion Builder, which includes many features customized for animating human-based characters.

A hardware solution that is available, though very expensive, called motion capture, enables game companies to record the actual physical motions of an actor wearing special hardware. This motion data can then be loaded into a 3D animation package and applied to a character.

Regardless of the features that are available, animators still create many character animations manually by studying video reels and observing the motions of real-life people.

# Rigging Characters to Move Realistically

The key to animating characters doesn't involve the actual character model, but rather a structure of bones that are positioned underneath the character. The character model is then attached to this bone structure, and the bones are animated, causing the model (or skin) to move with it. This process is known as rigging.

## Creating a skeleton that lies under the character

The first step in rigging a character is to create a set of bones. The number of bones that you need depends on the motions that you want your character to do. For example, if you plan on having your character point its finger, then you need to add bones for the fingers, but if the character's fingers remain in a fist for the entire sequence, then only creating a hand bone is sufficient.

### Structuring bones

The key to making bones work is that they need to be part of a structure. Each bone needs to be connected to the adjacent bones to form joints like the elbow and knee. When bones are in a structure, then moving one bone affects the surrounding bones and creates realistic motions. For example, the upper arm bone is attached to the forearm bone, and when the upper arm is moved, the forearm and the hand should follow.

Bone structures are often called skeletons.

Bone structures are organized into hierarchies. Hierarchies refer to objects as parent objects and child objects. A child object is attached to a parent and moves along with the parent. For example, the upper arm would be the parent, and the forearm would be the child, but the forearm in turn would be the parent to the hand object. The topmost bone in the hierarchy is known as the *root,* and moving it moves the entire structure.

In standard structure, each parent can have multiple children, but each child can have only one parent.

### Creating and editing bones

When creating bones with a bone tool, you simply need to drag from where the bone starts to where the bone ends. Bones typically look like long rectangular boxes that are tapered at one end. Bones are also created in multiples making it easy to create an entire hierarchy quickly.

After a bone is created, it can be selected and positioned using the same tools that are used to move other scene objects. You can also change the selected bone's parent and children.

When building a bone structure, you may be tempted to make the head or the torso the root object, but the pelvis is the best bone to set as the root. The head bends at the neck, and the torso bends at the waist, but the pelvis doesn't bend about anything, making it a good choice for the root.

### Positioning bones

After a bone structure has been created for the entire character, including bones and joints for every body part that needs to move, you want to position the bones within the character that they control. Place the bones inside the character, and scale and position them to match as closely as possible the body parts that they control.

Follow these steps to create a bone structure in Maya:

1. **Choose File ⇨ Open Scene, and open the Final character.mb file.**

   The Final character file is the character created in Chapter 9.

2. **Select the Animation menu set from the drop-down list at the top-left corner of the interface.**

   The Animation menu set includes all the commands that you need to create bone structures.

3. **Select the Skeleton ⇨ Joint Tool menu command to access the joint tool. Then click at the top of the upper leg, again at the knee, again at the ankle in the Front view, and finally at the end of the foot in the Side view. Then choose the Select Tool to exit the joint tool.**

   Each click with the Joint tool creates a new bone that is a child to the previous bone. With four simple clicks, you can create the entire bone structure for the character's leg.

4. **Repeat Step 3 to create bone structures for the other leg and both arms.**

   The bone structures for the arms also need four clicks each to make bones for the upper arm, the lower arm, and the hand.

5. **Use the Joint Tool again to create a bone structure for the character's spine, clicking the hip, the upper back, and the head.**

   The bone structure for the spine needs only three bones, but the arm and leg bone structures are tied in to this structure.

   When creating the bone structure for the back, be careful not to click the existing bone chains, or you will alter the hierarchy.

**6. Select the top bone for the arm, hold down the Shift key and select the joint at the neck, and then choose the Edit ⇨ Parent menu command.**

This command adds another bone to the structure between the arm and the spine, making the arm chain part of the back chain.

**7. Create parent bones for the remaining arm and the legs.**

Connect the top leg bone to the hip joint. After this step, the entire bone structure should be in place as shown in Figure 11-1.

**8. Select the File ⇨ Save Scene As menu command, and save the file as Bone structure.mb. Close the file when you are finished.**

All the examples in this chapter build from the preceding one. By saving the file at the end of each example, you can continue the next example where this one finished.

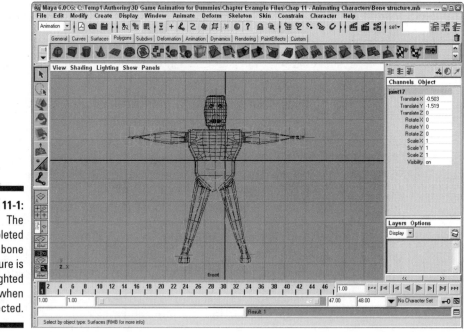

**Figure 11-1:**
The completed bone structure is highlighted when selected.

### Naming bones

When bones are created, they are given a unique name like "bone1" or "bone2." If you create a bone structure with 20 or so bones, then finding the right bone can be quite a task. To prevent this, you really should name each bone with a name that makes sense, like "left forearm." This makes finding and working with bones much easier.

Follow these steps to name all the bones in Maya:

1. **Choose File ⇨ Open Scene, and open the Bone structure.mb file.**

   This file is the same file that was saved at the end of the preceding example.

2. **Select the left hand bone by clicking the circular icon that represents its joint. Then click in the name field at the top of the Channel Box located on the right side of the interface, and type "l_hand."**

   Changing the name of the joint to something that makes sense helps when you try to find the bone later.

   When naming bones, be sure to include left and right designations, and always name the parts according to the character's right and left side, not the sides that you see in the Front view.

3. **Continue to select and name each bone in the entire bone structure.**

   When a bone is selected, all its child bones are also selected.

4. **Select the Window ⇨ Outliner menu command to open the Outliner.**

   The Outliner interface includes a hierarchical list of all objects in the scene. If you locate and click the pelvis root bone, you can expand the list to see the entire bone structure, as shown in Figure 11-2.

5. **Select the File ⇨ Save Scene As menu command, and save the file as Named bones.mb. Close the file when you are finished.**

   All the examples in this chapter build from the preceding one. By saving the file at the end of each example, you can continue the next example where this one finished.

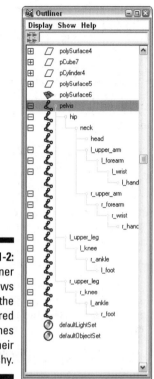

**Figure 11-2:**
The Outliner shows all the structured bones and their hierarchy.

# Setting constraints so the object doesn't move when it shouldn't

Each bone in a bone structure can be set with limits that define the extent that it can be bent, twisted, rotated, and slid. By specifying these constraints, you can ensure that a character doesn't accidentally move in a way that it shouldn't. And that's a good thing to keep in mind if you're ever animating a flock of flamingos. Their knee joints bend backward instead of forward like humans. Using constraints, you can make sure that your flamingos' knees bend the right way.

Although constraints can be set for each bone, they can also be disabled for certain bones as needed. For example, if you need to animate a character breaking his arm in a fight sequence, then you can disable or change the constraints for the arm bone to enable the painful animation to proceed.

# Controlling character motion with kinematics

Kinematics is a branch of physics that deals with the motion of connected objects. It is used to compute the motion of a bone structure. Standard bone structures work using a process called Forward Kinematics, which causes child objects to move with their parents and allows child objects to move independent of their parents.

When animating characters, the position of the very last child in the hierarchy is often what you're most interested in. Think of how you'd animate having a character open a door. The hand object would need to be placed on the door knob. Using Forward Kinematics would mean that you'd need to position the hand by rotating the upper arm and then the forearm to get the hand in the right position, which would be difficult.

Another kinematics solution that comes to the rescue is known as Inverse Kinematics, or IK for short. Inverse Kinematics enables the position of parent objects to be controlled by the position of a child bone known as the *goal*. Positioning the goal object makes all the parent objects follow, so you can animate a character reaching for the door knob.

In order for Inverse Kinematics to work, you need to define a series of bones called an IK chain that includes all the parent objects that need to move with the goal. IK chains always end with the goal object.

Follow these steps to enable Inverse Kinematics in Maya:

1. **Choose File ⇨ Open Scene, and open the Named bones.mb file.**

   This file is the same file that was saved at the end of the preceding example.

2. **Select and move the upper leg bone.**

   Moving the upper leg bone causes all the child bones to move with it.

3. **Select the Edit ⇨ Undo menu command to undo the previous movement. Then select and move the foot bone.**

   Moving the foot bone stretches it away from its parent bone, but this movement has no effect on the parent.

4. **Select the Edit ⇨ Undo menu command to undo the foot bone movement.**

   The purpose of this step is to show how the bones work without IK enabled, so the change is obvious.

5. **Select the Skeleton ➪ IK Handle menu command, and click the upper leg joint (the ball at the end of the bone) to select the parent for the IK solution. Then click the ankle joint for the same leg to select the goal object.**

   The selected IK chain changes color after the IK solution is applied. If you move the goal object, the knee bends, but it bends sideways.

6. **Change the Twist value in the IK Solver Attributes panel to the right side of the interface to 90 degrees.**

   This change orients the knee so it bends forward as it should.

7. **Select the ankle joint as the IK goal, and move it forward in the Side view.**

   The leg bones bend naturally forward at the knee as you'd expect, as shown in Figure 11-3.

8. **Select the File ➪ Save Scene As menu command, and save the file as IK enabled.mb. Close the file when you are finished.**

   All the examples in this chapter build from the preceding one. By saving the file at the end of each example, you can continue the next example where this one finished.

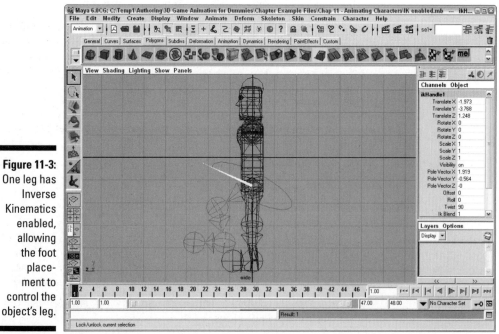

**Figure 11-3:** One leg has Inverse Kinematics enabled, allowing the foot placement to control the object's leg.

# Creating a Realistic Skin

A bone structure is only part of the rigging story. The other part is the actual character model that is affected by the bone structure or the character model. The character model that is applied to a bone structure is called a skin. The skin should be one combined object with no overlapping parts.

You can think of the skin as a glove that is placed over a hand. The glove doesn't move when it is off the hand, but when the fingers are moved underneath, the glove moves and bends along with the fingers. If there are any holes in the glove, they get stretched open as the fingers move. The same works for a skin over a bone structure.

## Skinning a character

Character models typically are created one part at a time, but to make a model into a skin, you need to combine all parts into a single object. If the model consists of any groups, you should dissolve these groups. Objects still can be attached to the skin, but all parts of the skin that move with the bones need to be able to bend and flex.

After a skin is attached to a skeleton, the second part of skinning is to make sure that the skin deforms well when the bones are moved. Each bone has an influence volume that defines the portions of the skin that moves with the bone. If these influence volumes are incorrect, then the skin can deform unrealistically when the bone is moved.

For example, if the influence volume for the upper arm includes part of the side of the character, then rotating the upper arm pulls the character's side

## A character's default pose

Most characters are modeled in a pose called the T-pose. This pose has the character's arms straight out with their palms facing down and their legs spread the width of the character's shoulders.

Although this pose may seem strange because the character will not likely assume this pose, it actually has a purpose. The T-pose has a minimum amount of deformation in the joints of the character. This enables you to rig and skin the character without having to worry about bones crossing one another or having the skin fold about the joint, such as the elbow joint.

out as the arm is raised, causing a funny-looking bump. To control these deformations, you can precisely control the influence volume. Attaching a skin to a skeleton

After a bone structure is created, it can be attached to the character skin that has already been created. The character model was created in the previous chapter, and all the various body parts were already combined into a single mesh, so the skin is ready to be attached to the bone structure. Some software programs make this a separate step, and others simply require that the bones be positioned within the skin.

Follow these steps to attach a skin to a bone structure in Maya:

1. **Choose File ⇨ Open Scene, and open the IK enabled.mb file.**

   This file is the same file that was saved at the end of the preceding example. Be sure to move the bones back into place before attaching the skin.

2. **Select the character model, press and hold the Shift key, and select the pelvis bone. Then choose the Skin ⇨ Bind Skin ⇨ Smooth Bind menu command.**

   The skin is now attached to the bone structure, so moving any of the bones moves the character model with the bone.

3. **Select the ankle joint with the IK chain attached, and move the ankle forward in the Front view. Then select and rotate one of the arms about its upper arm joint.**

   With the skin binding in place, the character model moves along with the bone movements, as shown in Figure 11-4.

4. **Select the File ⇨ Save Scene As menu command, and save the file as Attached skin.mb. Close the file when you are finished.**

   All the examples in this chapter build from the preceding one. By saving the file at the end of each example, you can continue the next example where this one finished.

## Setting a bone's influence

Surrounding each bone is an influence volume (called an envelope in several animation packages) that you can control. The skin that is within this volume moves along with the underlying bone, and the skin that is included in overlapping influence volumes are the areas of the skin where the bending is most extreme, such as at the elbow.

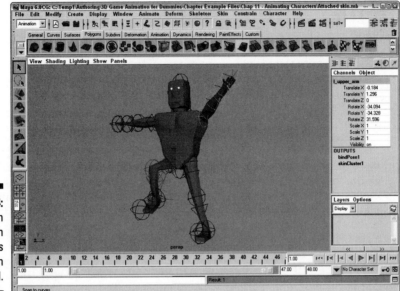

**Figure 11-4:**
The skin
moves with
the bones
when
attached.

The influence volume is initially set to surround each bone, and the closer the bone matches the skin for each body part, the more accurate the influence volumes are. If any portion of the skin isn't included within any influence area, then that portion of the skin is left behind when its bones are moved.

Influence volumes can be altered using controls to increase their radius on either end of the bone.

Another way to control which skin parts deform with the underlying bone is to paint the skin vertices using a paint brush. Select a bone and then paint the weight. Different colors depict the skin vertices' influence. It is important to have a gradual change between skin influences so that the skin moves realistically.

## Adding deformations to create muscle bulges

Another aspect of working with the skin object is that you can define deformations based on bone positions. This provides a way to make muscles bulge. For example, deforming the bicep muscle to bulge when the angle between upper and lower arm bones is shortened is a realistic deformation that you'd expect from a realistic character.

# Animating with Bones

After the process of rigging and skinning your character are completed, you can move onto the task on animating your character. Character animation at this level deals mainly with the movement of the body and its limbs. Later you can add refined animations to control other details such as the facial animation.

Character animation sequences are created by moving and rotating the skeleton joints. Keep in mind that just animating the main joints moving isn't enough: You need to look for places where secondary motion also takes place. For example, during a walk cycle, the legs move and the arms swing opposite each step. These are the primary motions, but secondary motions include the rotating of the hips and torso, and the swaying of the head from side to side.

Follow these steps to make the character jump in Maya:

1. **Choose File ⇨ Open Scene, and open the Double IK.mb file.**

   This file is the same file that was saved at the end of the preceding example, except it has been modified to include another IK chain on the opposite leg, and the arms have been moved to the character's side.

2. **Select the pelvis bone, move the entire character down, and then rotate the character forward slightly.**

   This positions the body in a crouching position prior to the jump.

3. **Select the IK goal for each foot separately, and move each foot upward so it is touching the ground. Then pull the feet in under the body in the Front view so the feet are under the body.**

   This is the starting pose for the action as shown in Figure 11-5.

## Loading a reference background

In Chapter 4, you loaded a sketch of the interface as a background and used it to trace the interface borders. The same technique can be used to load a reference video as a background image. This reference background can be used to line up the body positions of the modeled character to the video character.

For example, you can use a camcorder to record a person walking from the side view.

This taped video can be loaded into the 3D program as a background. Then you can animate the character's motion by simply lining up the character's arms, feet, and legs to the background video.

This technique can be used for any type of motion including spaceships, walking animals, or whatever you can capture as a video.

**Figure 11-5:**
The
character in
its starting
position.

4. **Select each joint that was moved or will be moved and choose the Animate ⇨ Set Key menu command (or press the S key) to create a keyframe.**

   The initial keyframe is set at frame 1. Keys need to be set for the pelvis, IK goals, and each shoulder and ankle joint. These are the joints that will be animated during this motion.

5. **Drag the Time Slider to frame 10.**

   This is the intermediate position for the jump: The body is fully extended at its maximum height.

6. **Select the pelvis bone and move the character upward and forward slightly. Then rotate the body so it is vertically straight.**

   Although the body is in position, you still need to position the arms and feet. Notice how the IK goals stay put as you move the body, causing the legs to straighten out.

7. **Select the IK goal for each foot separately and move each foot forward so the leg is straight under the torso. Then select the shoulder joint on each arm and rotate each arm so it is in front and slightly above the character. Finally, rotate the ankle joint of each foot so the foot is pointing downward.**

   When positioning the arms, each arm can be slightly different from the other to add some variety to the action. Figure 11-6 shows this intermediate position.

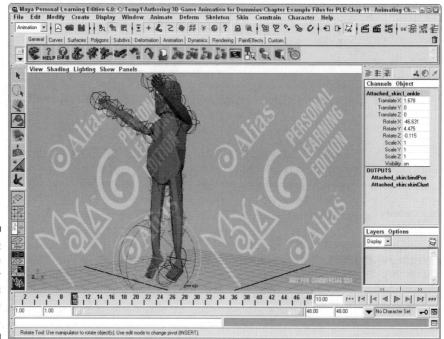

**Figure 11-6:**
The
character
in its
intermediate
position.

8. **Select each joint that was moved and choose the Animate ➪ Set Key menu command (or press the S key) to create a keyframe for each.**

   The intermediate keyframe is set at frame 10. Keys need to be set for the pelvis, IK goals, shoulder joints, and ankle joints.

9. **Drag the Time Slider to frame 20.**

   This is the final position for the jump, where the character lands in a forward position.

10. **Select the pelvis bone and move the character downward and forward slightly.**

    Although the body is in position, you still need to position the arms and feet. Notice how the IK goals stay put as you move the body, again causing the legs to bend behind the body.

11. **Select the IK goal for each foot separately and move each foot forward so the leg is under the torso and slightly bent. Then select the shoulder joint on each arm and rotate each arm downward slightly. Finally, rotate the ankle joint of each foot so the foot is flat on the ground.**

    The final position of the character should be slightly bent under the impact of the jump.

12. **Select each joint that you moved and choose the Animate ➪ Set Key menu command (or press the S key) to create a keyframe.**

The final keyframe is set at frame 20. Keys need to be set for the pelvis, IK goals, and each shoulder and ankle joint again.

**13. Drag the Time Slider to see the resulting motion.**

Figure 11-7 shows the final position of the character after completing the jump.

**14. Select the File ⇨ Save Scene As menu command, and save the file as Jumping action.mb. Close the file when you are finished.**

All the examples in this chapter build from the preceding one. By saving the file at the end of each example, you can continue the next example where this one finished.

# Integrating Motion Capture for the Ultimate in Realistic Motion

Motion capture is really the ultimate in character animation because it allows you to use data taken from the actual physical motion of the actor performing the motion. This technology allows game manufacturers to capture the signature motions of sports superstars and rock musicians.

## Lots of dots: Motion capture hardware

Here's how motion capture works: Thousands of tiny sensors are placed all over the actor's body at key points, such as the elbow, the wrist, the shoulders, and so on. Then several high-speed cameras are positioned about the actor to record the motion of each sensor. The position of each sensor during each slice of time is then saved into a format that can be read into a 3D animation package and applied to a character model.

To import the data correctly, each body part is named to correspond with the motion capture data. After the motion data is imported and matched up, clicking the play button makes the character's body parts follow the imported motion, and voilà, instant motion.

Motion capture data can be applied to any type of character. Even though a large football player was used to record the motion of a quarterback throwing a pass, the same motion can be applied to a small child throwing a ball or to a dinosaur throwing a caveman.

If you remember a few years back, the dancing baby was all the rage. This cute little animation was accomplished by applying motion capture data to a baby character model.

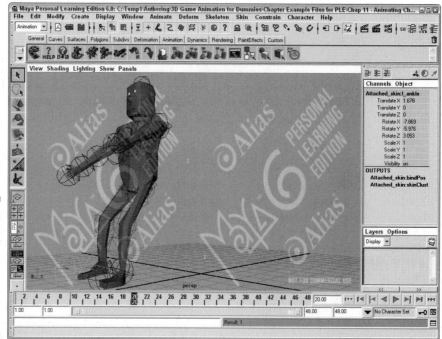

**Figure 11-7:**
The final position of the jumping action returns the character to the ground.

# Unique motion capture systems

Most motion capture systems deal with a single individual in a full-body suit, but other unique systems are available that allow entire groups of individuals or a pair of fighting characters to be captured at the same time.

Other systems capture only the facial motions of an actor, including his expressions and speaking patterns.

# Buying motion

The major drawback to motion capture systems is their cost. These state-of-the-art systems are expensive to use, but for budget-minded game companies, several other companies make available for purchase some of the motion sets that they've already captured.

If you need to animate a character performing a triple round-off pike back flip, then chances are good that it's available.

# Chapter 12

# Animating Facial Movements

● ● ● ● ● ● ● ● ● ● ● ● ● ● ● ● ● ● ● ● ● ● ● ● ● ● ● ● ● ● ● ● ● ● ● ● ● ● ● ● ● ● ● ● ● ●

## *In This Chapter*

▶ Learning to speak

▶ Morphing

▶ Handling eye movements

▶ Making custom facial controls

▶ Syncing facial movements with a soundtrack

● ● ● ● ● ● ● ● ● ● ● ● ● ● ● ● ● ● ● ● ● ● ● ● ● ● ● ● ● ● ● ● ● ● ● ● ● ● ● ● ● ● ● ● ● ●

*B*ones and inverse kinematics are great for animating a body full of joints and limbs, but they don't help much it you need a character's face to show a surprised expression. Sure, there's body language, but the subtle raising of a character's eyebrows and pulling in the corners of the mouth just can't be done effectively with bones.

For facial animations, you need to discover another dear friend that can help you out. This new friend is the morphing feature. Morphing keeps track of all the vertices for a character in a state called a morph target and then slowly moves the vertices between two morph targets as the animation progresses.

Using morph targets, you can make characters smile, grimace, and even speak. Morphing can also be used for other body parts as well. Hands, in particular, can benefit from the morphing features.

# Creating Morph Targets: The Character of a Thousand Faces

Just when you thought you were done with deforming characters, you've discovered that you need to create new deformations that can be used as morph targets. It is common for game companies to create libraries of deformed character faces that can be used as morph targets.

## Working on a clone

The gotcha with morphing features is that the objects contained within each morph target must have an equal number of vertices, so morphing doesn't work for changing a laser weapon into a nuclear detonator. The best way to create morph targets is to make a copy of an existing part and modify the clone to create a new morph target.

Follow these steps to create a morph target in Maya:

1. **Choose File ⇨ Open Scene, and open the Final character.mb file.**

    The Final character file is the character created in Chapter 9.

2. **With the head object selected, choose the Edit ⇨ Duplicate menu command to create a copy of the original head object. Then move the cloned head to the side of the original.**

    Creating a duplicate of the original object ensures that both objects have the same number of vertices.

3. **Choose the Vertex component mode, and select all the vertices that make up the lips in the Front view. Deselect the middle seven columns of vertices by dragging over them with the Ctrl key held down. Move the remaining vertices in the Y-axis upward, deselect the two innermost columns, and move the remaining vertices a bit further. Continue until each column of vertices gradually rises at each end of the mouth to form a smile.**

    Other deformation techniques are available, but this is a simple way to create a quick and easy smile by moving vertices. Figure 12-1 shows the simple smiling morph target.

4. **Select the File ⇨ Save Scene As menu command, and save the file as Smiling morph target.mb.**

    This file includes a morph target of a smiling head.

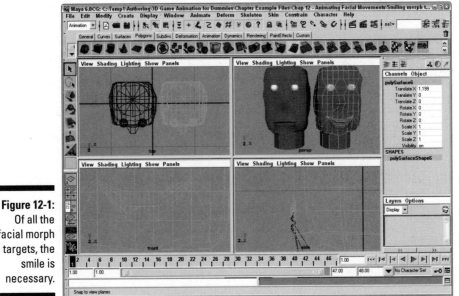

**Figure 12-1:**
Of all the
facial morph
targets, the
smile is
necessary.

# Creating a blend control

Doing all the work to create a morph target is only half the battle. When using morph targets, you need to be able to blend between the two morph targets to varying degrees. To make this easier for animating, creating a control like a slider is helpful and gives you better control over the animating between morph targets.

Because slider controls enable you to precisely control the amount of a morph target that is used, you should use an extreme example when deforming objects to create morph targets. Make a huge smile instead of a small one; you can then use the control to select a small smile or a huge smile, giving you two faces for the work of one.

Follow these steps to create a morph blend control in Maya:

1. **Choose File ➪ Open Scene, and open the Smiling morph target.mb file.**

   This file is the same file that was saved at the end of the preceding example.

2. **Select the smiling morph target, hold down the Shift key, and select the original face object (this selects them both). Then choose the Deform ➪ Create Blend Shape ➪ Option menu command.**

The Create Blend Shape Options dialog box opens, revealing the settings for the blend shape control. This menu can be found in the Animation menu set.

3. **Enter the name** Smiling **in the Name field, and click the Create button.**

    The Name field lets you name the blend control. When hundreds of these controls exist, you'll be glad you named each one.

4. **Select the Window ⇨ Animation Editors ⇨ Blend Shapes menu command.**

    A dialog box opens, offering available blend shape controls, including the Smiling control.

5. **Drag the Smiling control.**

    The original face object slowly morphs from its initial look to the smiling morph target, as shown in Figure 12-2.

6. **Select the File ⇨ Save Scene As menu command, and save the file as Blend control.mb.**

    This file includes a blend control for the smiling morph target.

After a blend control is created for all your morph targets, you can simplify the current view by hiding all the morph targets.

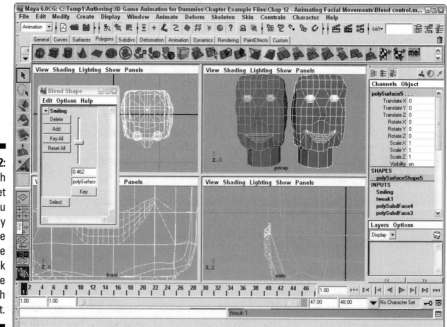

**Figure 12-2:** The morph target lets you gradually change between the original look and the morph target.

# Learning to Talk: Speaking the Basic Phonemes

Not only can morph targets be used for facial expressions like smiling and smirking, but by creating morph targets for all the basic phonemes, you can animate a character talking. A phoneme is the facial expression that occurs when making each of the possible speaking sounds.

As you can imagine, an amazing number of sounds can be made by the human voice. Luckily, many of these sounds use a similar expression, so the number of phonemes with unique expressions is much smaller.

A minimal set of phonemes needed to make characters able to speak includes the following:

- The *A* **sound** has the lips slightly apart.
- The *E* **sound** has the lips slightly apart and the corners of the mouth pulled back.
- The *I* **sound** has the lips apart further than the *A* sound.
- The *O* **sound** has the lips pulled together to form an *O* shape. How appropriate.
- The *U* **sound** has the lips apart and jutting forward.
- The *B, P,* and *T* **sounds** have the lips together and pulled in.
- The *CH* **sound** shows the teeth with the lips apart.
- The *TH* **sound** shows the tongue between the lips.
- The *S* **sound** is the same as the *CH* sound, but with the lips pulled further back.
- The *V* **sound** has the lower lip under the teeth.
- The *M* **sound** has the lips tightly together.

# Syncing Facial Movements with a Soundtrack

After all the morph targets are created for the different phonemes, the next task is synching the morph animation keys with the soundtrack. To do this, print out the waveform for the soundtrack and mark in pen where the different sounds are located. Then you can move the keys to align with these sounds and let the morph blend naturally between the different sounds.

Most 3D programs include features that enable the waveform for a sound-track to be displayed on the animation time line or in an interface where the sound and the keys are both displayed. Figure 12-3 shows a soundtrack wave-form displayed on Maya's time line at the bottom of the interface. This makes aligning keys with the soundtrack easy to do.

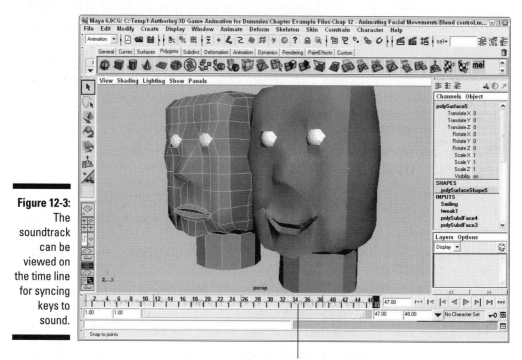

**Figure 12-3:**
The soundtrack can be viewed on the time line for syncing keys to sound.

Soundtrack waveform

# Building Controls for Handling Eye Movements

In addition to the mouth positions, the eyes are often used to add lots to a conversation. If eyes are created using a separate sphere for the eyeball, then you can easily change where the eye is looking by simply rotating the eyeball sphere, but because most characters include two eyes, the effort becomes double, and you run the risk of having a wandering eye.

Another technique for handling eye movements so they move together is to have both eyes aimed at a dummy, non-rendered object that can be moved to control the eye movement. This technique keeps the eyes together and pro-vides a single control for moving both eyes.

Follow these steps to create an eye movement control in Maya:

1. **Choose File ⇨ Open Scene, and open the Blend control.mb file.**

   This file is the same file that was saved at the end of the preceding example.

2. **Select the Create ⇨ Locator menu command to create a locator object.**

   The locator object is a simple point in space. It is a non-rendered object that merely marks a position in space.

3. **Select and move the locator object up in the Front view until it is between the eyes, and then move it in the Side view to be out in front of the eyes.**

   The locator object needs to be far enough in front of the eyes that the eyes can focus on the locator without looking cross-eyed.

4. **Select the locator object, hold down the Shift key, and select one of the eyeball spheres. Then choose the Constrain ⇨ Aim menu command. Repeat this command for the other eyeball sphere.**

   Both eyeball spheres are reoriented to aim at the locator object at all times. You can visually tell this because the axis for the eyeball points at the locator when the eyeball is selected.

   Be sure to select the objects in the correct order, with master first and then the slave, or the locator will be aimed at the eyeball instead.

5. **Select the Create ⇨ Polygon Primitives ⇨ Sphere menu command to create a new sphere object. Move the sphere to be directly in front of the eyeball sphere, and scale it to be a small dot in front of the eyeball.**

   This new sphere is added to the front of the eyeball as a makeshift pupil. This helps as you begin to move the eyes to see exactly where they are looking.

6. **In object mode, select the pupil sphere and choose the Lighting/ Shading ⇨ Assign New Material ⇨ Blinn menu command from the Rendering menu set. In the Attribute Editor that appears, drag the Color slider to the left to make the pupil sphere black.**

   Materials and textures typically aren't applied during the modeling process, but making this quick color change makes the pupil easier to recognize and position. The Lighting/Shading menu is found in the Rendering menu set.

7. **Select the pupil object, hold down the Shift key, and select one of the eyeball spheres. Then choose the Edit ⇨ Parent menu command.**

   By parenting the pupils to the eyes, the pupil spheres move with the eyeballs and stay in place.

8. **With the pupil sphere selected, choose the Edit ⇨ Duplicate menu command to create a copy of the pupil sphere. Then move the copy to the left in the Front view, and repeat the above step to parent this copy to its eyeball.**

   Both eyes should now have parented black pupil spheres in front of them.

9. **Move the locator object back and forth and up and down in the Perspective view.**

   Both eyes follow the locator as it is moved around the scene, as shown in Figure 12-4.

10. **Select the File ⇨ Save Scene As menu command, and save the file as Eye control.mb.**

    This file includes a locator object for the eyeballs.

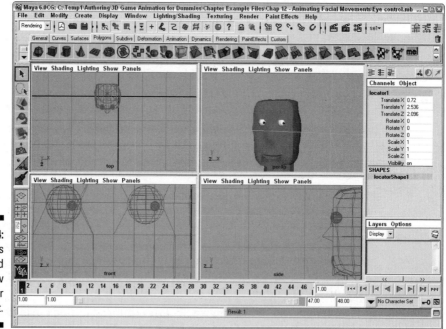

**Figure 12-4:**
The eyeballs were aimed to follow the locator object.

# Chapter 13

# Automating Reactions with Dynamics

**M**anually creating keyframes can be time consuming. It sure would be great if you could just place some solid 3D items in the scene, add some gravity, and click Go and have all the objects fall and bounce off each other automatically. Well, there is such a system. It's called dynamics.

*Dynamics* is the branch of physics that calculates the motion of several colliding objects. It is these calculations that have been added to 3D programs to make automatic keyframes possible.

Calculating dynamics requires that you define the properties of the objects in the scene and the forces that act on each object. These properties and forces can include mass (or weight of the object), stiffness, springiness, gravity, wind, and friction.

Before you give up animating with keyframes completely, be aware that dynamic simulations aren't completely accurate and can often cause more problems than they solve. The more complex a scene, the more chance you have for problems to arise. Calculating dynamic simulations also can take lots of time.

# *Incorporating Physics: I'm Glad I Don't Have to Calculate This by Hand*

Believe it or not, physics is your friend. Physics includes all the mathematical formulas needed to compute the exact position of objects in the scene as they collide with one another. Imagine a pool table. Hitting a pool ball into another transfers some of the energy from one ball to the next ball, causing it to speed away. By keeping track of the energy, speed, and position of each object, you can figure out where each object is going, and the software does all the work for you.

## Soft and rigid body objects

Dynamic simulations use two different types of objects: soft body objects and rigid body objects. Soft body objects are objects that transfer a minimum amount of energy when they collide with other objects. A pillow is a good example of a soft body object. Another aspect of soft body objects is that their surfaces easily deform when they collide with other objects.

On the other hand, rigid body objects are solid, and they transfer a maximum amount of energy when they collide with other objects like a pool ball. Rigid body objects maintain their surface when they collide with other objects.

## Special object types

In addition to soft and rigid body objects, the dynamic features can also define a couple of other special object types that can be involved in dynamic simulations.

One of these special types is cloth. Cloth is unique because it acts like a soft body object, but it is typically flat, allowing it to easily deform and mold around objects that collide with it.

Another special dynamic case is rope. Rope is another soft body object, but when stretched to its limit, it behaves like a rigid body.

Other specialized cases can include wheels, character bodies, and shattering objects.

## Making objects immovable

Some scene objects, such as the ground plane, can be set to be immovable. If all scene objects are subject to gravity, including the ground plane, then the ground plane would fall with the other objects, and nothing would ever collide.

By making certain objects immovable, you're essentially setting their mass values to be equal to the entire Earth. When you drop a bowling ball to the ground, there is an equal and opposite reaction on each colliding object causing the bowling ball to move the Earth, but its impact is so small given the weight of the Earth that it isn't detected.

Follow these steps to create a scene and designate dynamic object types in Maya:

1. **Select the Create ⇨ Polygon Primitives ⇨ Plane menu command to create a flat plane object. Then scale the plane object to fill the entire view.**

   This plane object is the ground plane for this simulation and is set to be immovable so all objects can collide with it.

2. **Select the Create ⇨ Polygon Primitives ⇨ Cylinder ⇨ Options menu command to open the Polygon Cylinder Options dialog box. Select the Edit ⇨ Reset Settings menu command to reset the cylinder settings. Then set the Radius and Height settings to 2.0 and 10, enable the X Axis option, and click the Create button.**

   This creates a long thin cylinder object and places it in the scene.

3. **Select the Create ⇨ Polygon Primitives ⇨ Sphere ⇨ Options menu command to open the Polygon Sphere Options dialog box. Select the Edit ⇨ Reset Settings menu command to reset the sphere settings. Then set the Radius setting to 3.0, and click the Create button.**

   This creates a simple sphere object and places it in the scene.

4. **Select the Create ⇨ Polygon Primitives ⇨ Cube ⇨ Options menu command to open the Polygon Cube Options dialog box. Select the Edit ⇨ Reset Settings menu command to reset the cube settings. Then set the Width, Height, and Depth settings to 10, 1, and 40, and click the Create button.**

   This creates a long thin cube object and places it in the scene.

5. **Select the Create ⇨ Polygon Primitives ⇨ Torus ⇨ Options menu command to open the Polygon Torus Options dialog box. Select the Edit ⇨ Reset Settings menu command to reset the torus settings. Then set the Radius setting to 3.0, and click the Create button.**

   This creates a simple torus object and places it in the scene.

6. **Move the cylinder object up in the Front view until it is just above the ground plane. Then move the cube object to be directly above the cylinder. Move the torus to be just above the cube object in the Front view and located at the end of the cube in the Side view. Finally, move the sphere to be above the cylinder in the Front view and position to the opposite end of the torus in the Side view.**

   All objects are now in position for the dynamic simulation, as shown in Figure 13-1.

   When positioning objects for a dynamic simulation, be careful not to overlap any object, or the collisions between objects cannot be detected.

7. **Select the ground plane object, and choose the Soft/Rigid Bodies ⇨ Create Passive Rigid Body menu command.**

   This command causes the ground plane to be immovable and rigid.

   The Soft/Rigid Bodies menu can be found within the Dynamics menu set.

8. **Select the cylinder, cube, sphere, and torus objects, and choose the Soft/Rigid Bodies ⇨ Create Active Rigid Body menu command.**

   This command causes the selected object to be made into active rigid body objects, which allows them to interact with and collide with other objects in the scene.

9. **Select the File ⇨ Save Scene As menu command, and save the file as Dynamic objects.mb. Close the file when you are finished.**

   This file includes several dynamic objects in position for a dynamic simulation.

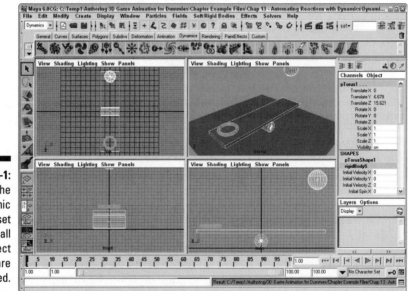

**Figure 13-1:** The dynamic scene is set up, and all the object types are defined.

# Defining Physical Properties Such as Gravity and Friction

Defining a general object type endows objects with certain characteristics and specifies which physical properties are needed to define the object.

# Defining object properties

Changing the physical properties for objects involved in a dynamic simulation can greatly alter the outcome. Think of a meteor model that is three times the size of a spaceship. If the weight properties are set correctly, then the simulation causes the spaceship to go flying when the two collide, but if the meteor object has a weight set to a fraction of the spaceship, then the meteor bounces off the spaceship when they collide. Without the proper properties, the resulting simulation appears fake and even humorous.

## Weight

No single physical property affects the motion of colliding objects more than an object's mass (or weight). Heavy objects push objects around more; lighter objects get pushed around more.

## Volume

Volume is a physical property that you can set, but it is determined by the size of the 3D object. An object's volume along with its mass are used to determine its density, which is the object's weight per volume.

## Surface friction

Surface friction is used to determine how easy the object slides across other surfaces. An object with a high surface friction, like sandpaper, moves slowly and stops quickly when coming in contact with other objects. An object with a low surface friction value, like ice, slides easily and for a long distance when it impacts another object.

## Air friction

Air friction defines how easily an object moves through the air. A rock has a low air friction value, causing it to fall quickly through the air. A feather has a high air friction value, causing it to move slowly through the air and be susceptible to wind forces.

## Springiness

You know what springs do: They bounce. Objects with lots of springiness bounce when they fall and strike the floor. Consider a clump a mud and a rubber ball that weigh the same and have the same volume. If they both fall to the floor, one rebounds, and the other simply sticks where it lands.

# Defining forces

Defining object properties is only part of the equation. In order for the objects to interact, they need some forces to push them around. Forces, such as wind and gravity, are typically defined for the scene and not for individual objects, but objects can be given forces as well, such as an initial speed.

### Gravity

Probably the most common force is gravity, which pulls all objects toward the ground. Gravity can be set to be stronger than normal or even set to a negative value, causing objects to be pulled to the sky.

### Wind

Wind force is typically the same as gravity. It is a single direction force applied to the entire scene. But wind differs from gravity in that it is typically generated using a scene icon that can be positioned to direct the wind.

### Torque

Torque is a force that causes objects in the scene to spin about their center axis. This force can be used to rotate objects in the scene, such as spinning a ninja star as it moves toward the enemy.

Follow these steps to define the acting forces and compute the simulation in Maya:

1. **Choose File ⇨ Open Scene, and open the Dynamic objects.mb file.**

   This file is the same file that was saved at the end of the preceding example.

2. **Select the sphere object, and in the Channel Box located on the right side of the interface, locate the Initial Spin X property and set it to 50. Then set the Mass value to 10 and the Bounciness value to 3.**

   These settings cause the sphere to spin initially when the simulation starts and to be ten times as heavy than the other objects and have three times the bounce.

3. **Select the cylinder, cube, sphere, and torus objects, and choose the Fields ⇨ Gravity menu command.**

   This command enables gravity that is set to its default value for all the selected objects.

4. **Locate the End Frame text field at the bottom of the interface, and enter a value of 200. Then drag the right end of the Range Line so all 200 frames are visible.**

   This gives the simulation more frames to work with so more interaction between the objects can be seen.

5. **Drag the current frame marker in the Timeline to the right to see the resulting dynamic animation.**

By dragging the frame marker, each frame of the dynamic simulation is calculated and displayed in the active view. For this dynamic scene, notice how the all objects drop to the ground floor where they collide with one another. Also notice how the weight of the sphere is enough to launch the torus object. The sphere object then continues to bounce higher and higher. Figure 13-2 shows one frame of the dynamic simulation.

6. **Select the File ⇨ Save Scene As menu command, and save the file as Dynamic simulation.mb. Close the file when you are finished.**

    This file includes the animation of all the dynamic objects colliding with one another.

**Figure 13-2:**
The dynamic calcula-tions are computed automati-cally for all objects in the scene.

# *Using constraints*

Allowing unrestrained motion typically sends objects flying all over the scene. If you need more control over the scene objects, you can use object constraints. These constraints limit the motion of objects by binding them together, allowing only certain motions.

The available constraints found in Maya include the following. You can apply each of these to the selected object or objects using the Soft/Rigid Bodies menu:

- ✔ **Nail Constraint:** Limits the motion of an object to rotating at a fixed distance from the nail point. The motion of a clock's pendulum is an example.

- ✔ **Pin Constraint:** Used to tightly bind two objects together, although the two objects are separated by a specific distance. A barbell weight is an example.

- ✔ **Hinge Constraint:** Also used to bind two objects together, but the objects can be connected to a point that forms an angle between the two objects. The objects can rotate about the point in between them, but the distance stays fixed. The movement of a book's cover opening and closing is an example.

- ✔ **Spring Constraint:** Applied to prevent the movement of an object away from a given point. This constraint is like attaching a bungee cord on the end of an object. As soon as the object moves too far away from the attach point, it springs back towards the attach point.

- ✔ **Barrier Constraint:** Attaches a plane that acts as a barrier to the selected object. The object stops or moves along the plane when the objects contacts the barrier. This saves the step of creating a separate, immovable ground plane.

Follow these steps to apply constraints to a simulation in Maya:

1. **Choose File ⇨ Open Scene, and open the Swingset.mb file.**

   This file includes a simple set of cylinders positioned to form a swingset.

2. **Select the Create ⇨ Polygon Primitives ⇨ Sphere menu command.**

   A sphere object is added to the scene at the center of the view panel.

3. **Select and move the sphere object below the top bar of the swingset and over to the side.**

   This positions the sphere so it can swing below the swingset as though using the force of gravity.

4. **With the sphere selected, choose the Soft/Rigid Bodies ⇨ Nail Constraint menu command.**

   This adds a nail constraint to the sphere at its center. The nail constraint appears as a single point, but a line connecting the sphere and the nail constraint appears if you move the constraint away from the sphere.

5. **Drag the nail constraint point to the center of the cylinder at the top of the swingset.**

   The position of the nail constraint point is the point about which the sphere rotates.

6. **Select the sphere object and choose the Fields ⇨ Gravity menu command. Move the gravity icon beneath the center of the swingset.**

   This command adds a gravity field to the center of the scene, which pulls the sphere towards the ground.

7. **Set the total number of frames to 200, and click the Play Animation button.**

   The sphere is animated rotating under the swingset about the nail constraint, as shown in Figure 13-3.

8. **Select the File ➪ Save Scene As menu command, and save the file as Swinging sphere.mb. Close the file when you are finished.**

   This file includes an animation of the sphere swinging under the swingset.

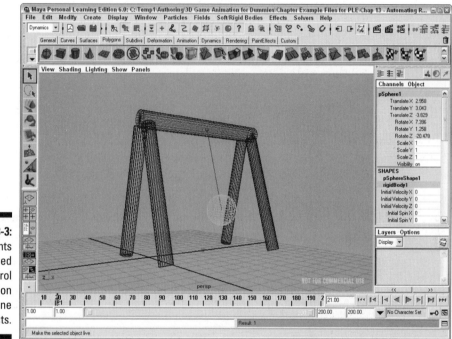

**Figure 13-3:**
Constraints can be used to control the motion of scene objects.

# Part IV
# Animating Game Cut Scenes

The 5th Wave    By Rich Tennant

"Why don't you try blurring the brimstone and then putting a nice glow effect around the hellfire."

## In this part . . .

Animated game elements have to be kept within certain limitations so that the game engine isn't overworked, slowing down the game. But, when you are animating cut scenes, this limitation is removed, and you can finally pull out your high-resolution models and scenery.

This part addresses animating scene elements, a method for creating special effects using particles, and the process of rendering the final animation.

# Chapter 14

# Animating Scene Elements

*V*ideo games traditionally weren't meant to have an ending. They were designed to be perpetual, quarter-eating machines making money from now to infinity, but as video games improved, it became apparent that, like movies, video games would stay popular only for a finite length of time.

So then video games started to include different ways to hook players into coming back. One of the first ploys was to include cute animations between levels, such as those offered by Pacman.

From simple animations, simple storylines began to develop, such as saving a princess from a sinister gorilla named Donkey Kong. One of the first huge storyline successes was a simple game called Dragon's Lair. The game was a huge hit until everyone reached the end, but the message was clear: Storylines can be used to hook players. Game fanatics would pump hundreds of quarters into a game just to see the game ending.

Over time, storyline games have developed into their own unique game genre that is gathering the talent that until now has been reserved for Hollywood. Many games, like James Bond, are using popular actors for speaking and acting roles.

Creating game cut scenes is now a necessity for a game and for animators; they provide a great opportunity to create animations without polygon count or texture size limits, just like Hollywood.

# Using Cut Scenes: All the Stuff That Happens Between Game Levels

Cut scenes are those animation sequences that appear before the game starts, between game levels, and at the conclusion of the game as a way to incorporate a storyline into the game.

Turning the game control over to the player doesn't exactly move the game's storyline along at a quick pace, but dividing the game into levels gives game creators a chance to present cut scenes that tell the story. These cut scenes are often the player's reward for finishing a level and completing a goal.

 For game players who revisit a level several times, be sure to detect whether the game player clicks any of the controller buttons as a way to skip a cut scene. Nothing is more annoying to players than forcing them to watch the same cut scenes over and over before allowing them to play.

## The pregame show

When the game is first loaded, several animations are used to show the game play in action. These can be created by simply capturing someone playing the actual game. Be careful not to reveal any secrets when showing off the game play. Also, switch between different levels to show a variety of the game content.

The pregame animations should include a title screen that shows instructions for continuing, such as "Press the start button." The title screen can be animated also.

Another common practice during the pregame is to use the animations to introduce the characters, enemies, goals, or weapons. By presenting this information before the game starts, you don't need to introduce it during cut scenes.

## Introducing the game

When the game is first started, an introductory animation that introduces the story can be played. This animation, along with the ending, should be captivating and get the player excited about taking on this mission. It can also be used to explain how players progress through the various levels and why they are playing the game.

## Explaining the game

Following the introduction animation, a tutorial-based animation with limited player control tasks can be presented. This is a helpful way to explain how the different controls work and allows the player to test these controls before encountering an enemy.

## Tell a story with animation

Before each cut scene storyboard is completed, you need to determine the total number of cut scenes that you have available. Then you need to divide the story into logical animation sequences that move the story along.

# Presenting High-Resolution Images: What to Do After the Animations Are Finished

In addition to cut scene animations, several other high-resolution images may be needed.

## Rendering backgrounds

Rendered background can add lots to a game scene, including details that appear 3D without adding to the total game polygon count. Rendered backgrounds have a specific resolution that they must use.

## Rendering a title screen

Another commonly rendered screen is the title screen, which includes characters, art, and the game logo.

## Rendering marketing materials

Because animators have access to all the scene objects, characters, and environments and they have the ability to render scenes, it is common for the marketing department to request images that can be used for the game box, instruction manuals, and Web site graphics. Each of these requests requires different resolutions for the final images.

# Animating Cut Scenes: No Limits

When working on cut scenes, you don't need to worry about any of the typical limits that are imposed on animating for the game because cut scenes are run directly from the game's media and through a game engine. This gives you a chance to animate things like cameras and materials.

## Modeling for cut scenes: I can use NURBS!

If you've modeled any characters or scene objects with too many polygons that you needed to cut down, be sure to save the high-res version because you can include them when creating cut scenes and you can let the players see what you really wanted the character to look like.

In addition to the high-res models, you can also use other modeling techniques such as NURBS and patches. These additional modeling types open a whole new arsenal of objects that you can model.

Follow these steps to model a raindrop using NURBS in Maya:

1. **Choose the Create ⇨ NURBS Primitives ⇨ Sphere menu command to add a NURBS sphere to the scene.**

   The NURBS sphere appears in the center of the view panel. Notice how the NURBS sphere is composed of curved lines instead of polygonal faces.

2. **Right-click the sphere object and select Control Vertex from the pop-up menu.**

   The control vertices (CVs) for the NURBS sphere appear around the sphere object. By moving these points, you can reshape the NURBS object.

3. **Select the single CV at the very top of the sphere object and move it upward, away from the sphere.**

   Moving this single CV forms a sharp point at the top of the sphere.

4. **Drag over the second horizontal row of CVs in the sphere and move them upward.**

   This rounds out the top of the raindrop.

5. **Drag over the third horizontal row of CVs in the sphere and scale the CVs in towards the center of the sphere slightly.**

   Scaling the third row of CVs causes the upper end of the raindrop to be more narrow, as shown in Figure 14-1.

   You can change the resolution of the NURBS surfaces displayed in the view panel using the 1, 2, and 3 keyboard keys. 1 shows NURBS surfaces at the lowest resolution, 2 at a medium resolution, and 3 shows them at a highest resolution.

6. **Select the File ⇨ Save Scene As menu command, and save the file as NURBS raindrop.mb. Close this file when you are finished.**

   This file includes a simple raindrop created by moving some control vertices for a NURBS sphere object.

**Figure 14-1:**
NURBS
surfaces
flow better
and are
generally
smoother
than
polygon
objects
because
they are
made from
curves.

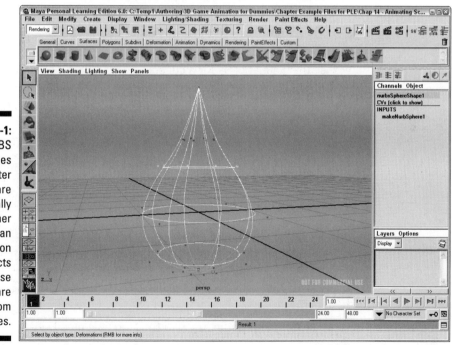

# Animating cameras: I finally have a chance to control the camera!

One aspect of game animation that you never have to worry about when working with a game engine is animating the camera. For 3D games, the camera is set by the player, but for cut scenes, you can control the camera all by yourself.

Moving cameras are great for certain instances, such as a car chase or an overhead flyby of an area, but for most scenes, moving cameras aren't recommended and can actually detract from the scene. As a general rule, animate the camera moving only if you have a good reason to do so.

Follow these steps to animate a camera flying down a tube in Maya:

1. **Select the Create ⇨ CV Curve Tool menu command, and click in the Side view to create a smooth wavy curve.**

   This curve is used to make a tube that you can use to create a waterslide-like effect using a moving camera.

2. **Select the Create ⇨ NURBS Primitives ⇨ Circle menu command to create a perfect circle.**

   Because this animation is for a cut scene, you have no problem using NURBS primitives.

3. **With the circle object selected, choose the Edit ⇨ Duplicate menu command several times to create eight circle objects.**

   These circles can be used to create a loft profile using the drawn curve.

4. **Use the Move and Rotate tools to position the circles perpendicular to the path at regular intervals in the Side view.**

   The circles should be placed along the curve so they are visible in the Side view.

5. **With the Select tool selected, press and hold the Shift key and choose each placed circle in order from the beginning of the curve to the end. Then select the Surfaces ⇨ Loft menu command.**

   Each of the circles is connected with edges that make a tube running the length of the curve.

   The Surfaces menu can be found in the Modeling menu set.

6. **With the tube object selected, choose the Lighting/Shading ⇨ Assign New Material ⇨ Blinn menu command. Then, in the Attribute Editor that opens, click the Map button to the right of the Color attribute, and choose the Checker option in the Create Render Node palette.**

This assigns a checker pattern material to the tube object, making it easy to detect movement as you move down the tube.

The Lighting/Shading menu can be found in the Rendering menu set.

7. **Select the View ⇨ Select Camera panel menu command for the Perspective view. Then press and hold the Shift key, and select the curve path in the center of the tube. Then choose the Animate ⇨ Motion Paths ⇨ Attach to Motion Path menu command.**

If you're having trouble selecting the center curve, you can easily select the camera and the path from the Outliner interface. Just choose the Window ⇨ Outliner menu command to open the Outliner, and select both with the Ctrl key held down. The items are highlighted when selected.

Using this command attaches the camera to the curve as a motion path, causing it to be animated moving along the path.

The Animate menu can be found in the Animation menu set.

8. **Drag the current frame marker in the Timeline to see the animated camera in the Perspective view.**

To see the applied texture, press the 6 key when the Perspective view is active.

When you drag the current frame marker, the animation plays back in the Perspective view, as shown in Figure 14-2.

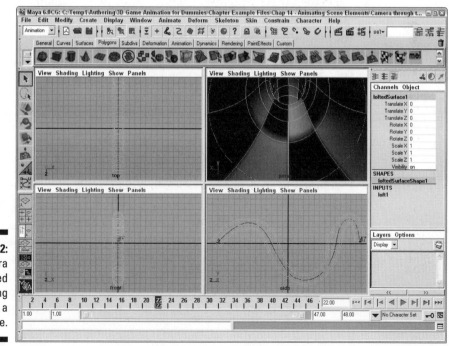

**Figure 14-2:**
A camera animated flying through a tube.

9. **Select the File ⇨ Save Scene As menu command, and save the file as Camera through tube.mb. Close this file when you are finished.**

   This file includes a tube with a camera animated flying through its center.

# Animating lights (and not just a flashlight)

Many scenes use static lights that don't move, but lights can also move in the scene. Moving lights can have a dramatic impact, or they can be subtle like the flickering of a candle.

To animate a light, you can move it about the scene just like an object, or you can change its attributes: Fade a light over several different frames, or change its color. Animated lights can also cast unique shadows that grow longer.

Follow these steps to animate a light moving back and forth in Maya:

1. **Choose File ⇨ Open Scene, and open the Chair on ground.mb file.**

   This file includes a simple scene with a chair positioned on a ground plane, and a light fixture above that has been animated to swing gently back and forth.

2. **Select the Create ⇨ Lights ⇨ Point Light menu command to add a light to the scene.**

   The new light appears in the center of the view.

3. **Move the light until it is positioned within the light fixture in frame 1. Then hold down the Shift key and select the light fixture and choose the Edit ⇨ Parent menu command.**

   By parenting the point light to the light fixture, the point light moves along with the animated fixture.

4. **Select the point light object, open the Attribute Editor, and, in the Shadows section, enable the Use Depth Map Shadows option.**

   This turns shadows on for the selected light.

5. **Select the Render ⇨ Render Current Frame menu command. Then drag the Time Slider to frame 25 and render another frame.**

   Notice how the shadow has chair's shadow has changed between the two rendered images. If the entire animation were rendered, the shadow would move as the light moves, even though the chair stays still. Figure 14-3 shows a single rendered frame.

6. **Select the File ⇨ Save Scene As menu command, and save the file as Animated light.mb. Close this file when you are finished.**

   This file includes an animated light that casts the shadow of a stationary chair.

**Figure 14-3:** Animating lights can change the scene dramatically.

# Animating textures: Just like television

Textures have parameters, and parameters can be easily animated. To animate a material parameter, simply set the initial parameter value, set a keyframe (keyframes and basic animation techniques are covered in Chapter 10), then change the frame and the parameter, and set another keyframe. The software interpolates the values for all the frames between these two keyframes, so you can make an object slowly turn from blue to white over 20 frames or make a ghost object slowly become fully transparent over 50 frames.

Another way to animate textures is to replace the texture image with a movie. By loading a movie that loops, such as a flickering flame, the animation can run indefinitely without having to change the texture.

Follow these steps to create an effect by animating a material in Maya:

1. **Choose File ⇨ Open Scene, and open the Camera through tube.mb file.**

   This file is the same file that was saved at the end of the preceding example.

2. **Select the tube object, and then choose the Window ⇨ Attribute Editor menu command to open the Attribute Editor to the right of the interface. Then select the Blinn1 tab at the top of the Attribute Editor.**

   The Attribute Editor opens all the nodes for the selected object. Each node is presented as a tab across the top of the Attribute Editor.

3. **Click the map icon to the right of the Color attribute in the Attribute Editor to open the Checker1 node. Then select the place2dTexture1 tab at the top of the Attribute Editor.**

   The place2dTexture1 node controls the placing of the checker texture on the tube object. By animating its attributes, you can make the checker texture spin about the tube.

4. **With the current frame marker at frame 0 on the Timeline, right-click each of the Repeat UV values and select the Set Key pop-up menu command.**

   The Repeat UV values are highlighted orange to show that the value is controlled by an animation key.

5. **Drag the current frame marker on the Timeline to frame 25, set the Repeat UV values to 32, and right-click to set keys for these values.**

   Setting a key at frame 25 causes the tube checker material to change from a value of 4 at frame 1 to a value of 32 at frame 25. This effect makes the checker text look like it's spinning.

6. **Drag the current frame marker on the Timeline to frame 48, set the Repeat UV values back to 4, and right-click to set keys for these values.**

   Setting the Repeat UV values back to 4 causes the spinning texture to stop halfway through the animation and reverse direction.

7. **Drag the current frame marker in the Timeline to see the animated camera in the Perspective view.**

   When you drag the current frame marker, the animation plays back in the Perspective view, as shown in Figure 14-4. Notice how the checker texture has changed.

8. **Select the File ⇨ Save Scene As menu command, and save the file as Spinning texture.mb. Close the file when you are finished.**

   This file includes a camera animated flying through a tube with a texture animated spinning within it.

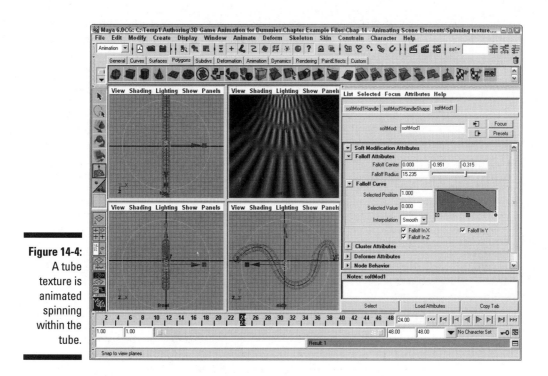

**Figure 14-4:**
A tube
texture is
animated
spinning
within the
tube.

# Chapter 15

# Animating with Particles

*I*magine receiving a storyboard for the next cut scene and discovering that it includes a scene of the character struggling to walk through a dust storm. Well, you now know how to animate characters walking and struggling, but how in the world do you create a dust storm?

The answer lies with thousands of small objects called particles. A *particle system* is a collection of small shaded objects that act together as a group with a degree of randomness. These systems may be used to create smoke, fire, and yes, even dust storms.

Particle systems are great for adding all sorts of special effects, but keeping track of all those small pieces can really take lots of computing power. This means that using them within a game engine is difficult, but they work well for cut scenes when you aren't limited by the number of polygons the scene can handle.

You can create special effects such as dust storms within a game engine using animated 2D texture maps and programmed pixel manipulation, but they lack the realism of full-blown particle systems with hundreds of thousands of particles.

# Creating Special Effects with Particles: A Treat for All the Pyromaniacs

Particle systems can be used for a wide assortment of cases. A simple particle system featuring snowflake-shaped objects can be used to animate a winter scene; a can of spray paint can be animated with particles that shoot out from its nozzle; or bright, glowing embers can be projected from the top of a firework.

Particles can come in many different shapes. They can be small cubes, simple points, spheres, or flat planes that always face the camera. The size and randomness of the particle's size are configurable.

Particles can also have materials and random materials to add variety to the system. Particle materials can also be animated to change over time.

All particles have a life span that determines how long the particles stay around in the scene.

## Creating smoke and dust

The key to creating a good smoke and dust particle effect is to create enough particles that each individual element can no longer be identified. Smoke and dust can affect the lighting in the scene.

Be sure to disable highlights for any material that is applied to smoke and dust particles.

## Creating fire

Fire can be created by simply endowing particles with a glowing material that radiates into the world. Making the particle material semi-transparent gives the flames the consistent look.

## Creating clouds

Another way to use particles is to create clouds. Hundreds of semi-transparent particles clumped together can create wonderfully realistic clouds.

Follow these steps to create a fire effect in Maya:

1. **Select the Create ➪ Polygon Primitives ➪ Sphere menu command to create a sphere object. Then scale the sphere object to fill the entire view.**

   This sphere object provides an object to which you can apply a fire effect.

2. **With the sphere selected, choose the Effects ➪ Create Fire menu command.**

A fire emitter object is added to the center of the sphere object.

The Effects menu can be found within the Dynamics menu set.

3. **Drag the current frame marker in the Timeline to see the flames rise from the sphere object.**

   The rising particles are random in nature and displayed as circles in the Perspective view, as shown in Figure 15-1. Each particle has a glowing transparent material applied to it. Each of these settings can be configured, but the fire effect is common enough that it is made available as a preset.

   Other effect presets include Smoke, Fireworks, and Lightning.

4. **Select the Render ⇨ Render Current Frame menu command to render the scene.**

   Particle effects such as fire can be seen only when rendered. This command renders the scene in a separate window. Figure 15-2 shows a rendered fire effect.

   The Render menu can be found within the Rendering menu set.

5. **Select the File ⇨ Save Scene As menu command, and save the file as Sphere on fire.mb. Close the file when you are finished.**

   This file includes a simple sphere with a fire particle effect applied to it.

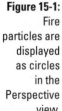

Figure 15-1:
Fire
particles are
displayed
as circles
in the
Perspective
view.

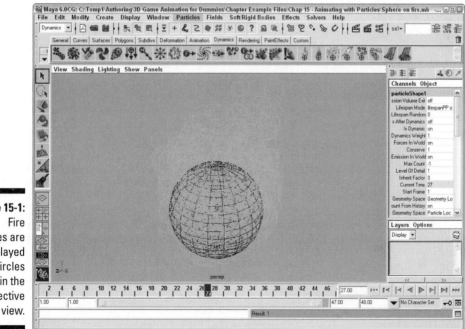

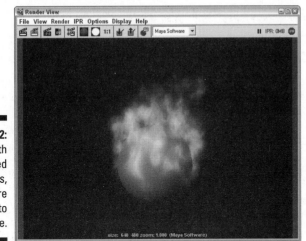

**Figure 15-2:**
With rendered fire effects, the sphere appears to be on fire.

# Pinpointing a Particle's Starting Location with Particle Emitters

When creating a particle system, you first need to define the source of the particles. This object is where all the particles originate and is called an emitter. Emitters are typically non-rendered icons that are added to the scene, but a scene object, such as the edges of a snow globe, can also be made into an emitter.

When the emitter object is selected, all the particles emitted from the selected emitter are also selected, and the settings for the particle system are made available.

## Using emitter types

The first particle property to be set for emitters is the direction in which the particles move when first created. This can be determined by a setting or by the shape of the emitter. Omni emitters send particles forth in all directions from a central point, directional emitters focus the particles to a specific direction or cone-shaped area, and volume emitters confine the particles to a certain volume.

# Using an object as an emitter

Any selected object can be specified as an emitter. When an object is selected as an emitter, particles are emitted from every object vertex.

Follow these steps to create a particle emitter in Maya:

1. **Select the File ⇨ New menu command to reset the current scene.**

    Resetting the scene deletes all current objects and starts a new file.

2. **Select the Particles ⇨ Create Emitter ⇨ Options menu command to open the Emitter Options dialog box. Then select Directional as the Emitter Type, and click the Create button.**

    A directional type emitter is added to the scene, but no particles are visible yet. Particles are emitted as the frames progress, so no particles exist at frame 1. Remember that the Particles menu is in the Dynamics menu set.

3. **Select the Create ⇨ Polygon Primitives ⇨ Cube menu command to create a cube object. Then move the cube object to the right in the Perspective view.**

    This cube object gives you an object that you can make into an emitter object.

4. **With the cube selected, choose the Particles ⇨ Emit from Object menu command. In the Attribute Editor, change the Emitter Type to Omni.**

    The cube object is now an object emitter, and the Omni emitter type causes the particles to move in all directions from each corner.

    The Particles menu can be found within the Dynamics menu set.

5. **Drag the current frame marker in the Timeline to see particles being emitted from both the directional emitter and the sphere object.**

    The emitter releases particles in a steady straight stream, but the sphere object releases particles from every face creating a swarm of particles engulfing the sphere, as shown in Figure 15-3.

6. **Select the File ⇨ Save Scene As menu command, and save the file as Particle emitters.mb. Close the file when you are finished.**

    This file includes a simple directional emitter and a cube used as an emitter.

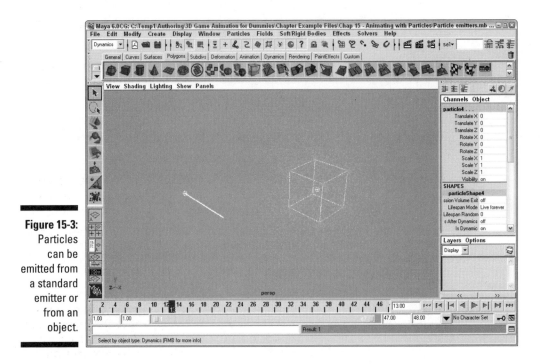

**Figure 15-3:**
Particles
can be
emitted from
a standard
emitter or
from an
object.

# Configuring Particle Systems: Randomness Is the Name of the Game

With a particle system selected, you can use many different settings to control how the particles move about the scene. For each of these settings, you have options to define the amount of randomness that is applied to each setting. For example, setting the size of particles to be random creates a realistic aspect for the particle system.

## Setting particle rate

Regardless of the direction, you can set the particle rate, which is the number of new particles that are generated each second. Rates of 100 are common, but for an animation of only 10 seconds, 1,000 particles are emitted into the scene for each emit point. If you use a cube as an emitter with eight corners, then 8,000 particles are emitted every second, which is 80,000 particles for the 10-second animation.

Particle systems can include hundreds of thousands of particles, which can quickly overwhelm your system. Be aware of the number of particles that you're generating before setting the figure too high.

## Setting particle life span

One way to control the total number of particles in a scene is to set the life span of the particles. The life span value is the number of frames for which the particle stays around before disappearing. Smoke particles, for example, float off and eventually disappear.

## Setting particle shape and size

Particles can be set to use several different default shapes, including points, dots, spheres, cubes, and 2D plane elements that always face the camera. For each of these shapes, you can also set the particles size. Just because it's a particle doesn't mean it can't be as large as other objects in the scene, but large particles consume the view.

## Spawning new particles

As if all the emitter particles weren't enough, you can also select to have each particle spawn new particles when it dies, when it collides with another object, or after so much time. Spawning new particles enables you to create sparks when bullets strike a metal surface and other effects.

If you read the warning on controlling the particle rate, then you probably realize that using the particle spawn feature can multiply the total number of particles very quickly.

## Changing particle materials

When the particle set is selected, you can apply or edit the material that is applied to the entire particle set. Using transparency helps make all the particles appear as flames or clouds. Although the material is applied to every particle, you can set the material to be random using the particle system's settings.

Follow these steps to configure a particle system in Maya:

1. **Choose File ⇨ Open Scene, and open the Particle emitters.mb file.**

   This file is the same file that was saved at the end of the preceding example.

2. **Drag the Timeline to make some particles appear from each emitter. Then click the particles from the cube object.**

   Selecting a single particle selects the entire particle set. Note that the cube object, however, is not selected.

3. **Select the Window ⇨ Attribute Editor menu command to open the Attribute Editor on the right side of the interface, and click the particleShape tab at the top of the Attribute Editor. Locate and open the Render Attributes section, and change the Particle Render Type to Spheres. Click the Current Render Type button, and change the Radius value to 0.15.**

   With the cube's particle system selected, you can open the Attribute Editor to gain access to the particle system's properties, including the shape, which is changed to spheres.

4. **Click the particles from the directional emitter to select them.**

   Selecting a single particle selects the entire particle set.

5. **With the Attribute Editor still open, click the Emitter tab at the top of the Attribute Editor. Locate and open the Distance/Direction Attributes section, and change the Spread value to 0.5. Then, in the Basic Emission Speed Attributes section, change the Speed value to 5.0.**

   Increasing the Spread value causes the straight line of particles to be spread randomly as they leave the emitter; increasing the Speed value causes the particles to move quicker and travel more distance per frame, as shown in Figure 15-4.

6. **Select the File ⇨ Save Scene As menu command, and save the file as Changed properties.mb. Close the file when you are finished.**

   This file includes a simple directional emitter and a cube used as an emitter with new particle properties.

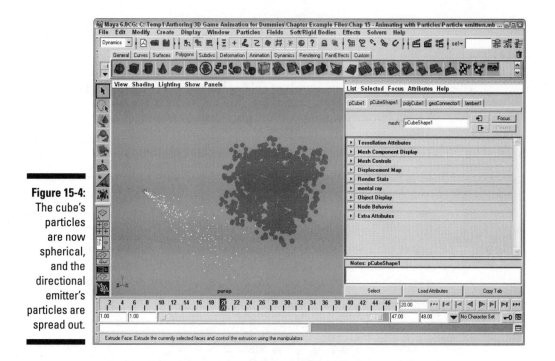

**Figure 15-4:**
The cube's particles are now spherical, and the directional emitter's particles are spread out.

# Creating a Blizzard: Combining Particles with Dynamics

Particles systems are tied closely to dynamic simulations, and all dynamic forces can be used to influence the motion of the particles. Collisions can also be enabled for particles, giving you the ability to animate a swarm of bugs bouncing off the front of a car.

Follow these steps to add forces to a particle system in Maya:

1. **Choose File ⇨ Open Scene, and open the Changed properties.mb file.**

   This file is the same file that was saved at the end of the preceding example.

2. **Select the particle system that is coming from the cube emitter, and then choose the Fields ⇨ Vortex menu command.**

A vortex force field is added to the scene, but its magnitude value is so small compared to the particles that it doesn't really affect the particle system.

3. **Select the Window ➪ Attribute Editor menu command to open the Attribute Editor on the right side of the interface, and click the vortexField tab at the top of the Attribute Editor. Locate and open the Vortex Filed Attributes section, and change the Magnitude value to 1000.**

   This increases the power of the Vortex field in the scene.

4. **Drag the frame marker in the Timeline at the bottom of the interface.**

   The cube emitter's particles are affected by the Vortex field, causing them to swirl about and out of view, as shown in Figure 15-5. Notice that the other particle system is unaffected by the Vortex.

5. **Select the File ➪ Save Scene As menu command, and save the file as Vortex particles.mb. Close the file when you are finished.**

   This file includes a particle system being impacted by a Vortex force field.

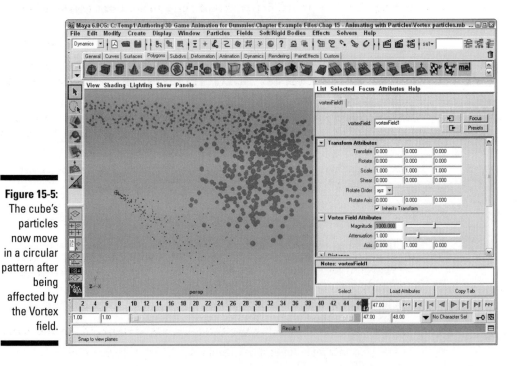

**Figure 15-5:** The cube's particles now move in a circular pattern after being affected by the Vortex field.

# Creating a Custom Particle with Instanced Objects: When Simple Shaped Particles Aren't Enough

Animating a swarm of bees emerging from a hive and chasing a character would be a nightmare if you had to manually animate every bee, but using a particle system makes easy work of it. Just animate one bee, and create a particle system with the correct motion. Then replace the particles with the bee object, and the bees are ready to chase the pesky character.

 Okay, I'll apologize before I say it again, but remember my warning about not overwhelming your system. A simple model like a bee can easily include 100 polygons, and if a particle system generates 200 particles, then we're talking about 20,000 polygons.

Follow these steps to create a particle system using a custom object in Maya:

1. **Select the Create ⇨ Polygon Primitives ⇨ Torus menu command to create a torus object.**

   This torus object is used as the custom object to replace the particles.

2. **Select the Particles ⇨ Create Emitter ⇨ Options menu command to open the Emitter Options dialog box. Select Omni as the Emitter Type, and click the Create button.**

   An omni type emitter is added to the scene, but no particles are visible yet. Particles are emitted as the frames progress, so no particles exist at frame 1.

3. **Select the Particles ⇨ Instancer (Replacement) ⇨ Options menu command to open the Particle Instancer Options dialog box.**

   The Particle Instancer Options dialog box includes a list where you can choose the object to replace a particle system, which can be several separate objects.

4. **Select the torus object in the Perspective view, click the Add Selection button in the Particle Instancer Options dialog box, and then click the Create button.**

   All particles are switched to use the torus object.

5. **Drag the frame marker in the Timeline at the bottom of the interface.**

   The particles are now flying donuts, as shown in Figure 15-6.

6. **Select the File ➪ Save Scene As menu command, and save the file as Torus particles.mb. Close the file when you are finished.**

This file includes a particle system made of torus objects.

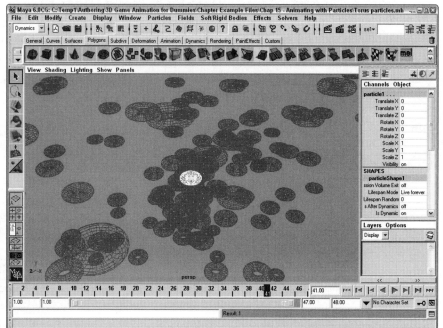

**Figure 15-6:**
All the particles are replaced with torus objects.

# Chapter 16

# Rendering an Animation

● ● ● ● ● ● ● ● ● ● ● ● ● ● ● ● ● ● ● ● ● ● ● ● ● ● ● ● ● ● ● ● ● ● ● ● ● ● ● ● ● ● ● ● ● ● ● ●

## In This Chapter

▶ Exploring the rendering options

▶ Raytracing images for realism

▶ Cartoon rendering

● ● ● ● ● ● ● ● ● ● ● ● ● ● ● ● ● ● ● ● ● ● ● ● ● ● ● ● ● ● ● ● ● ● ● ● ● ● ● ● ● ● ● ● ● ● ● ●

*R*endering a game happens in real time, but when creating cut scenes, you need to render the animations using the rendering features included with your software. Understanding the various options enables you to judge between the quality and speed of the rendering process.

When modeling and building games, you should take care to keep the models trim and within the designed guidelines, but just because these restrictions aren't imposed for cut scenes doesn't mean that you can enable every feature.

A software render engine is like a race car: It comes with a perfectly good engine, but if you want to get even more power, you can replace the engine with a larger, more powerful one. Different rendering engines have different abilities, from creating ultra-realistic scenes to making cartoon-rendered scenes.

## Creating Test Renders: Try It before You Buy It

Rendering an entire animation at a production-quality setting can take some time. Before you take the time to render the entire animation, you should do some spot checking to make sure that the scene and the render settings are correct.

## Using the Render View window

When rendering an image or an animation, you typically have the choice of rendering directly to a file or rendering to a preview window that is only temporary. The Render View window is mainly used for rendering quick test images. Many scene details such as bump and reflection maps aren't visible until the image is rendered, so creating a test render of a single frame in the Render View window helps you to check the material settings before wasting a whole day rendering a mistake.

Follow these steps to render to the Render View window in Maya:

1. **Select the File ➪ New menu command to reset the current scene. Open or create a scene to render.**

   For this chapter, I'm using a simple scene that I created.

2. **Select the Rendering menu set from the drop-down list at the top left of the interface.**

   Each menu set includes a unique set of menus.

3. **Right-click in the Perspective view to make it the active view.**

   The Render View window renders whichever view is active.

4. **Choose the Render ➪ Render Current Frame menu command.**

   This command opens the Render View window and renders the current frame for the active view, as shown in Figure 16-1.

5. **Select the File ➪ Save Scene As menu command, and save the file as Mushroom scene.mb. Close the file when you are finished.**

   This file includes a rendered scene.

**Figure 16-1:** The Render View window renders and displays the current scene using the default settings.

# Rendering an area

For complex scenes, even the test renders take some time. Another feature that most software programs include is the ability to render only a designated area within the Render View window.

For example, if you've changed the bump map settings on a character, then you need to see only a portion of the render to check whether the settings are correct. Using the Render Area feature, you can drag within the Render View window to select just the area that you want to render and only that portion will be updated.

Follow these steps to render a region in Maya:

1. **Choose the File ⇨ Open Scene menu command, and open the Mushroom scene.mb file.**

    This file is the same file that was saved at the end of the preceding example.

2. **Right-click in the Perspective view to make it the active view.**

    The Render View window renders whichever view is active.

3. **Choose the Render ⇨ Render Current Frame menu command.**

    This command opens the Render View window and renders the current frame for the active view. Keep the Render View window open during the next steps.

4. **In the Top view, select the ground plane object and choose Window ⇨ Attribute Editor to open the Attribute Editor.**

    All the nodes for the ground plane are shown in the Attribute Editor.

5. **Select the lambert2 material tab at the top of the Attribute Editor. Then click the map button to the right of the Color attribute. Click the color swatch for the Rock Color attribute, and change the color to white.**

    The material for the ground plane changes.

6. **In the Render View window menu, choose the Render ⇨ Render Region menu command.**

    A red box appears within the Render View window, and the area within the box is rendered with the new material for the ground plane, as shown in Figure 16-2.

7. **Select the File ⇨ Save Scene As menu command, and save the file as Render area.mb. Close the file when you are finished.**

    This file includes a rendered scene with a new rendered area.

**Figure 16-2:**
The Render
View
window
allows you
to render
just a given
area.

# Selecting a view and range

Before a rendering begins, you can choose which view is rendered, including camera views. You also have options to render the entire animation range or the current frame. By selecting and rendering only a single, specific frame within the animation, you can quickly check how the scene looks.

# Making animation previews

Good animation is all about timing, and sometimes the view panes fail in showing the timing correctly. Before rendering a final animation, you should create a preview animation and let others look at it. Most 3D packages include the ability to render a preview, but if yours doesn't, you can create a preview by rendering the animation at half or quarter size.

Follow these steps to make an animation preview in Maya:

1. **Choose the File ⇨ Open Scene menu command, and open the Render area.mb file.**

   This file is the same file that was saved at the end of the preceding example.

2. **Right-click in the Perspective view to make it the active view.**

   The Render View window renders whichever view is active.

3. **Choose the Window ⇨ Playblast ⇨ Options menu command to open the Playblast Options dialog box. Set the Display Size to From Window and the Scale value to 1.0. Then click the Playblast button.**

   This command starts creating an animation preview using the preview settings in the active view. After it's completed, the animation is opened and played in the default media player, as shown in Figure 16-3.

4. **Select the File ⇨ Save Scene As menu command, and save the file as Animation preview.mb. Close the file when you are finished.**

   This file includes a rendered scene and an animation preview.

**Figure 16-3:**
The Playblast feature lets you create animation previews.

# Exploring the Rendering Options

Before initiating a render job for an animation that includes more than 2,000 frames, you'd better make sure that all the render settings are what they should be. Nothing is worse than waiting an entire day for a render job to complete only to realize that you forgot to enable a crucial setting.

## Selecting a format

If you decide to render to a file, you can choose which image or video format to use in the Render Settings dialog box. Although images are typically rendered using an image format like TIF or Targa and video is rendered using a video format like AVI or Quicktime, most 3D software lets you render animations to an image format. Each frame is saved as a separate image file with the image name and frame number attached to each file.

Rendering animation frames to individual images requires that an image-editing package like Adobe's Premiere is used to assemble the images into a final animation file, but it gives you chance to manually look at the results while the animation is still in the process of being rendered. It also gives an easy way to manually edit the frames.

## Setting resolution

Along with specifying the file format, the Render Settings dialog box includes options for setting the resolution of the final rendered images. Most game companies have very strict resolution requirements with specific aspect ratios, depending on where the animation will be shown. Aspect ratio is the ratio of width to height. If the aspect ratio is incorrect, then the image can still be used, but it is distorted or cut off in order to fit.

Before rendering an animation, double-check the resolution settings because the wrong resolution takes extra time to render.

## Using network rendering

Most 3D packages include the ability to render images and animations using a network. By installing a minimum installation of the software, you can use the computer's resources to render images when the computer is idle, such as at night and over weekends. This is a great way to speed up the rendering cycle immensely without adding lots of cost.

# Adding Effects at the Last Minute

Most 3D software packages include some special rendering effects that can be specified and added in at render time.

All these render effects have an impact on the total render time.

## Enabling anti-aliasing

When dealing with pixel-based images, you run the risk of having jagged lines in your image. These jagged edges occur when square, dark pixels are placed next to lighter-colored pixels in a lower resolution image.

Anti-aliasing is a process that smoothes these jagged edges (or artifacts) by reducing the color of neighboring pixels to make a more gradual transition from the harsh dark colors to the lighter colors. This smoothing effect makes the image appear softer and removes the jagged lines.

Figure 16-4 shows two rendered examples that have been zoomed in to show the fine detail. The image on the left was rendered using a low anti-aliasing setting; the image on the right was rendered using a high anti-aliasing setting.

**Figure 16-4:**
Higher
quality
images are
possible
using the
anti-aliasing
settings.

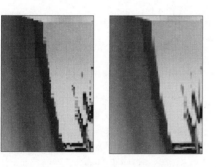

## Using the depth of field effect

A depth of field effect causes objects in the 3D scene to appear clearly at a position where the camera is focused and gradually blurs all other objects, depending on their distance from this central focus point. For example, if you have several cars in a row, you could focus on the shiny red one in the middle by making it the center of focus. All other cars gradually appear more blurred the further they are from this center-focused car.

# Adding atmospheric effects

Atmospheric effects such as fog or haze can be added during the rendering process. Fog can be a simple coloring of the entire scene, or it can appear in layers where you can define the thickness, such as cloud cover with an airplane rising above it.

# Adding motion blur

Objects that are in motion can be blurred to show their speed. This effect is called motion blur, and the amount of blurring applied to an object depends on the object's speed.

Follow these steps to render the scene with motion blur in Maya:

1. **Choose the File ➪ Open Scene menu command, and open the Animation preview.mb file.**

   This file is the same file that was saved at the end of the preceding example.

2. **Select the Window ➪ Rendering Editors ➪ Render Globals menu command to open the Render Global Settings dialog box.**

   The Render Global Settings dialog box opens, containing all the render options for the current scene.

3. **Click the Software Render tab, locate and open the Motion Blur section, and enable the Motion Blur option. Then set the Motion Blur Type to 3D and the Blur by Frame setting to 6.**

   This activates the motion blur option and uses the six frames surrounding the current frame to blur the rendered image.

4. **Right-click in the Perspective view to make it the active view.**

   The Render View window renders whichever view is active.

5. **Choose the Render ➪ Render Current Frame menu command.**

   This command opens the Render View window, renders the current frame for the active view, and includes the motion blur applied to the snake in the grass, as shown in Figure 16-5.

6. **Select the File ➪ Save Scene As menu command, and save the file as Motion blur.mb. Close the file when you are finished.**

   This file includes a rendered scene with the motion blur option enabled.

**Figure 16-5:**
The motion
blur option
blurs any
objects in
the scene
that are
moving.

# Raytracing Images for Realism

Another render option available within the Rendering Settings dialog box is to enable raytracing. Raytracing is a method of computing lighting effects that is very accurate. It works by casting light rays into the scene and following them as they bounce around the scene. The results can be noticed especially around shadows, transparent glass, and reflective materials.

The drawback to raytracing is that rendering a scene using raytracing can take a long time. The length of time really depends on the number of transparent and reflective objects in the scene.

Follow these steps to render the scene with raytracing in Maya:

1. **Choose the File ⇨ Open Scene menu command, and open the Motion blur.mb file.**

   This file is the same file that was saved at the end of the preceding example.

2. **Select the Window ⇨ Rendering Editors ⇨ Render Globals menu command to open the Render Global Settings dialog box.**

   The Render Global Settings dialog box opens, containing all the render options for the current scene.

3. **Click the Software Render tab, locate and open the Raytracing Quality section, and enable the Raytracing option.**

   This activates the raytracing option.

4. **Right-click in the Perspective view to make it the active view.**

   The Render View window renders whichever view is active.

5. **Choose the Render ⇨ Render Current Frame menu command.**

   This command opens the Render View window and renders the current frame for the active view using the raytracing option. The results are especially visible in the crystals, as shown in Figure 16-6.

6. **Select the File ⇨ Save Scene As menu command, and save the file as Raytracing.mb. Close the file when you are finished.**

   This file includes a rendered scene with the raytracing option enabled.

**Figure 16-6:**
The raytracing option makes shadows, glass, and reflections very accurate.

# Cartoon Rendering: Saturday Morning Will Never Be the Same

Along with all the various rendering options is the ability to use different rendering engines to render the scene. The different rendering engines can give the scene a whole different look and feel. Some of these engines are made to give ultra-real effects; others create a less-than-real result.

One common rendering engine enables the scene to be rendered as a cartoon using vectors instead of shaded objects. This provides a different look for the rendered images that may fit a certain style.

Follow these steps to render the scene as a cartoon in Maya:

1. **Choose the File ⇨ Open Scene menu command, and open the Raytracing.mb file.**

   This file is the same file that was saved at the end of the preceding example.

2. **Select the Render ⇨ Render Using ⇨ Maya Vector menu command.**

   This command changes from the default renderer to one that renders the scene as vectors resulting in a cartoon-looking result.

3. **Right-click in the Perspective view to make it the active view.**

   The Render View window renders whichever view is active.

4. **Choose the Render ⇨ Render Current Frame menu command.**

   This command opens the Render View window and renders the current frame for the active view using the vector renderer. The results are especially unique, as shown in Figure 16-7.

   Maya, Personal Learning Edition, doesn't include the option to use the vector renderer.

5. **Select the File ⇨ Save Scene As menu command, and save the file as Cartoon scene.mb. Close the file when you are finished.**

   This file includes a rendered scene with the vector renderer enabled.

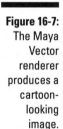

Figure 16-7:
The Maya
Vector
renderer
produces a
cartoon-
looking
image.

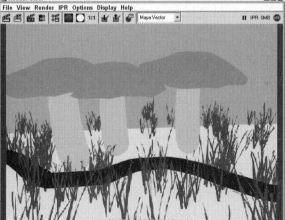

# Part V
# The Part of Tens

# In this part . . .

This book uses Maya, Personal Learning Edition, for its examples, but there are many other tools available that are used in the game production pipeline. This part takes a closer look at some of the main tools used to create games.

This part also looks at jobs that are available for individuals wishing to work in the game industry. You'll also find valuable suggestions on how to work your way into a desired position.

This part also includes three appendixes. The first shows the final step of the game development process: Plugging game content into the game engine. The second appendix is a glossary of common terms, and the third is a directory of popular animation schools.

# Chapter 17

# Ten Types of Tools Used by Game Companies

*I*f you go to a game production company, you'll typically find the illustrators using Illustrator, the digital artists using Photoshop, and the 3D modelers using Maya or 3ds max. You can see that one job equals one software package.

But if you were to look deeper into the skills of the individual employees, you might find that the 3D animator is also the local expert on Photoshop, the compositor used to work as an audio engineer, and the director knows all kinds of tricks for using all the various packages.

Artistic people who work on computers are extremely creative and tend to spread their skills among several different creative realms including art, music, cartooning, sculpting, and even architecture. So it is not uncommon for a single individual to be very skilled in several different software packages.

This is a huge benefit for the game company because these individuals can easily jump in to work on several different aspects of a game.

Of all the various types of software that are available, several types of packages are found in abundance within game development companies. Mastering these software packages gives you the skills you need to land a job with a game company.

Often, just being aware of some of the more expensive packages, such as the facial animation and motion capture systems, helps you as you discuss opportunities with game companies.

The products listed in this chapter are the most popular packages typically used by game companies, but please be aware that other packages exist, many of which are more cost-effective.

# Introducing Your New Best Friend: 3D Modeling, Rendering, and Animation Tools

Of all the different software tools, game animators spend most of their time mastering a single 3D modeling, rendering, and animation package. These packages are complex and powerful pieces of software that take years to master.

Although many 3D modeling, rendering, and animation packages are available, you will probably master and be most comfortable with one specific package and initially seek a career using that specific package. However, if the game company where you end up working uses a different package, you shouldn't worry. The underlying concepts used by all these packages are roughly the same, but their interfaces and approaches account for the major difference.

Many schools teach several different packages and require students to be proficient in two or more of these packages in order to make them more marketable to game companies.

Some companies offer tools that are specific to a single 3D task, such as modeling or rendering. For example, Rhino3D is a powerful modeler that can render images, but its main purpose is to model objects. Renderman is a rendering engine that can't be used to model or animate.

# Maya

Maya, created by Alias, is a great piece of software to learn because people who can use it are in high demand. Maya is used frequently to create movies, commercials, and games.

Three different flavors of Maya are available:

- ✔ **Maya Complete:** This is the base package including everything you need to model, render, and animate scenes.
- ✔ **Maya Unlimited:** This is an advanced package including modules for working with hair and cloth simulations.
- ✔ **Maya, Personal Learning Edition:** This is a free version available on the Alias Web site. It includes all the same features as Maya Complete, except it renders a watermark on all images.

Maya runs on Windows, Linux, and Macintosh systems. You can learn more about Maya at the Alias Web site: www.alias.com.

# 3ds max

3ds max is made by a company named Discreet. It is a very common package within the gaming industry and includes a number of features that are especially helpful for game creators.

For character animation, 3ds max includes a module known as Character Studio that enables you to animate complex characters by simply placing the character's footsteps throughout the scene.

3ds max is available only for Windows XP. Additional information on 3ds max can be found at the Discreet Web site: www.discreet.com.

# Softimage XSI

Softimage XSI was developed and is owned by Avid, the makers of high-end video editing systems. If you work for a company that uses Avid systems, then Softimage XSI is probably part of its pipeline.

Softimage is actually one of the older 3D packages available, and its experience is apparent. Softimage software is used extensively in the film industry and is gaining ground in the gaming industry also. Softimage XSI also comes in several flavors, including the following:

- ✔ **Softimage XSI Foundation:** This is the base package including modules for creating characters, cloth simulation, and particle effects.

- ✔ **Softimage XSI Essentials:** This is a mid-range package that includes all the features of the base package along with compositing and paint modules, network rendering, and dynamics.

- ✔ **Softimage XSI Advanced:** This is the high-end offering including an advanced behavioral animation system, advanced cloth simulation, and hair and fur modules.

Softimage runs on Windows and Linux systems. You can find more information at www.softimage.com.

## Lightwave

NewTek's Lightwave is another popular 3D package that has a split interface. Lightwave objects are created in NewTek's Modeler interface, and all scenes are laid out and animated in NewTek's Layout interface. This split interface approach actually removes a level of complexity from the software by not stacking all the modeling features on top of an already complex animation interface.

Lightwave is available for Windows, Linux, and Macintosh systems. More information can be found at Newtek's Web site: www.newtek.com.

# Remembering Your Old Friends: 2D Painting and Drawing Tools

All the 3D packages include interfaces for creating 2D shapes and painting images, so why would you still need to learn these 2D packages? The answer lies in their impressive feature lists. When creating and editing images, using Photoshop is often much quicker than using the tools available in the 3D package.

Another reason to use these packages is that other departments use graphics. For example, the marketing department probably uses Illustrator to design its logos. You don't need to recreate objects such as logos when another graphic designer has already done the work.

2D packages are often used to create textures and skins for scene objects and characters. They are also used to paint backgrounds, interface designs, and all the concept art.

Illustrator and Photoshop aren't the only drawing and painting packages available, but they represent the main tools that are accepted by the industry.

## Photoshop

Adobe's Photoshop is the industry standard for image editing and painting. It is commonly used to create object textures and maps. Photoshop is also used frequently to create backgrounds.

Photoshop information can be found at Adobe's Web site: www.adobe.com.

## Illustrator

2D drawings can often provide the starting point for modeling 3D objects, and all the 3D packages listed above can import Illustrator shapes. Logos and game titles are frequently created using Illustrator, as are any cartoon-based graphics that may appear in the game. Another place where Illustrator is commonly used is to design the interface.

Illustrator information can be found along with information on Photoshop at the Adobe Web site at www.adobe.com.

## Painter

Painter is another common 2D painting program that is used extensively today. It is currently developed by Corel and offers one of the best natural medium simulating interfaces around. Information on Painter can be found at www.corel.com.

## Z-Brush

Z-Brush is a unique painting interface that lets you actually pull, push, and move paint strokes in 3D. These abilities make it possible to create some rather interesting effects and textures. You can learn more about Z-Brush's unique features at the Pixelogic's Web site: http://pixologic.com.

# Getting a Little Extra Realism: 3D Rendering Systems

Each of the 3D modeling, rendering, and animation systems listed above is a complete end-to-end system, but these packages can also utilize plug-in modules that extend their functionality.

One such module that can be replaced is the rendering system used to render the final image or animation. By adding a new rendering system, you can change the final look of the animation, making it more realistic or more cartoonish — depending on the rendering system and its settings.

## Brazil Rendering System

The Brazil Rendering System is a high-end rendering system that gives users precise control over the shaders used to render objects. You can learn more about the Brazil Rendering System at www.splutterfish.com.

## Mental Ray Rendering System

Another common plug-in rendering system available as a default option in both 3ds max and Maya is Mental Ray. This rendering system includes support for advanced lighting solutions. You can learn more about the Mental Ray Rendering System at www.mentalimages.com.

# Putting All the Pieces Together: Compositing Packages

Compositing is the process of adding multiple rendered images together into an edited scene. Compositing images usually takes place during post-production after all the scenes have been rendered. Compositing software provides a way to edit rendered images and animations after the renderings are completed.

Many different compositing packages are available, each with strengths and weaknesses.

## After Effects

Created by Adobe, After Effects works easily alongside the other Adobe products such as Photoshop and Illustrator. One key advantage to After Effects is that, like Photoshop, After Effects can import and use plug-ins to add more special effects to an already powerful compositing package.

To find more information on After Effects, visit Adobe's Web site: www.adobe.com.

## Combustion

Combustion is another popular compositing package made by Discreet, the same company that developed 3ds max, making this package a good choice for 3ds max users.

Combustion information can be found on the Discreet Web site: www.discreet.com.

## Digital Fusion

Another excellent compositing package is Digital Fusion, created by Eyeon. One key feature of Digital Fusion is its ability to batch render multiple sequences at once over a network. You can find more information on Digital Fusion at www.eyeonline.com.

# Removing What Shouldn't Be There: Video Editing Tools

For editing animation sequences, adding sound, and creating demo reels, you need to know how to use a video editing package. Most 3D animation packages include features that can do these types of edits for you, but a separate video editing package makes the process easier and enables you to work with the animation sequences after they've been rendered.

## Premiere

Of all the available video editing packages that are available, Adobe's Premiere offers the most features, including the ability to plug in separate transition effects. Premiere also works seamlessly with other Adobe products. You can learn more about Premiere at Adobe's Web site: www.adobe.com.

## Final Cut Pro

Final Cut Pro is another popular video editing package that can work with several different formats. You can learn more about this package at Apple's Web site: www.apple.com.

# Taking Your Designs Online: Web Creation Tools

3D objects and animations are beginning to appear in many places on the Web, and several tools can make including 3D effects and animations easy work.

## Flash

Macromedia's Flash is a helpful piece of software if you are planning to take your illustrations to the Web. Flash uses vector-based graphics, which results in small file sizes. These smaller files are much quicker to download than larger pixel-based images. Another advantage of Flash is that the graphics can be made interactive. Information on Flash is found at Macromedia's Web site: www.macromedia.com.

## GoLive

Adobe's GoLive product is another excellent tool used to create and manage entire Web sites. You can learn more about GoLive at Adobe's Web site: www.adobe.com.

# Making Your Voice Heard: Audition, an Audio Editing Tool

Dialogue and sound effects are other critical pieces to the gaming puzzle that require software to capture and edit audio files, including character dialogue and sound effects.

Adobe's Audition is a fairly new, full-featured, multi-track recording and editing package. If you're dealing with animation audio, it is another critical piece to the production pipeline. More information on Audition can be found at Adobe's Web site: www.adobe.com.

# Animating Characters the Easy Way: Motion Capture Systems

Many games that include human actions such as sports games are produced more cost-effectively using motion capture software to capture the animation data needed to animate the human characters.

These motion capture systems include software and hardware to capture the motions of a target actor performing an action in the real world. The process works by attaching small devices at key points on the actor's body. The positions of these devices are recorded as the action is performed, and the data is fed into a computer, where the positions are applied to the 3D character.

A key benefit of these systems is that they can capture the subtle motions of specific individuals such as a famous baseball or football player who would be difficult to mimic using manual animation techniques.

The prohibitive factor in the use of these systems is their cost, but the cost is decreasing each year, and the technology is improving. Many companies also make the individual motion capture data available for purchase.

## Vicon Motion Systems

Vicon Motion Systems creates motion capture systems that are noted for their precision and accuracy. You can learn more about its systems at www.vicon.com.

### Motion Analysis

Motion Analysis creates the software and hardware necessary for motion capture systems. You can learn more about its systems at `www.motion analysis.com`.

## Animating a Talking Face: Lip Synching Systems

Synching dialogue tracks to facial animations can be a tricky animation task requiring many hours. Luckily, several packages exist that make this task much easier by simplifying the process. Some packages can even generate the facial animations automatically as the actor speaks.

### LifeStudio: HEAD

The LifeStudio: HEAD package, created by Lifemode Interactive, is used extensively by many game development companies. You can find more information on this product at `www.lifemi.com`.

### LipSync

LipSync is another popular lip synchronization package used by game companies. You can learn about this product at `www.speechanimation.com`.

## Speaking the Programmers' Language: 3D Programming Tools

If you're working with animation, then you're confined to the artistic side of the company, but you still need to work with programmers. If you understand a little about the tools they work with, you can speak their language.

3D programmers work with unique sets of code that interacts with the game hardware to reproduce 3D effects. Two major programming interfaces are used in games.

## DirectX

DirectX is a technology developed by Microsoft that is used to program 3D. You can learn more about it at the Microsoft Web site: www.microsoft.com.

## OpenGL

Another common 3D programming interface is OpenGL. This graphic language is also widely supported by hardware manufacturers and is used by 3D programmers. You can learn about OpenGL at www.opengl.org.

# Chapter 18

# Ten Creative Jobs in the Animation Industry

**G**ames have become big business, and they are no longer created by a single person with a good idea. Games are created by teams of people, and each person is responsible for his or her little piece of the puzzle.

Some of these positions are entry-level positions, and others require many years of experience. Experience in the game industry typically is measured in the number of game titles shipped. Another good measure of success is the success of the games that you've shipped. It is much more impressive to list a few successful titles to your credit than to list many disappointing titles.

These jobs represent the creative side of the game development world, but keep in mind that the other side of the aisle includes game programmers, and that category can encompass several different positions as well.

# Producer/Director

Game producers are the executive-level managers who keep track of project time lines and budgets. They have some limited input into the games, but they keep track of the games as a business. Producers typically hold advanced degrees in business such as a Master of Business Administration (MBA).

Game producers are under lots of pressure to ensure profits to the company shareholders, and they push very hard to get the correct people in place as department heads who can produce successful games.

The director is the individual who runs the day-to-day operations of the game development. Unlike the producer, the game director, is generally a creative, artistic type who is concerned with how the game looks, feels, and plays.

Directors have the final say on the game design and concept. They spend most of their time managing the various departments, but very little time actually creating and animating themselves.

Game directors are typically the most experienced individuals on game development teams, having more game titles to their credit. A director's experience is typically obtained in the trenches, working his way up from one of the key departments. Directors have a passion for creating the best game possible and will fight with the producer to get the right people, tools, and content.

The ultimate success of the game falls squarely on the director's head, and his approval is typically needed for all major game design and artistic decisions.

# Game Designer

Game Designers are charged with piecing together all the different ideas that are used to create the game and creating the game design documents. Chapter 2 covers creating those documents. The design documents for games are typically designed with input from a variety of team members.

Although the overall responsibility for creating the design documents lies with the lead game designer, the game designer also uses additional writers to help create storylines and dialogue, animators to complete the storyboards, and programmers to detail the flow of the game and any technical issues.

After the design documents are completed, the game designer remains engaged as a consultant for the remainder of the project. At every step of the development process, questions arise that challenge the design, such as how the enemies attack each other.

Game designers, like the director, have worked their way through the ranks in a game studio. They also are more experienced than some other people on the game development team.

Game designers are individuals who have tons of ideas and are extremely creative in their approaches and in how they look at things. Game designers build a reputation over time for the types of games they have successfully designed, and they take lots of credit for the success of a game.

# Game Artists

Game artists are members of the art department and can consist of beginning artists, senior artists, and the art department manager. Several artists can be assigned to a specific section of a game, and they work closely together to complete all the necessary art for the title. Working in teams lets the artists learn from one another and check one another's work.

The first task tackled by artists is to design and create the volume of concept art that gives the game its look and feel. These images can be drawn using a computer, but they are often drawn using traditional medium.

After game production begins, artists shift gears into creating all the artwork that the game will require. This artwork is divided among artists that specialize in different types of art including texture art, background art, and matte maps, among others. The specialty of an artist is decided by the artist's experience and skill.

Texture artists are tasked with creating the textures and maps that are wrapped about objects and characters. This work is typically completed on a computer using a package such as Photoshop. Texture artists need to be excellent artists, and their job often includes drawing and painting images on paper as well as a computer.

Backdrop artists create backgrounds and backdrops for the scene. These backgrounds can include actual game backgrounds as well as backgrounds for cut scenes. Backgrounds are also typically created using a program like Photoshop.

Another common task for artists is to paint matte maps. These maps are used to hide certain background objects such as a modern-looking home or power lines in the background image.

Game artists are typically experts in painting and drawing using traditional mediums and software packages such as Photoshop. Having school experience from an artistic program can help hone your skills.

# 3D Modeler

A modeler is the one who creates all the objects and characters that exist in the game world. The modeler typically is an expert at a specific modeling package and understands the structure of objects. The software typically used by 3D modelers can include 3ds max, Maya, Softimage XSI, or Lightwave, but other special-purpose modeling packages exist, such as Rhino3D and Poser, which is used to create and pose human figures.

3D modelers are also typically assigned to build the level environments, which can be built using 3D modeling tools or using proprietary building tools that are common for building mods.

In addition to levels, some modelers specialize in building characters. To build characters, you should have an excellent grasp of anatomy and be able to build controls for deforming muscles.

One of the trickiest tasks for a 3D modeler is to create a 3D object that is within the required polygon threshold. Real-time characters that are animated and controlled by the game's rendering engine need to be built using a designated number of polygons, so the size of the object won't overload the game engine and slow down the game.

This task of building low-polygon models that still look good can be difficult, but several software tools exist to help in this task, including optimization features and certain mapping techniques to move the polygon details to the texture map.

After objects are built, a 3D modeler needs to map textures created by the art department about the object using various mapping techniques.

Another common task performed by modelers is to rig their characters. Rigging a character is the process of adding bones and other controls that the animator can use while animating the objects and characters. To correctly rig a character, the modeler needs to work closely with the animator to build the exact controls that the animator needs in order to give the character its personality, such as a slider that controls how much the character clenches his fist or how a bunny wiggles its ears.

# Lighting Director

After all the game levels, objects, and characters are complete, the lighting director takes over to add lights to the environment. By defining the lighting solution, the lighting director creates the atmosphere for the game.

Lighting directors need to understand how different lights can change the mood of the environment. From a dark, creepy corridor with monsters hiding in the corners to a bright meadow at noon, the lighting director accomplishes the ambient feel by strategically placing lights throughout the scene.

A lighting director also places the lights for all animated cut scene environments and works with animators to ensure that all characters are properly lit throughout the game.

This is a specialized position focused on one specific key aspect of the game, and the person in this position needs to have a detailed understanding of the lighting process and effects.

After a lighting solution is created, light maps can be pre-rendered and applied as maps to the environment objects. This saves the game engine from having to compute the lighting solution for static objects during real-time game play.

# Animator

Animators take the finished models and environment and make them move through the scene. They are responsible for all the motion for the entire game, which can include object and character motion, story cut scenes, and interface interactions.

Animators need to work closely with artists and modelers to ensure that the objects and characters are the right dimensions and color depth and have the right controls to animate the characters correctly.

The animation department, like the art department, typically includes several levels of animators from beginning animators to senior animators and an animation department manager. Because animations are representative of the final action seen in a game, animators also work with the director and often require the director's approval.

One specific type of animator is a character animator who focuses on animating characters.

Because animators must have a good grasp on all aspects of animating, this is another key position that includes many years of experience for the senior positions.

Another creative branch of the game process deals with the game audio, which can include background music, dialogue, and sound effects. These positions are very creative, but have been excluded from this list because they are uniquely different. However, audio engineers need to work closely with animators. Typically, the animations are completed first with a simple timing audio track, and the final sound is recorded while the animation is being viewed to ensure a synched audio track.

## Special Effects Artist

The special effects artist is the person who adds all the cool explosions, destructions, and effects that are outside of the characters and objects. These effects are usually created using particle systems.

Special effects is another type of animation, but they are based on physical effects that are simulated in the computer. These special effects are included within the game itself, within cut scenes, and even within the interface and can include simple effects from glows that surround an object to lightning strikes to smoke from the end of a gun.

Another common special effect involves advanced dynamics such as water effects, the motion of hair and fur, and the flowing of cloth about objects and characters. 3D packages such as Maya and 3ds max include features that enable these types of effects, but custom plug-ins are often used in many cases.

Special effects artists have a background in physics and natural phenomenon and have learned the tricks required to simulate these effects using 3D packages and programming.

## Tester

When the first rough build of a game level is completed, the build is delivered to the quality assurance (QA) department for testers to look over. Testers play the game as a customer would and look for problems.

These problems may include technical difficulties such as sounds and graphics that are missing, animation sequences that are erratic, and serious problems like game crashes and dead ends.

Each problem is reported back to the appropriate department for fixing, and new builds are delivered regularly to the QA department as "bugs" are fixed.

Different testers are assigned to look for different types of problems, and the QA department must sign off on a build before it can be released.

Before a final product is shipped to stores, a broader test cycle, known as a beta test, is completed using an external group of testers. This beta test cycle typically finds many additional problems that weren't found internally.

# Grunt

Every game company has several individuals who are used to complete all the necessary undefined tasks on a project from getting pizzas for late-night programming sessions and coffee for the early morning staff meetings to running the CD case proofs to the printer.

These individuals may not create any content that actually appears in the game, but their names are listed in the credits because games couldn't be created without their help. Their titles are typically vague such as Director's Assistant, Game Gopher, and Staff Aide.

Although these positions may not seem very important, many of these individuals gain a detailed understanding of the tasks required to ship a game title and move up the ranks to various positions within the company.

# Trainer

You may have heard someone say, "some people do, and others teach." Another common position or responsibility is to teach and train others in the skills you've already mastered.

Trainers can appear within a game company as individuals who have the skills and patience to work with the inexperienced talent and bring them up to speed with the game development process.

Teachers and trainers are also found within animation schools, colleges, and universities sharing their talents with the numerous students seeking to break into the game industry.

# Chapter 19

# Ten Ways to Land a Job as a 3D Game Animator

**S**o you want to work as an animator. Well, you need to have some talent, you must be creative, and you must work hard, but this isn't all. You can have a good work ethic, tons of talent, and creativity bubbling out your ears and still not land a job animating.

Video games are popular and becoming more so all the time. As more and more people are playing them, more people are deciding that this is the type of job they want to do full time. Although the demand for 3D game animators is large, the competition is also incredible.

To help you in your quest, I've included a list of ten things to get you on your way.

# Gaining the Necessary Experience: First Things First

When you first approach a company about an animation job, the first thing it wants to see is some animation you've done. Real-world experience is required, and if you don't have any, you won't get very far.

The first step in landing an animation job is to animate. This can be done on paper as cartoons, on video, or using the software covered in this book. The key is to try your hand and show some creativity. As you animate, you should see some improvement over time. The skills you gain help you along the way.

In many ways, animating for games is exactly the same as animating movies, the only difference being its final destination. The steps outlined in this section are geared toward landing a job in the game industry, but similar steps can be used to obtain an animating job in the movie industry also.

## Developing software skills

Although animating on paper may be a good place to start, all major game producers work on computers sooner or later, so you need to develop software skills.

The first choice is to select a software package to work with. Lots of software packages are used within the game industry. See Chapter 17 for more information of the types of packages that are used.

The various game companies use different animation software, but the underlying concepts used to create animation are similar; differences occur in the interface. After you are skilled in one animation package, transferring your skills to another package is simply a matter of learning a new interface.

Animation software is typically pretty expensive, so obtaining the software is typically beyond the range of animators who are just starting out, but you can still get some experience in the following ways:

- **Use trial versions:** Most animation software programs offer limited trial versions of their software that you can use to get familiar with the package. Check how long the trial is good for, and use it for its full timeframe.

- **Academic versions:** Some software companies, including Adobe, offer academic versions of their software at a reduced price to students. Using these offers can help you get the skills you need at a price you can afford.

✔ **Use school computer labs:** Many school computer labs include copies of the software that you can use to complete school projects and gain skills.

✔ **Obtain an education license:** Some software such as the version of Maya covered in this book are available in an educational release specifically created to be free or at a low-cost for the purpose of enabling students to learn their software. These software versions typically have several features disabled, such as the ability to save files.

# Getting involved in creating games

Most game company job postings include a requirement asking applicants to have shipped at least one game title. Gaining this experience can be a real gotcha because you can't get the experience of shipping a game title until you work for a game company, and you can't work for a game company until you ship a game title. Several solutions are available to solve this conundrum.

## Creating shareware, freeware, or Web-based games

You can create your own game title. Many game creators started out by creating shareware or freeware titles. Even if the game is simple, you can learn lots in the process. The Web is replete with Flash-based and simple JavaScript games, and every little game you're involved in gives you experience that you can claim on your resume. If you go this route, make sure the games represent your best work.

## Build custom game levels and mods

Another good way to get some experience creating games is in building custom levels for your favorite games. Games such as Quake, Unreal, and Doom include tools that you can use to create custom game levels with unique content. Levels that are well designed with creative graphics that push the game in new directions get noticed by game companies and add to your experience.

## Offering to help on a game

If you scan the Web, you can find many other people who are interested in gaining game experience just like yourself. Groups of these individuals often band together and work over the Internet to create a game using the talents of several individuals. These groups create games using volunteer time and can be very rewarding, in addition to helping you gain the valuable experience that you need.

## Getting a game company internship

Some game companies offer summer internships that provide an excellent way to see the inner workings of a game company, but obtaining these positions may be difficult because competition is pretty fierce. If you can get one of these exclusive positions, then you'll be on a fast track to a career as a game animator.

## Studying games

Imagine going in for an interview with a game company and having the interviewer ask what your favorite game is. If you can't answer this question with a 30-minute conversation, then you probably should look to another industry for work. Game players, creators, and companies are extremely passionate about what they do because they love games. They love playing them and creating them.

If you're looking to work in the game industry, you should be aware of every good, successful game out there. You should know why some games work and why others fail. You should be able to identify what makes a good game and look for ways to make a good game great.

As you study games, be sure to cover a variety of games by playing PC games, online games, and console games. You should own at least one console system.

Studying games doesn't mean that you need to buy every game out there, although some of you would love to do that, I'm sure. Most PC and online games offer games with one or two levels that you can play for free.

As you play your favorite games, look at how the art appears and how objects are animated. Look for flaws and places where you could do a better job. Play a variety of games to understand what their appeal is. The more game playing experience you have, the better you fit in with people who do and love the same things.

# Finding Animation Programs and Schools

Just like any other career, the real way to land an animation job is to go to school. The competition for animation jobs is fierce, and even though the number of jobs is increasing, you really need to distinguish yourself in order to get the position you want.

Unlike many other careers, attending an animation school isn't necessary. If you have an amazing talent, you can get hired directly without a college degree, but attending an accredited school and taking the time to earn a degree are perhaps the best ways to show employers that you are serious about animation. Even with an amazing talent, you can improve your skills by attending an animation school.

Many colleges and universities offer animation programs that you can enroll in, but locating these programs can be tricky. These programs can be found in the Arts, Computer Science, Design, Architecture, and Film departments. I've even seen these programs offered in an Engineering department.

Every college and university offers classes in drawing, painting, and even animation, but try to seek out a school that doesn't only offer animation classes, but has a full-fledged program in animation. Schools that specialize in animation have a broader number of classes, which prepare you better.

Another path for obtaining the animation skills you need is to enroll in the programs offered by several schools across the country that specialize in 3D animation. These schools represent some of the strongest programs for learning the skills needed to land your dream job. You can find a short list of these specialized schools in Appendix B.

## *Knowing which degree to earn*

Before enrolling, check out the actual degrees that are offered. Some degrees are equal to a two-year associate's degree, and others are four-year Bachelor of Science or Bachelor of Art degrees. The more specific the degree is to your career goal, the better tailored the courses will be to you. For example, some schools offer a degree in Character Animation, which would get you much closer to animating in a game company than a more generalized Animation degree.

Game companies typically hire based on talent rather than the type of degree you have. If the skill level obtained with a focused two-year program is as good as what you would obtain from a four-year program, then you can use the two additional years improving your skills working for a game company instead of completing the additional requirements for a Bachelor's degree.

On the other hand, obtaining a Bachelor's degree puts you in a better position to move to other types of jobs both inside and outside the gaming industry, including management positions. Much of the extra time spent to obtain a Bachelor's degree is spent taking general education requirements that don't directly apply to animation.

These types of degrees are available at colleges and university around the world:

- ✔ Digital Entertainment
- ✔ Game Design
- ✔ Industrial Design
- ✔ Multimedia and Web Design
- ✔ Animation
- ✔ Media Arts
- ✔ Graphic Design
- ✔ Character Animation
- ✔ Visual Effects
- ✔ 3D Design
- ✔ Game Arts
- ✔ Visual Communications

Be careful of your degree choice because a degree in Multimedia and Web Design teaches you skills needed to create animations for the Web, but this is a long way from creating high-end 3D game graphics. The best degrees for creating 3D game animation are Animation, Visual Effects, 3D Design, and Game Arts.

## Knowing which courses to take

Perhaps a better indication than the program name is the types of courses that the degree requires. To get a better feel for what the program entails, check the available courses that are offered as part of the program.

Before enrolling in a program, locate several recent graduates from the program you are thinking of attending, preferably people who are working in the game industry, and ask them their opinion of the program they completed. Recent graduates who are working in the game industry will give you a better idea of the quality of the program and the best courses and instructors to take than the promotional material available for the program.

The types of programs that you should look for teach these types of courses:

- ✔ Traditional animation techniques
- ✔ Math and physics
- ✔ Storytelling and storyboarding

- ✔ Drawing
- ✔ Color theory
- ✔ 2D sprite animation
- ✔ 3D software courses for Maya, 3ds max, Lightwave, and/or XSI
- ✔ Lighting
- ✔ Special effects
- ✔ Compositing
- ✔ Pre- and post-production
- ✔ Anatomy
- ✔ Character animation
- ✔ Cinematography

Another benefit of attending an animation school is that many schools have placement centers with gaming company contacts, which can help you land a job with these companies.

# Showing Off: Creating an Awesome Demo Reel

After you've got some experience and schooling under your belt, you need to create some really good animation and show it off. A demo reel is the business card of the animation world, and it says lots about you, such as your style, flair, and the type of animations you like to do.

A great demo reel is the first and greatest way to distinguish yourself from all other applicants. Your demo reel needs to include your best work and be an impressive piece of work that makes anyone who views it say, "Wow, this stuff is great."

A demo reel is typically short at three minutes or less. A demo reel longer than this will lose the interest of the person viewing it. Remember that every piece needs to be your best work and your own work.

Avoid putting any uncredited models, sound, or textures within your demo reel. Nothing gets you rejected quicker than borrowing someone else's work. If you worked on an animation with someone else, be sure to explain exactly which parts you did.

## Creating a demo reel

A demo reel doesn't need to include complete works, just impressive snippets edited together. After you've decided on the pieces that you want to include in your demo reel, use some video-editing software to stitch the various pieces together.

Adobe's Premiere is one such video-editing software package, but other free or inexpensive video-editing software packages can also be used.

Be sure to include a variety of animations and modeling and texturing examples, but lean toward those pieces that show the type of work that you're interested in doing.

Place your absolute best piece right at the beginning of the demo reel. If you can grab the attention of the viewers in the first 10 seconds, then they will be more interested in viewing the rest of the reel. If you save your best work for the last of the reel, then the rest of the reel may never be seen.

The demo reel doesn't need to include music to accompany the edited animation pieces, but if the original animation includes any sound effects or dialogue, make sure that those are included and edited to be smooth. Don't cut off any dialogue in mid-sentence.

After the edits are complete, save the entire thing as a single file that is easy to find in the root directory of the DVD or CD. Make it an executable or playable using a standardized format such as Windows Video (AVI), QuickTime (MOV), or DIVX. Don't place the file within a folder so the viewer needs to search for it, and don't include multiple files on the disc.

When it's completed, show your finished work to several people and get their feedback. The more educated eyes that examine the demo reel, the better you can anticipate the types of responses that the game companies will give.

As a final step, burn your demo reel to a DVD or to a less expensive CD-R. CDs are less expensive, but DVDs are more universal. Be sure to check with the game company to which you are sending the tape to see what format it prefers.

Some companies still accept and prefer video tapes. To save your demo reel to a VCR tape, simply hook up your VCR player to your video card using the TV Out port and record the demo reel.

## Labeling a demo reel

Don't forget to label your demo reel, but don't overdo the labeling or packaging. Game companies are interested in the contents of the demo reel, not in the cool graphics on the label or whether the DVD is purple. The demo reel should include your name, phone number, and e-mail address so the game company can contact you if it is interested.

It is also a good idea to include a shot list with the demo reel. This shot list can describe the snippets that are included in the demo reel and credit any ancillary materials that you used to create the demo reel.

You can include your contact information as part of the demo reel, but be sure to include it on the demo reel's case as well as the actual DVD or CD.

## Sending out demo reels

Many game companies say on their Web sites that they are always looking for new talent and accept demo reels continuously. If you look under the Careers section of a game company's Web site, you can find out where to send the demo reel and the accepted formats.

Be sure to include a cover sheet and a copy of your resume, so they can review your experience in addition to your animation skill. Don't expect the game companies to return your demo reel.

Another popular way to submit demo reels is to attend a conference such as the Game Developer's Conference. At such conferences, many game companies are in the exhibition hall accepting demo reels for available positions.

# Establishing a Web Presence

Although not as important as a demo reel, a Web site is also a great way to make your work visible. With an established Web site, you can direct people to your work without having to send them an actual DVD. You could just give them a business card that includes your Web site or direct them there using an e-mail message.

There is a gotcha with Web sites, though. If you don't present the material with good design or in a format that is too optimized, the viewers may not see your best work.

If you've never built a Web site, then don't sweat it. The hardest part of creating a Web site is compiling good content, and you already have that from your demo reel.

## Securing a domain name

The first step is to locate an Internet domain name. Search for a name that isn't already taken that still identifies you personally. You may need to use a .net suffix to find a good match. You can register your domain name in one of several different places. The registration cost is typically charged per year and isn't very expensive.

The best Internet addresses are ones that are easily remembered, but be sure to make it specific to you.

The more expensive part of maintaining a Web site is paying hosting fees, which is the cost of some space on a server where you can place your Web site files. If you have an Internet Service Provider (ISP) account, check with your ISP first. Most ISPs offer a limited amount of server space that you can use as part of your account.

## Building an amazing Web site

Web sites can be built using several different software packages, including Microsoft's FrontPage, Adobe's GoLive, or Macromedia's Dreamweaver. Several free or inexpensive Web site construction packages are also available, or you can learn to edit HTML code and build the site from scratch using a simple text editor.

As you lay out your Web site, use a design that is professional and creative and expresses your personal style. The design should reflect the quality of your artistic abilities. If a hiring manager sees a jumbled Web site with poor design, he may be reluctant to look deeper for your animation files.

If you search the Web for 3D artists, you can find many great examples of Web sites created by other 3D artists. These Web sites are great for giving you ideas for your own site and giving you an idea of the competition you are up against.

Another benefit of having a Web site is that you can include full-length animations for those who want to view them, but be careful. As with the demo reel, you should include only your best work and include credits when necessary.

One of the trickiest aspects of presenting your images and animations is to optimize them so they are quick to download from the Web, but they retain their quality. You can handle this dilemma in several ways:

- **Include thumbnails:** Thumbnail images show a small image or a portion of the image that can be accessed by clicking the thumbnail. Thumbnails offer viewers a chance to see a representation of the image before downloading to see the full image.

- **Use an optimized video format:** Certain formats such as QuickTime, Flash, and DIVX are optimized for the Web to retain the quality of the animation without sacrificing quality. These formats usually require that a player is downloaded before the animation file can be viewed. Be sure to include a link where the player can be downloaded and installed.

- **Display as grayscale:** One way to decrease the size of images for sample viewing is to save the images as grayscale images and link these images to a full-color version. This dramatically reduces the size of the image file, but if you don't have good control over your lighting, the grayscale image could reveal a weakness.

- **Use the JPEG or PNG format:** Many image formats are available for saving images on the Web, but you should save your rendered images using the JPEG or PNG formats. The GIF format can represent only 256 * colors and shouldn't be used for rendered images. Also, check the optimization settings for the JPEG format because significant optimization can destroy the image quality.

## *Adding your work to an online gallery*

If creating and maintaining a Web site sounds like too much work, an alternative is to create a user account with a 3D art Web site. Many of these sites let you post your work in galleries that are viewable by others. These sites also let other users comment on your work and vote for their favorite images and animations.

The following sites include galleries for 3D artists:

- 3D.ARTISTS (www.raph.com)
- Highend3D (www.highend3d.com)

- CG Channel (www.cgchannel.com)
- 3D Total (www.3dtotal.com)
- Renderosity (www.renderosity.com)
- Ultimate 3D Links (www.3dlinks.com)
- 3D Cafe (www.3dcafe.com)
- 3D Commune (www.3dcommune.com)
- 3D Up (www.3dup.com)
- 3D Gate (www.3dgate.com)
- 3D Ring (www.3d-ring.com)
- CG Focus (www.cgfocus.com)
- 3D Ark (www.3dark.com)
- CG Talk (www.cgtalk.com)

The Web sites listed above are community sites offering much more than just artist galleries. They are also a great resource for news and information, user tutorials, and job postings. I suggest that you join one of these communities and become active in all it has to offer.

In addition to these sites, you can also find galleries for specific software and specific schools.

# Getting Feedback and Exposure

As your skills begin to gel, you'll want to get some feedback on your animations and gain some exposure. By building a reputation, you can get noticed by some game companies, and new opportunities may open up.

## Entering Web animation contests

The Web is full of sites that offer all kinds of news, resources, and information about games, game companies, and developing your skills. Several Web sites occasionally offer contests where you can submit your work.

The prizes for these contests vary, but more important than the prizes are the reputation and exposure that follow and the ability to place a line on your resume stating that you won first place in a notable animation contest.

Even if you don't win, these contests typically offer a way for viewers to give you feedback on your work. This feedback is essential to helping you to improve your animation skills. You can also gain a feel for what your animations need to be by comparing your entry to the winning entry.

## Entering animation festivals

Another place where you can get your animations noticed is by entering your animation in many of the animation festivals that are available. These festivals typically have very tight submission deadlines, but sitting in an auditorium when hundreds of people are applauding your work can do tons for your confidence.

These animation festivals are held throughout the world on all different levels. Some festivals focus on a specific type of animation, such as science fiction or cartoons. Some are specific to geographic locations, such as the Manchester Film Festival or the Phoenix Film Festival. Some are open only to certain classes of people, such as the many student film festivals.

You can find a comprehensive list of current animation and film festivals at the Animation Industry Database Web site: www.aidb.com.

# Improving Your Skills

After you have the some animation experience, don't sit back and wait for a job. You must continue to improve your skills. Don't think that after you get out of school, you won't need to study ever again. Learning is lifelong process, and if you continue to learn and develop, you'll always be sharp in your work.

## Learning from books

You have plenty of chances to learn. Books, like this one, provide excellent chances to improve your skills at your own pace. Thousands of books have been written on animation, and I'm sure you haven't read them all.

Find the types of books that you learn best from, and use them to improve your skills. You can also concentrate on other areas besides just animation, such as drawing, lighting, special effects, and cinematography.

## Training by video

Another form of training that is becoming more popular is training by video. These training modules show how to complete specific tasks and are great for gaining familiarity with a certain product.

## Using Web tutorials

Many people learn the best by doing, which makes tutorials an efficient way to learn. Many Web sites, including those listed earlier in this chapter, include tutorials for learning everything from creating a metallic-looking texture to animating the walk cycle for a spider.

## Attending workshops

Training sessions held at conferences and elsewhere are great places to make new friends and learn new skills. These workshops often cost money to attend, but frequently the software companies offer workshops to introduce new features for their recently released software. Attending these sessions can give you a leg up on the software's newest features.

## Joining a user group

Many software companies have organized user groups that have frequent meetings. These user groups provide a great way to meet with other users and learn from them.

# Attending Animation Conferences

Attending conferences is an excellent way to meet the right people and make connections. Conferences also often include an exhibition hall where several game companies are present for you to discuss job openings, present demo reels, and turn in applications.

Attending conferences can be very expensive, but most conferences look for people to volunteer; when you do so, you receive full access to the conference for a minimal number of hours of volunteer work.

These conferences are frequently attended by 3D animators, game developers, and digital artists:

- ✔ **Electronic Entertainment Expo (E3):** Held annually in May, this conference is the place where all new games are announced and is probably the best conference for budding game animators to attend. You can find more information at www.E3expo.com.

- ✔ **Game Developer's Conference (GDC):** Held annually in March, this conference focuses on game development including game animation. You can get more information at www.gdconf.com.

- ✔ **Siggraph:** Held annually in August, this conference is the International Conference on Computer Graphics and Interactive Technologies. This conference also includes many game companies. You can find more information at www.siggraph.org.

- ✔ **National Association of Broadcasters (NAB):** Held annually in Las Vegas, Nevada, in April, this conference focuses on video broadcasting, editing, and animation. You can find more information at www.nab.org.

- ✔ **Annecy:** Held annually in June, this conference is the International Animated Film Festival. It is frequently held overseas. You can find more information at www.annecy.org.

- ✔ **DV Expo West/East:** Held annually in December, this conference focuses on digital video. You can find more information at www.dvexpo.com.

# Joining a Professional Organization

Another avenue for making contact is through a professional organization. Conferences typically offer a registration discount to members of certain professional organizations. The fees for these organizations usually aren't very expensive, and they often offer discounted rates for students.

You may be interested in joining these organizations:

- ✔ **International Game Developer's Association (IGDA):** Membership to this organization is required in order to attend the GDC conference. More information can be found at www.igda.org.

- ✔ **Association of Computer Machinery, Special Interest Group on Graphics (ACM-SIGGRAPH):** This organization sponsors the Siggraph conference every year and publishes a magazine with interesting articles in the field of computer graphics. You can find more information on this organization at www.siggraph.org.

- ✔ **Graphic Artists Guild (GAG):** The Graphic Artists Guild is organized into local chapters and committees spread across the world. You can find information at www.gag.org.

# Knowing the Right People

You've heard people say, "it's not what you know, but who you know," and the same holds true for animation jobs. Knowing the right people can make all the difference.

You can meet the right people in lots of places, including these:

- **School classmates:** Keep in contact with any friends you make while attending school because some of them could end up with great game companies, and having someone on the inside can help you secure a position.

- **Conference attendees:** Many good connections can be made at conferences, including people who work in the Human Resources department. These people can tell you exactly what you need to do to land the job you want with their company. Conference speakers are also good contacts, but be respectful and specific with your questions.

- **User group attendees:** Attending a local user group introduces you to many people who are in the same position as yourself, but user groups also include some people who work in the professional sector who can give you advice.

- **Online forum contacts:** Participating in online forums is a great way to meet people who can help you in your pursuit of a job.

# Working Your Way Up

If you're looking to get hired as a game director right out of school, then you had better start your own game company. Advanced positions such as game director aren't starting positions and are typically reserved for individuals who have worked their way up through the ranks excelling in every aspect of their job.

## Getting your foot in the door

Another path to animating is to get hired with a game company in a high-turnover job such as technical support and watch for an opening that you qualify for. By learning how a company works and where the openings are, you can prepare yourself and have an inside track for obtaining the exact position you want.

A game tester is a good example of the type of job that is easier to obtain without lots of experience, yet a game tester can learn a great deal about the types of errors that keep a good game from becoming a great game. Game testers who excel in their position get promoted to testing lead and then to testing manager. From this position, you can move into a beginning animator position as your skills improve.

## Getting on a beta test team

If you want to work with a game company, but don't happen to live close to one, you can join the ranks as a beta tester. Working as a beta tester lets you sample new games in their raw form before they hit the shelves, but don't think that this lets you impress your friends with insights into the new game before it is released. Game companies require that you sign a Non-Disclosure Agreement (NDA) before you can be accepted as a beta tester. This NDA prevents you from talking to anyone about the game before it is released.

Beta testers typically aren't paid for their work.

Don't think that being a beta tester is a great way to play games for free. Beta testing software is hard and often frustrating work. Imagine spending days moving through levels only to have the game crash just as you meet the final boss and then spending lots of time reporting bugs.

But if you approach a beta test with a desire to learn about the game company, you can use the opportunity to show your value. To excel as a beta tester, learn how to find the obscure bugs and be active in the beta forum. If you distinguish yourself as an awesome beta tester, then you'll have someone who can vouch for you when you apply for a position with that company.

Another huge advantage to beta testing games is that it helps you to understand at least part of the process involved in creating games and helps you to learn of some difficulties that are commonly encountered when building a game. Game animators who have some experience as testers are often more successful in producing content without problems when the game goes into a testing phase.

## Starting as a junior animator

Even animation departments are segregated into different ranks including junior animator and senior animator. Some game companies have as many as six levels of animators. The way to get ahead is with experience typically measured in the number of games that you've shipped.

The assignments given to junior animators aren't as critical as those given to senior animators. But, with each promotion comes more responsibility.

The types of assignments given to the junior members of the team can include animating simple scene objects, game titles, credit scenes, and interface elements. The senior animator's tasks can include advanced character animations, cut scenes, and special effects.

## Making an internal move

After working for a game company on several shipping titles, you may find yourself getting anxious for new challenges. Most game companies post new job opportunities internally before searching for external candidates. As you work in your current position, keep a close watch on other positions that you would be interested in pursuing. When other positions become available, apply for the position, but make sure that your current workload can be covered before leaving your current team.

# Being Persistent

I've frequently heard of individuals who earned a coveted position with a company because they simply refused to give up. They kept working on their animation skills, accepting feedback, using it to improve their skills, and working until they finally achieved the animation skills that were exactly what the specific game company needed.

The advice to be persistent doesn't mean that you should consistently contact a hiring manager for a game company annoyingly, but if you are professional and open, then you may get the feedback that will help you the next time around. However, being persistent in this instance applies to improving your skills.

We've all heard the advice, "if first you don't succeed, try, try again." Well, in the animation field with so many resources available, if you keep trying and working, you can achieve anything you want. The key is to be persistent.

# Appendix A

# Using Game Engine Tools

*A*fter you've created all the various game animation pieces, you can simply dump all the content in the game programmers lap and walk away, right? Well, not exactly. Game programmers are great at producing code that defines how the various game objects interact, but game artists are in demand during the programming phase to check how the game is coming together. For example, during the programming phase, game artists are typically asked to look at the results to see if the environment looks right, if all animations are seamlessly working together, and if the character's motion is correct.

In addition, several game engines include interactive tools that can be used to create some game elements and environments such as skyboxes and terrains automatically. Using these tools to populate your game environment is a task better suited to artists than to programmers, so you'll probably be asked to assume some of these responsibilities using the various game engine tools.

It is worth your time to look at the game engine tools that are included with the game engine your programmers use. Any art pieces that can be created using a game engine tool get you that much closer to completing your art assets.

## Selecting a Game Engine

The game engine that you use really depends on the game studio that you end up working for. Some game engines are fairly inexpensive to play around with, but require a license in order to distribute games.

## It's a mod, mod, mod, mod world

Mods are custom levels created for games that can be loaded and played using the game's game engine. Game players love mods because they give players a chance to be creative and to make their own levels for their favorite games. Game companies love mods because they can greatly extend the appeal and life a game. If many mods are available, then a game player keeps playing the game even after he's finished all the normal levels. These custom levels are frequently shared over the Web, enabling game players all over the world to access additional content.

The key to mod creation lies in the hands of the game engine creators. To enable mod development, a game engine must be able to load custom levels. Game companies frequently take the time to develop custom mod tools in order to make the development of additional levels easier for game hobbyist.

Many of the biggest game companies write their own game engine designed to give their game that unique stylized look that is different from all other games on the market. This includes recent successes like Id Software's Doom 3, Epic's Unreal Tournament 3, and Value's Half Life 2.

There are hundreds of different game engines to choose from and each has their advantages and disadvantages. Many game engines have been developed and abandoned along the way, but several have remained strong and are continually being updated.

The current available game engines represent thousands of hours of development time, but they also enable complex games to be created in a fraction of the time. For a game market that is demanding more and more games, using a game engine to produce games more quickly makes a lot of sense.

The drawback to using a standard game engine is that you run the risk of similarity to other games that use the same engine, but a strong, unique game design coupled with some creative artistic vision makes your game unique enough to be noticed.

Each game engine also has some cost associated with it. This cost is charged per seat (depending on the number of people you have using it) and also as a license, which costs a fraction of each game sold.

The license fees associated with the various game engines vary quite a bit. Before deciding on a game engine for your production, check the licensing structure for your planned game. Some game engines are more favorable for smaller game productions.

Some popular game engine choices include the following:

- ✔ **RenderWare:** One of the oldest and most popular 3D game engines, RenderWare is used in many games including Sonic Heroes, Grand Theft Auto, Tony Hawks, and Burnout. More on RenderWare can be found at `www.renderware.com`.

- ✔ **Unreal Engine:** Created by the team that produced Unreal Tournament, this game engine is used for creating many next-generation console and PC games including Splinter Cell, Harry Potter, and Rune. For more on this game engine, visit `www.unrealtechnology.com`.

- ✔ **Quake Engine:** The Quake Engine has been used to produce games including Doom, Quake, and Medal of Honor Allied Assault. It has been updated for the release of Doom 3. For more information on this engine, check out `www.idsoftware.com`.

- ✔ **Gamebryo:** Used to create games including Sid Meier's Pirates, Dark Age of Camelot, and Elder Scrolls III, this game engine is used by several different studios. Information on Gamebryo can be found at `www.ndl.com`.

- ✔ **Jupiter by Touchdown Entertainment:** This game engine is used to create console games such as Tron 2.0 and F.E.A.R. More on this advanced game engine can be found at `www.touchdownentertainment.com`.

- ✔ **Glacier by IOI Technology:** This game engine is used to create games including Hitman: Contracts and Freedom Fighters. More on this advanced game engine can be found at `www.ioi.dk`.

- ✔ **Torque Game Engine:** The Torque engine was used to create Tribes 2. It is available for the PC, Macintosh, and Linux. It is a great choice for starting out. More information on the Torque game engine can be found at `www.garagegames.com`.

## Hey! This software is already opened — open source

As you begin to peruse the vast number of game engines listed on the Web, you'll find several that are listed as open source. Open source software is a different take on software development. Instead of having a single company develop the software for the purpose of selling it to make a fortune, open source software is created by teams all over the world that work together receiving little or no pay to build software that is sold for little or no money.

The goal of an open source project is to use the synergy of the community to produce something that wouldn't be possible otherwise. It's a community effort that teaches big business a thing or two about software development. Open source projects offer a great way to get your hands on some excellent software inexpensively and also a great place to learn and gain some skills.

# Using Game Engine Tools

Many game engines include interactive tools that make it possible to create and edit game environment without having to manually code the changes. These tools include everything from terrain editors and texture editors to physics simulators and procedural animation interfaces. The available tools differ with each different game engine.

The output for most of these game engine tools is code that the programmer can piece together to create the final game. In some cases, having an understanding of game programming (or having a programmer who can assist you) really helps. Remember that the game engine was created for programmers and not necessarily for artists.

In the sections that follow, the Torque game engine and its available tools are covered. This is only one of many possible solutions, but it is representative of the game engines and tools that are available.

The available tools found in the Torque game engine that are of use for game artists and designers include:

- **GUI Editor:** Used to build a simple user interface, this tool gives you access to all sorts of buttons, switches and dialog boxes.
- **Mission Editor:** Used to create and paint terrains, to place and position 3D objects, and to control environment settings like the sky, sun, and fog.

# Creating a User Interface

A game's user interface is the first look that a player has with a game and makes the first impression, so it needs to be impressive and easy-to-use. Chapter 4 covered the process of creating a user interface, but this section looks at the specific tool found in the Torque game engine for creating a user interface.

The GUI Editor can also be used to create a Heads-Up Display (HUD) for the game. A HUD comprises the controls that are visible while the game is being played, as shown in Figure A-1. It can include information such as checkpoints reached, current weapon and ammo status, and player health. To create a HUD, you need to access the GUI Editor inside of a mission.

**Figure A-1:**
The text at
the top of
the screen
and the
speed-
ometer in
the lower
right are
examples
of the HUD
interface
controls.

## Accessing the GUI Editor

The GUI Editor can be accessed while a game skeleton is being run. This enables you to work within the game as you are playing it. As examples of these various editors, Torque includes two sample game examples that you can run to see the various editors.

Follow these steps to access the Torque game engine's GUI Editor:

1. **After installing the Torque game engine, locate and run the FPS Starter Kit program.**

   The default installation of the Torque game engine makes two demo applications available — the First Person Shooter (FPS) Starter Kit and the Racing Starter Kit. Both of these applications are simple demo games that provide access to the various editors.

2. **Press the F10 key to access the GUI Editor.**

   The FPS Starter Kit opens with a simple title screen that includes several interface buttons. By clicking the F10 key, the title screen is surrounded with several panels and buttons, as shown in Figure A-2.

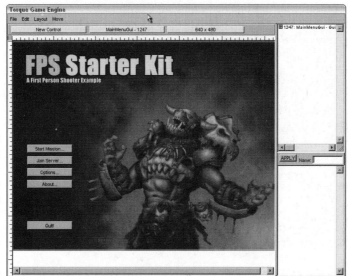

**Figure A-2:**
Pressing the
F10 key
accesses
the GUI
Editor from
the demo
application.

## Creating a new GUI page

The three buttons at the top of the GUI Editor are for selecting new interface controls (the left), for opening the existing interface controls (middle), and for switching between the various resolutions (the right).

The panels to the right are used to select and edit existing controls. The top right panel displays a hierarchical list of all the controls on the current interface page. When a control is selected, all its properties are displayed in the lower right panel. By changing these property values, you can alter the control's look and behavior.

You can drag the border between the right panels and the preview pane on the left if you want to see more of the properties.

Follow these steps to create a new interface page using the Torque game engine's GUI Editor:

1. **With the GUI Editor open, select the File ➪ New GUI menu command.**

    A simple dialog box, shown in Figure A-3, opens, allowing you to name the new GUI element and specify a Class. The name and class values are used by programmers to interact with the new element.

    When entering values that programmers will use, such as an element's name and class, don't include spaces or special characters: These may cause problems with the programming code.

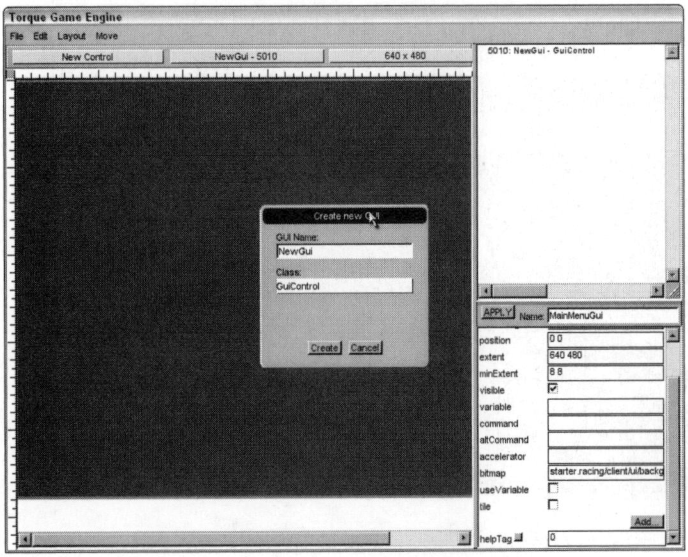

**Figure A-3:**
New GUI
elements
are named
to be
referenced
by the
program-
ming code.

2. **Accept the default Name and Class values and click the Create button.**

   The new interface element has no background, but its name appears in the hierarchy panel in the upper right.

3. **Click the New Control button at the top of the interface to select the GuiChunkedBitmapCtrl item from the pop-up menu.**

   This adds a new control to the newly create interface element. This control can load a background for the interface page.

4. **With the interface control selected, enter the directory for the background interface image in the bitmap field in the lower right panel. Then copy the background interface image into the specified directory.**

   The default directory for the Torque game engine examples is starter.fps/ client/ui/background. For this example, I've replaced background.jpg with alamobackground.jpg. You can click the Apply button to make the selected image appear.

5. **Change the size of the background image by dragging the image handles in the preview panel or by setting the extent field values to 800 600.**

   After changing the background image's size, the interface is displayed in the preview pane as shown in Figure A-4.

6. **Select the File ⇨ Save GUI menu command and save the new interface panel as NewGui.gui.**

   The new interface element is saved to the default directory where the Torque game engine is installed.

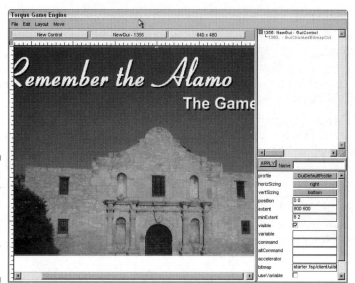

**Figure A-4:**
A new
background
image can
help define
the user
interface.

# Adding controls and commands to a GUI page

The GUI Editor includes a wealth of various interface controls including file dialogs, AVI panels, borders, check and radio boxes, a clock, fade in and fade out bitmaps, menus, text panes, scroll bars, and so on. Each of these controls can be selected from the New Control pop-up menu in the upper left of the editor.

Follow these steps to add a new interface button to an existing interface page using the GUI Editor:

1.  **With the NewGui page still open, click the New Control button again and select the GuiButtonCtrl item from the pop-up menu.**

    A new button is added to the page in the upper-left corner. The default name of this button is simply Button.

2.  **Drag the button beneath the game title.**

    The button can be moved by dragging it or by changing its Position property values.

3.  **With the button selected, enter Begin Game in the Text property.**

    Changing the Text property changes the text that appears on the button. Click the Apply button to update the preview pane.

4. **Enter the programming command needed to start the game in the Command field.**

   The Command field can hold a programming command that is executed when the button is clicked. This command could be to open another GUI element or to begin the game. The user interface page now includes a button that executes a command, as shown in Figure A-5.

   The programming commands will be different depending on the game engine that you use, but for the Torque game engine, the command to open another GUI element is Canvas.setContent(GuiElementName); and the command to start the demo mission is SM_StartMission( );.

5. **Select the File ➪ Save GUI menu command and save the interface panel over the existing one.**

   The new interface element is saved to the default directory where the Torque game engine is installed.

The GUI Editor can be closed at anytime by pressing F10 again.

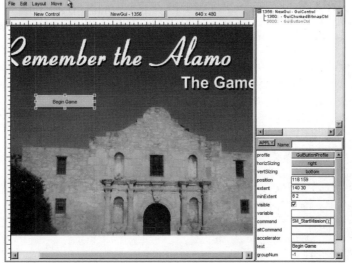

**Figure A-5:** GUI controls like buttons can be used to execute programming commands.

# Using the Mission Editor

The other editor available as part of the Torque game engine is the Mission Editor. This editor is the main editor used to build game levels. Using it, you can create and texture a game terrain, add and edit 3D objects to the scene, and define environment properties like sky, sun, and fog.

The Mission Editor deals with three different types of 3D models. These models include:

- ✔ **Terrains:** Terrains are created using a height map and can be interactively edited using the Mission Editor. Terrains can also be textured by blending as many as six different textures.

- ✔ **Interiors:** Interiors are larger objects such as buildings that allow the game player to enter and move around inside. They are saved using the DIF format and have a fairly accurate collision object. Interiors are created using the Quake Army Knife (QuArK) tool.

- ✔ **DTS Shapes:** DTS Shapes are smaller models that are placed in the scene such as weapons, game characters, and vehicles. These objects are saved using the DTS format. They also have a simple bounding box collision object. DTS Shapes can be created by using a plug-in to convert standard 3ds max or Maya models to the .DTS format.

A collision object is a simple object that surrounds an object that is used to determine if two objects collide with one another. Collision objects don't need to be as accurate as the actual model.

Figure A-6 includes examples of each of these model types. The surrounding hills are part of the terrain. The house is an Interior model that you can enter and move about, and the character and trees are both DTS Shapes.

In addition to the 3D model formats, you also need textures. These textures can be saved using the BMP, JPG, and PNG formats.

**Figure A-6:**
This game sample includes terrains, Interiors, and DTS Shapes.

## *Accessing the Mission Editor*

The tool that makes level editing possible for the Torque game engine is called the Mission Editor, and it's accessed, like the GUI Editor, using a sample of the game or one of the demo applications.

Follow these steps to access the Torque game engine's Mission Editor:

1. **After installing the Torque game engine, locate and run the Racing Starter Kit program.**

   Before you can access the Mission Editor, you need to load a mission and be inside the game.

2. **Click the Start Mission button. Then click the Launch Mission button.**

   The Start Mission button opens a separate dialog box where you can select which mission to load. After selecting the default mission, clicking the Launch Mission button loads the game engine and begins play just like a real game.

3. **Inside the game, press the F11 key to access the Mission Editor.**

   When the Mission Editor is opened, the game objects are still visible in the preview pane, but two additional panels also appear on the right, as shown in Figure A-7. Using these panels, you can select and edit the various scene objects.

 Even though the Mission Editor is opened, you can still maneuver about the scene as a player. You can use the right mouse button to control the player's orientation while the editor is open, the W key to move forward, and the S key to move backward.

The top-right panel of the Mission Editor includes a hierarchical list of all the scene objects. Using this list, you can select specific objects to edit. When a scene object is selected, its properties are listed in the lower right panel. By entering new values, you can alter an object's position, orientation and visibility in the scene. Clicking the Apply button after making a change to a property value updates the scene.

The Mission Editor includes several different editing modes. Each of these modes can be selected from the Window menu. The available modes include the following:

- ✔ **World Editor:** The World Editor is used to place and edit scene objects. In World Editor mode, all objects are labeled with an ID.

- ✔ **World Editor Inspector:** The World Editor Inspector displays all the properties for the selected object. These properties can be edited to change the object's look and behavior.

✔ **World Editor Creator:** The World Editor Creator lets you place new objects listed in several different categories in the scene.

✔ **Mission Area Editor:** In this mode, you can change the size or the play area.

✔ **Terrain Editor:** The Terrain Editor lets you adjust the terrain shape by moving areas up or down.

✔ **Terrain Terraform Editor:** The Terrain Terraform Editor lets you make global changes to the terrain using fractal and erosive patterns.

✔ **Terrain Texture Editor:** This mode lets you globally apply textures based on the terrain slope.

✔ **Terrain Texture Painter:** The Terrain Texture Painter lets you select a texture and paint it over the surface with an interactive brush.

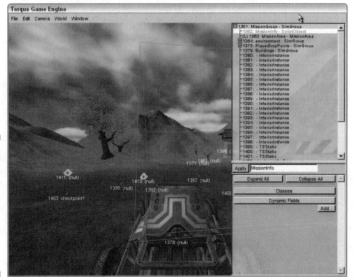

**Figure A-7:**
Pressing the
F11 key
accesses
the Mission
Editor from
the demo
application.

## Creating a terrain

Creating game terrains is easy enough to do in the various 3D packages, but the Torque game engine includes a tool that allows you to raise and lower a game terrain as you move about the world. This is extra convenient because it lets you make design decisions as you test play the game. For example, driving through an off-road racing course, you can quickly change the slope of a hill that is too steep to climb or add some bumps through a long straight stretch of road.

Follow these steps to edit the shape of the existing terrain using the Mission Editor's Terrain Editor:

1. **With the Mission Editor open, select the Window ⇨ Terrain Editor menu command.**

   This enters the terrain editing mode. In this mode, the mouse becomes a brush that you can move over the surface of the existing terrain. The red areas represent the areas of maximum change and the green areas represent the areas of lesser change. When the Terrain Editor is selected, two new commands appear — Action and Brush.

   The Brush menu includes options for setting the brush's size, shape, and edge hardness.

2. **Select the Action ⇨ Add Dirt menu command and drag in the scene at the places you want to raise up.**

   The Add Dirt command adds hills to the terrain under the brush area. Figure A-8 shows a terrain that has been raised.

3. **Select the Action ⇨ Excavate menu command and drag in the scene at the places you want to lower.**

   The Excavate command lowers areas to the terrain under the brush area. The Action menu also includes options to Flatten, Adjust Height, and Smooth areas.

**Figure A-8:**
The Terrain Editor mode can be used to alter the surface height.

# Adjusting the Terraform

Terrains can also be created from a 2D bitmap image where all light areas are raised and all dark areas are lowered. The Terrain Terraform Editor mode lets you create different terrains by blending together different 2D bitmaps. These bitmaps can include fractal, turbulence, smooth, and erosion patterns. You can even load a custom bitmap image and use it to create a terrain.

The 2D bitmap for the current terraform is shown in the lower left corner of the editor. You can change the current bitmap by clicking the Operation button and selecting a new terraform type from the pop-up list. Multiple operations can be added together for different effects. For example, you can use a Fractal pattern to create a lot of jagged peaks and then use a Smooth pattern or an Erosion pattern to wear down the jagged peaks.

Figure A-9 shows a terrain created with the Rigid MultiFractal pattern. This pattern caused the peaks to have sharp points and steep slopes. You can also set the parameters for each pattern, including the Water Level for the General operator.

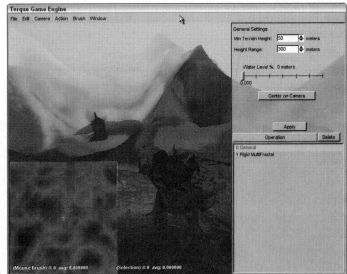

**Figure A-9:**
The Terrain Terraform Editor mode lets you create a terrain from a 2D bitmap pattern.

Follow these steps to edit the terrain pattern using the Mission Editor's Terrain Terraform Editor:

1. **With the Mission Editor open, select the File ➪ New Mission menu command.**

   The entire terrain is replaced with a new terrain that has a single homogenous texture applied.

2. **Select the Window ➪ Terrain Terraform Editor menu command.**

   This enters the terrain terraform editing mode.

3. **Click the Operation button and select the Smooth Ridges/Valleys option. Then set the Iterations value to 2.**

   The Iterations value determines how many times the calculations are computed. Using an Iteration value of 2 gives you a nice smooth series of hills and valleys.

4. **Select the General operation from the lower-right panel. Then change the Height Range value to 60 and set the Water Level to 0.0.**

   By making the Height Range value just over the Minimum Terrain Height value, you end up with a series of small rolling hills and no water. The landscape looks like a bleak desert environment, as shown in Figure A-10.

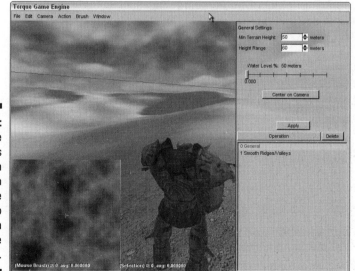

**Figure A-10:** The parameters for each operation can be altered to create even more variety.

# Texturing the terrain

After a terrain is deformed to your liking, you can load and apply textures to the landscape by simply dragging the mouse over the terrain surface. Several different textures can be used.

The Mission Editor includes two different methods for placing textures. The Terrain Texture Editor lets you specify different textures to be used at different elevations. This method is great if you want to create sand on the beach and rocks and snow at the higher elevations. Figure A-11 shows an example of this mode to add grass to the lower elevations.

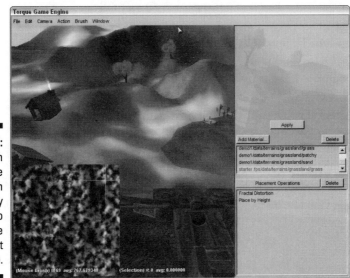

**Figure A-11:**
The Terrain Texture Editor can apply textures to the entire terrain at once.

The second method is the Terrain Texture Painter mode. Using this mode, you can select from a panel of different textures and paint areas under the brush with the various textures. The best method is to use a combination of the two. Apply default textures using the terrain elevation as a guide and then add the detailed textures using the paint method.

Follow these steps to paint textures on an existing terrain using the Mission Editor:

1. **With the Mission Editor open, select the Window ⇨ Terrain Texture Painter menu command.**

   This enters the terrain texture painting mode. In this mode, you can select a texture from the panel to the right and paint the texture using the terrain brush. The Brush menu includes settings for altering the brush's size, shape, and edge hardness.

2. **Select the Action ⇨ Paint Material menu command to enable texture paint mode.**

   Terrain shape can be changed while in Terrain Texture Painter mode if the Action ⇨ Paint Material option isn't selected.

3. **Select one of the textures from the panel to the right and drag with the brush in the scene to paint the texture.**

   Multiple textures can be overlapped as you paint in the scene and new textures can be loaded by clicking the Add button in the right panel. Figure A-12 shows the current scene with several interesting painted textures.

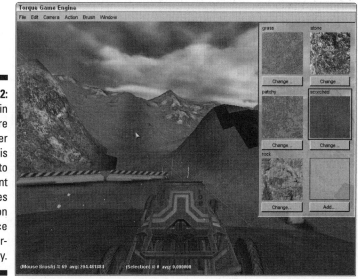

**Figure A-12:**
The Terrain Texture Painter mode is used to paint textures directly on the surface interactively.

# Populating the environment

The next step in creating a game environment is to populate the world with different physical models. These models can include buildings, scenery, and props. After you've placed them, you can easily move these objects about the scene.

Object placement is controlled using the World Editor mode of the Mission Editor. The World Editor Creator mode offers links to the available objects that can be placed in the scene, and the World Editor Inspector shows the properties for the selected object, allowing you to fine tune its placement.

Follow these steps to add new objects to the scene using the World Editor mode:

1. **With the Mission Editor open, select the Window ➪ World Editor Creator menu command.**

   This enters a mode where you can add new objects to the scene. The top-right panel displays a hierarchical list of scene objects and the lower-right panel displays an organized list of new objects that can be added to the scene.

2. **In the lower-right panel, expand the Shapes/Vehicles category and click the Default Car object.**

    By clicking this object, a new car is added to the scene. The location of the new object is determined by the option set in the World menu. The available options can drop the new objects at the Origin, the Camera's location, below the Camera, at the Screen Center, at the Centroid, or to the Ground.

    If you look closely at the upper right panel in the World Editor, you'll notice several items that aren't scene objects. In addition to objects, the scene can also include other items that have positions in the world such as a spawn location, which marks where the player starts and check-point triggers, causing message to appear when the player crosses them.

3. **With the new car object selected, select the Window ⇨ World Editor Inspector menu command.**

    When an object is selected, a bounding box is displayed around the entire object, and the object is highlighted in the upper-right panel. When the World Editor Inspector mode is enabled, all properties for the selected object are displayed in the lower right panel.

4. **Change the value of the Scale field to 3 3 3 and click the Apply button.**

    The new car object is increased in size, as shown in Figure A-13.

**Figure A-13:** Scene objects can be altered by changing their property values.

# Moving objects

With new objects added to the scene, you can move them about by changing the Position property in the lower right panel, but an easier way to move object is to drag them within the scene.

When an object is selected, it's highlighted by a bounding box, but three axes are also displayed at the object's origin. If you move the mouse over one of these three axes, then the axis will be highlighted, and you can drag the object in the direction of the selected axis.

Follow these steps to move objects in the scene using the World Editor mode:

1. **With the Mission Editor open, select the Window ➪ World Editor menu command.**

   This enters a mode where you can select and move objects in the scene.

2. **Navigate in the scene until you're close to a tree object. Then click the tree object to select it.**

   The selected tree is surrounded by a bounding box, and the X-, Y-, and Z-axes extend from the point at the tree's center.

3. **Move the mouse cursor over the Y-axis and drag the tree to the left.**

   When the mouse cursor is over the Y-axis, the axis becomes highlighted, and dragging the mouse causes the tree to move along the Y-axis in the direction that you're dragging.

4. **Move the mouse cursor over the Z-axis and drag the tree downward until it is in contact with the ground again.**

   The repositioned tree is now in its new position, as shown in Figure A-14.

# Defining the Scene Environment

You can also use the Mission Area Editor mode to specify the game area. In this mode, a small 2D overhead view of the scene is displayed in the upper right corner of the interface. Within this view, a rectangular box denotes the game area. The V-shape is the player's current position.

Clicking the Edit Area option lets you change the size of the game area using handles placed at each corner, as shown in Figure A-15.

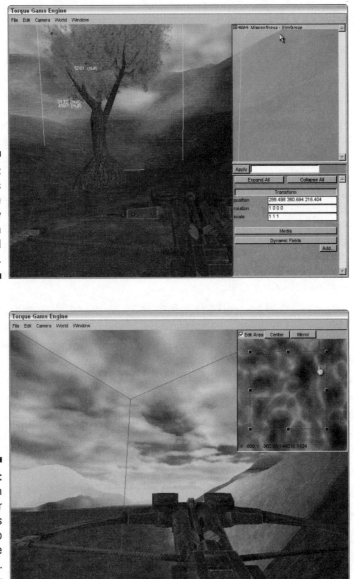

**Figure A-14:** Objects can be interactively moved in the World Editor.

**Figure A-15:** The Mission Area Editor mode is used to define the game area.

The Torque game engine also includes several different options for controlling the look and actions of the environment including the sky, the sun, the grass, and various weather conditions. By changing the sky's colors, cloud density and movement, you can add a wealth of detail to the game.

Follow these steps to change the scene's environment using the World Editor mode:

1. **With the Mission Editor open, select the Window ⇨ World Editor Inspector menu command.**

   In this mode, you can change the properties of the different environment settings, including sky, sun, clouds, and fog.

2. **In the upper-right panel expand the MissionGroup/environment category and click the Sky object.**

   By clicking this object, all the properties for the sky become accessible in the lower-right panel.

3. **In the lower-right panel, expand the Clouds category, change the cloudSpeed2 value to 0.02, and click the Apply button.**

   Changing the cloudSpeed2 value causes some clouds to move quickly in the sky. This is just an example of the editing that is possible with clouds.

4. **In the upper-right panel, expand the MissionGroup/environment category and click the Sun object.**

   By clicking this object, all the properties for the sun become accessible in the lower-right panel.

5. **In the lower-right panel, expand the Misc category, change the elevation value to15, and click the Apply button.**

   Changing the elevation value lowers the sun to the horizon, as shown in Figure A-16. Notice also how this also affects the scene lighting.

**Figure A-16:**
Scene environment properties can also be altered by changing their properties values.

# *Loading Maya Files into the Game Engine*

Game engine tools are useful for creating levels and populating the levels with standard objects that ship with the game. These objects are good for testing your game and for prototype, but sooner or later, you'll want to use your own custom models to give the game a unique style.

Unique models can be created using many different 3D packages including Maya, which has been covered in this book, but game engines very rarely use the default Maya files or the files from any standard 3D package. Instead, they use a custom format. These custom formats are typically highly optimized for the particular game engine.

One such custom 3D format is the DTS format. The game engine only recognizes this format, so the native Maya files need to be converted to this format before they can be loaded into the game engine.

To convert your models and animations from the format used by your 3D software package into something that the game engine can use, you need to load a conversion plug-in. These plug-ins run natively within the 3D package and can convert the DTS file format. The converted DTS format can then be loaded and used within the game engine.

## *Installing a DTS Export Utility*

For Maya, there are several different MEL scripts that can convert files. One such script is the DTS Exporter Utility, written by Danny Ngan. This script can be downloaded from the following link, `http://dannyn1.web.aplus. net/torque/maya2dts`.

Follow these steps to install and access the DTS Exporter Utility for Maya:

1. **After downloading the file, locate and copy the dtsUtility.mel file into the My Documents/Maya/scripts folder, and restart Maya.**

   Mel files are simple scripts that extend the functionality of Maya. They are installed by simply placing the script file in the scripts directory.

2. **Type dtsUtility on the command line in Maya and press the Enter key.**

   The command line is located under the Range Slider at the bottom of the Maya interface. It is used to enter textual commands into the interface. Pressing the Enter key automatically executes whatever command is entered into the command line.

3. **After executing the mel script, the DTS Utility panel appears.**

   The DTS Utility panel, shown in Figure A-17, includes all the controls needed to convert and export the selected model to the DTS format.

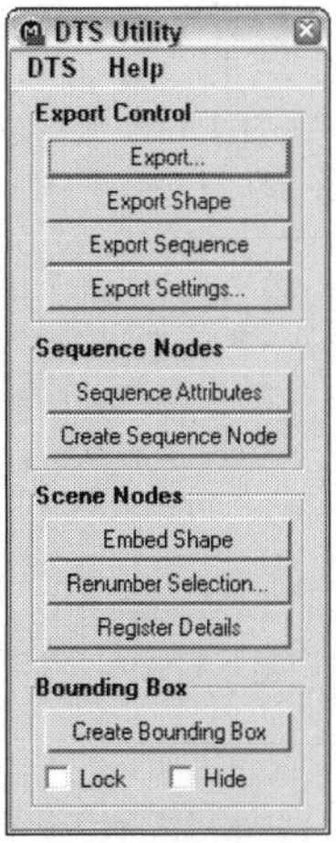

**Figure A-17:** The DTS Utility panel includes buttons for exporting the selected model to the DTS format.

# Changing default units

Before continuing, you can save a lot of headaches later on if you check the units that are used for Maya. The Torque game engine has units set so that one unit equals one meter, but Maya's default units has one unit set to one centimeter. If you don't change this, then your models will appear very small when loaded in the Torque game engine.

Follow these steps to access Maya's default units:

1. **Select the Window ⇨ Settings/Preferences ⇨ Preferences menu command.**

   The Preferences dialog box opens.

2. **Click the Settings option from the list on the right.**

   The General Application Preferences panel appears, including the Working Units section.

3. **Change the Linear units from centimeters to meters.**

   The other settings can remain at their default setting, as shown in Figure A-18.

4. **Click the Save button at the bottom of the dialog box.**

   Clicking the Save button saves this change as the new default.

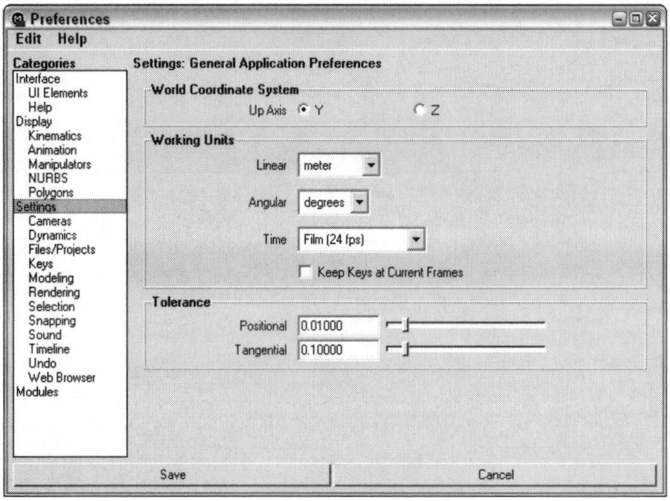

**Figure A-18:**
The
Preferences
dialog box
includes a
setting for
changing
the default
units.

# Exporting a Maya object

Each custom format has its own unique requirements, and the DTS format is
no exception. Before an object can be exported to the DTS format, it must be
surrounded completely by a Bounding Box object. This bounding box object
needs to be named 'bounds' and marks the edges of the exported object.

The DTS Exporter Utility includes a button that makes creating a bounding
box object easy. Simply click the Create Bounding Box button, and one is created and named automatically.

Clicking the Export button opens a file dialog box where you can name the
exported file.

Follow these steps to export a Maya object to the DTS format:

1. **Select the Create ➪ Polygon Primitives ➪ Sphere menu command.**

   A simple sphere object is added to the center of the scene.

2. **Click the Create Bounding Box button in the DTS Utility panel.**

   A bounding box object is added to the scene that surrounds the selected
   Maya object, as shown in Figure A-19.

3. **Click the Export button in the DTS Utility panel. Name the file simple ball.dts.**

   A file dialog box opens where you can name the exported file.

4. **Select the DTS Export option from the Files of Type field and click the Export button.**

   The file is saved to the designated directory.

If there is a problem with the export command, then a text file named dump.dmp will be placed in the export directory. This file will have information about why the export has failed.

## Viewing exported objects

A terrible time to find out that an exported DTS file has problems is when you're trying to load it into the game engine. Garage Games offers another tool, created by David Wyand, that enables you to view the exported DTS file before tying up the game engine. You can find more information about this tool at www.garagegames.com.

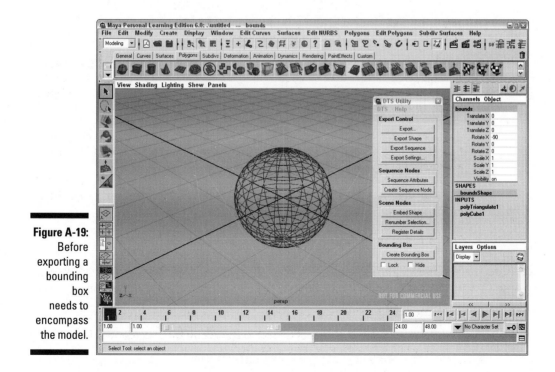

**Figure A-19:** Before exporting a bounding box needs to encompass the model.

The Torque ShowTool lets you load and view DTS files using a number of different shading methods. You can also see the effect of dynamic lights and textures on the loaded objects.

Follow these steps to view a DTS model in the Torque ShowTool:

1. **Open the Torque ShowTool.**

   The ShowTool interface includes a view window that can be panned, rotated, and zoomed.

2. **Click the Project Directory button at the top left of the interface.**

   This button lets you select the directory where the DTS files are saved.

3. **Click the Load DTS button.**

   All the available DTS files in the specified project directory are displayed.

4. **Locate the Simple ball.dts file and click the Load button.**

   The file is loaded into the ShowTool and displayed in the view window.

5. **Use the buttons in the upper-right corner of the view window to navigate about the loaded DTS model.**

   The view navigation buttons include Center, FOV, Rotate, Pan, and Zoom.

6. **Click the Display Properties button to the left of the view window.**

   A panel of options appears in the view window.

7. **Click the Render tab and choose the Day_0007 option from the EMap list.**

   The loaded model is displayed with a sample texture, as shown in Figure A-20.

## Exporting textured objects

The DTS format also supports texture maps. These maps can be applied using the typical methods in Maya. When the file is exported, the texture file should be placed along with the DTS file in the same directory. Texture files can be either JPEG or PNG files.

Standard materials, shaders, and procedural textures, such as the Checkboard in Maya, will not be exported with the DTS format. Only textures applied as an external file may be exported.

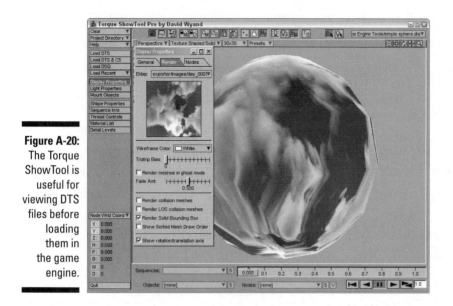

**Figure A-20:**
The Torque
ShowTool is
useful for
viewing DTS
files before
loading
them in
the game
engine.

Follow these steps to view a DTS model in the Torque ShowTool:

1. **Select the File ⇨ Open Scene menu command and load the Rock.mb file.**

   This file is a simple sphere that has been randomly moved in all directions to create a rock object. This rock also has a texture spherically mapping to its surface. The texture file is rock.png.

2. **Click the Create Bounding Box button in the DTS Utility panel.**

   A bounding box object is added to the scene that surrounds the selected Maya object.

3. **Click the Export button in the DTS Utility panel. Name the file Rock.dts.**

   A file dialog box opens, allowing you to name the exported file.

4. **Select the DTS Export option from the Files of Type field and click the Export button.**

   The file is saved to the designated directory.

5. **Open the Torque ShowTool and click the Load DTS button.**

   All the available DTS files in the specified project directory are displayed, including the exported Rock.dts file.

6. **Locate the Rock.dts file and click the Load button.**

   The file is loaded into the ShowTool and displayed in the view window including the rock texture, as shown in Figure A-21.

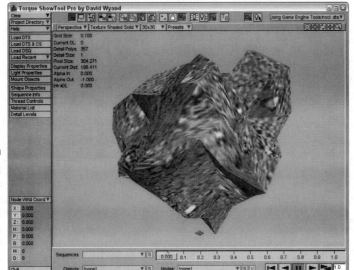

Figure A-21:
Textures
can be
exported
along with
the DTS
model.

# Exporting animation sequences

When a model is saved as a DTS file, none of its animation sequences are saved with it. Animation sequences can be saved using another format known as .DSQ. A single model can have many different animation sequences associated with it.

Each animation sequence file has several attributes associated with it. Using these attributes, you can set the beginning and ending frames, whether the animation loops, and the frame rate.

In order for the exporter to work, you need to rename your sequence node so it starts with 'Sequence_'.

Follow these steps to export an animation sequence:

1. **Create a simple ten-frame animation of the rock rotating.**

   This can be done simply by pressing the S key to create a key, dragging the Time Slider to frame 10, rotating the rock object, and then pressing the S key again.

2. **Click the Create Sequence Node button in the DTS Utility panel.**

   This command creates a sequence node for the selected object. The attributes for this node are displayed in the Channel Box.

3. **In the Channel Box, set the node name to Sequence_anim1, and set the Start and End Frame values to 1 and 10.**

Changing these attributes limits the animation to the first ten frames only. The Cyclic attribute is also set to On, which causes the motion to be repeated.

4. **Click the Export Sequence button in the DTS Utility panel. Name the file Asteroid.dsq.**

   A file dialog box opens, allowing you to name the exported file.

   **TIP**

   If the sequence node is created, then you can also use the Export button to export both the shape and sequence at the same time.

5. **Open the Torque ShowTool and click the Load DSQ button.**

   All the available DSQ files in the specified project directory are displayed including the exported Asteroid.dsq file.

6. **Click the Play Animation button to see the saved sequence.**

   The animated sequence is played showing the rock tumbling over and over, as shown in Figure A-22.

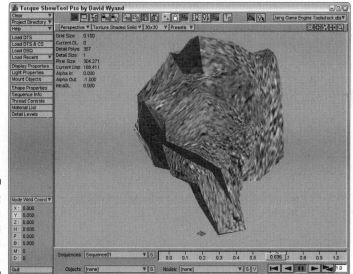

**Figure A-22:**
Animation sequences are saved as DSQ files.

# *Making models available in the Mission Editor*

After a model has been saved to the DTS format, you can add it to the resources that get loaded into the game engine. This enables you to use the World Editor Creator mode to add the new models to the current scene.

This process is easy: You simply need to find where the DTS files are located on your hard drive and copy the files to that location.

Follow these steps to make a converted DTS file accessible in the Mission Editor:

1. **Locate all the converted DTS files and copy them.**

   If the model file includes a texture, be sure to copy the texture file also.

2. **Locate the data directory where the Torque game resources are found.**

   For the FPS Starter Kit example, the sample DTS files are found in the example/starter.fps/data/shapes folder. This was easy to find because this folder includes all the same objects that are currently available in the World Editor Creator mode.

3. **Within the Shapes folder, create a new folder named 'custom'. Then copy the converted DTS files into this folder and restart the FPS application.**

   With all DTS files copied into this folder, you simply need to restart the demo application to see the new models.

4. **With the Mission Editor open, select the Window ⇨ World Editor Creator menu command.**

   The lower-right panel displays an organized list of new objects that can be added to the scene.

5. **In the lower-right panel expand the Static Shapes/starter.fps/data/ Shapes/custom category and click the Rock object.**

   By clicking this object, the converted DTS model is added to the scene.

6. **With the new rock object selected, drag the object axes to move the rock into position.**

   The rock is added to the scene, as shown in Figure A-23.

## Creating Interiors

The Torque game engine allows models that a player can move inside of to be added to their games, but these Interiors must be created using a tool and a format that was developed for the game Quake, by id software. The format for these interior models is the .DIF format. This format is unique because it offers an efficient way to compute collisions between objects.

The tool used to create .DIF files is the QuArK tool. The tool's name stands for Quake Army Knife. It is an open source map-editing tool that is available for free and can be downloaded from `http://dynamic.gamespy.com/~quark/`.

Figure A-24 shows the QuArK editing interface. This tool is used to build models for several games including Quake, Hexen, Sin, and others. It also includes a preset for the Torque engine. The package comes with an effective help file for learning to use the interface.

**Figure A-23:** Converted DTS files can be added to the current scene.

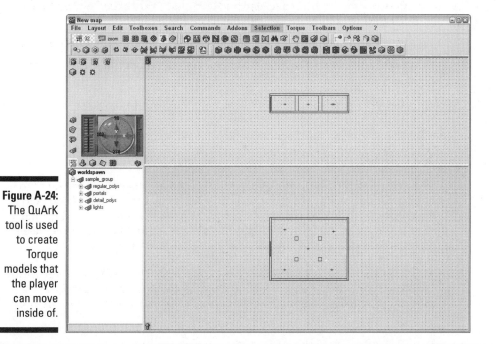

**Figure A-24:** The QuArK tool is used to create Torque models that the player can move inside of.

# Appendix B
# Glossary of Animation Terms

**2D graphics**

A type of graphics that are drawn on a single flat plane. These graphics are generally flat and are missing the element of depth.

**3D graphics**

A type of graphics that are created using a three-dimensional coordinate system. 3D graphics include a sense of depth created by surface shading and shadows.

**3ds max**

A 3D modeling, rendering, and animation software package made by Discreet.

**alpha channel**

A channel of data included with a bitmap image that holds transparency information.

**ambient light**

Created by light that is deflected off walls and objects; provides overall lighting to the entire scene and keeps shadows from becoming completely black.

**animation**

The process of simulating motion by displaying many separate images in succession.

**animation graph**

A graph that plots an object's value as a function of frames.

**animation loop**

A sequence of animation frames that are designed to repeat indefinitely using a minimum number of frames.

**animation path**

A line or curve that is used to define the path that an object follows during its animation.

**anti-aliasing**

The process of removing *artifacts* by softening the transition between colors.

**art design**

The process of designing the look and feel of a game including its heroes, enemies, props, scenery, and levels.

**artifacts**

Jagged edges caused by the square pixels where the material color changes from the object to the background.

**artificial light**

Usually reserved for indoor scenes where light bulbs provide the light.

**aspect ratio**

The ratio of an image's width to its height.

**atmospheric effects**

Effects such as fog or haze that are added to a scene during the rendering process.

**attenuation**

A property that determines how light fades over distance.

**baked texture**

A texture that is created by combining several textures on different channels into a single file. These baked textures can include pre-computed reflection, light, and bump effects.

**Bézier curve**

A type of curved line where the curvature of the line is controlled by control vertices and handles.

**blur**

The effect that results from smearing or smudging a scene, image, or object.

**bone system**

A hierarchy of bone objects used to define the skeletal structure of a character.

**bounding box**

A non-rendered box that completely surrounds a selected object and defines its extents.

**bump map**

A type of material map that defines areas to be modified by comparing the intensity of the pixels in the map.

**camera**

An object that can be positioned within a scene to provide a unique viewpoint.

**cartoon rendering**

A rendering option that outlines all objects and fills them with solid colors to look like a cartoon. Also called Vector rendering.

**character**

A figure in the game that is endowed with life which the game player can interact with.

**child object**

An object that is linked to and controlled by a *parent object*.

**compositing**

The process of combining several different images into a single image. Each element of the composite is included as a separate event.

**constraint**

A definable limit imposed on objects in a scene that prevents them from moving in certain directions during animation.

**controllers**

Affect the position, rotation, and scaling of objects in preset ways. Also, *plug-ins* that set the keys for animation sequences.

**cut scene**

An animation segment that plays in between game levels. Cut scenes are typically used to introduce the game and to tell a story as the game progresses.

**demo reel**

A CD or DVD that shows off your skills by presenting a sampling of your best animation work.

**depth of field**

An optical effect where the camera focuses on a specific point in space and all objects at a distance from this point are blurred.

**diffuse color**

The main color radiated by an object under normal white light.

**Dope Sheet**

An interface that shows all animation keys as cells in a spreadsheet in Maya. The Dope Sheet is useful for aligning keys to certain events and sounds.

**dummy object**

A non-rendering object that can be linked to structures to make the structure easier to animate.

**dynamics**

A branch of physics that deals with forces and the motions they cause.

**ease curve**

A curve that is applied to a function curve that softens the curve's shape, causing animations to ease into and out of a position.

**emitter**

An icon that looks like a plane or a sphere and defines the location in a *particle system* where the *particles* all originate.

**end effector**

The object included at the end of an IK chain that controls the movements of the chain.

**extents**

The maximum dimension along each axis.

**extruding**

A modeling action that raises a selected face from its surface and connects the face to its original position with new faces created at each edge.

**falloff**

A light property that defines how quickly the light intensity decreases with distance. Popular light falloff options are linear, cubic, and quadratic.

**field of view**

A measurement of how much of the scene is visible; directly related to the *focal length*.

**focal length**

The distance between the film and the camera lens.

**follow object**

An object that defines the motion of an applied IK solution.

**forward kinematics**

A default *hierarchy* established using the Link tool, where control moves forward down the hierarchy from *parent object* to *child object*. Causes objects at the bottom of a linked structure to move along with their parents.

**fps**

Frames per second, a frame rate measurement.

**frame**

A single image taken from an animation sequence.

**frame rate**

The rate at which images are displayed to produce an animation. Common rates are 30 fps (NTSC), 25 fps (PAL), and 24 fps (film).

**function curve**

Displayed in the Track View, these editable curves display the animation values as a function of time.

**game design**

The creative process of defining how a game works and its characters, story, and goals.

**game design document**

A document or set of documents that provide a detailed explanation of the game's concept and design.

**gamma settings**

A means by which colors can be consistently represented, regardless of the monitor that is being used.

**gamma value**

A numerical offset required by an individual monitor in order to be consistent with a standard.

**ghosting**

An animation setting that makes a set number of copies of the animated object appear before or after the object.

**HSB**

A common color definition system that includes values for hue, saturation, and brightness.

**hardware**

The components that make up the physical computer system.

**hierarchy**

The complete set of related *parent* and *child* objects.

**hotspot**

The portion of a spotlight where the light intensity is at a maximum.

**IK solver**

An *inverse kinematics* solution that can be applied to a linked hierarchy of objects that define how the objects move relative to one another.

**Illustrator**

A popular 2D drawing software package made by Adobe.

**in-betweens**

The frames that exist between a beginning and ending keyframes.

**index of refraction**

The amount that light bends as it goes through a transparent object.

**inverse kinematics system**

A method of defining the connections between parts for easier animation. Enables *child objects* to control their *parent objects.*

**keyframe**

A definition of a specific object state that exists during an animation.

**kinematics**

A branch of mechanics that deals with the motions of a system of objects. In Maya, these systems are defined by links between objects.

**lens flare**

An effect that occurs naturally when you point a camera at a bright light source. Lens flares can include a series of bright circles, streaks, and glows.

**level-of-detail**

The technique of displaying a high-resolution version of a model when it is close to the camera and displaying a low-resolution version of the model when it is further away from the camera.

**light object**

An object that defines the position and attributes of a scene's light.

**Lightwave**

A 3D modeling, rendering, and animation software package made by NewTek.

**linking**

The process of attaching one object to another so that they move together.

**lo-polygon model**

A polygon model that uses a minimum number of polygons.

**map**

A bitmap image that is pasted on an image.

**mapping coordinates**

Define how a map should be positioned and oriented on the surface of an object.

**materials**

Surface properties that are applied to an object which can include the surface's color, transparency, reflectivity, and specularity.

**matte object**

Causes any geometry object behind it to be invisible, but allows the background to be seen.

**Maya**

A 3D modeling, rendering, and animation software package made by Alias.

**Maya, Personal Learning Edition**

A free version of Maya's popular 3D modeling, rendering, and animation software that can be used for non-commercial purposes.

**mesh object**

An object type that consists of interconnected polygons.

**modeling**

The process of building 3D objects using a 3D software package.

**morphing**

An animation technique that changes a model to an altered copy of the same model over a given number of frames.

**motion blur**

A method for displaying velocity by blurring objects in proportion to their speed.

**motion capture**

A technique for recording the actions of a physical actor that can be superimposed onto a 3D model.

**natural light**

Used for outside scenes; uses the sun and moon for its light source.

**normal**

A vector that is perpendicular to the polygon face used to determine lighting for the face.

**NURBS**

An acronym that stands for Non-Uniform Rational B-Spline.

**NURBS modeling**

A modeling method that uses spline curves to represent objects. NURBS modeling is used to create smooth, flowing, organic-appearing models.

**omni light**

A type of light that sends light equally in all directions from a central point.

**onionskin**

A semi-transparent layer that displays a faint image of adjacent animation frames.

**opacity**

The amount that an object refuses to allow light to pass through it, typically measured as a percentage. The opposite of *transparency.*

**opaque objects**

Objects that you cannot see through, like rocks and trees.

**orthographic view**

Displayed from looking straight down an axis at an object, which reveals only one plane and shows the actual height and width of the object.

**out-of-range type**

Defines how an animation continues beyond the specified range.

**parent object**

An object that controls any secondary objects, or *child objects,* linked to it.

**particle**

A small, simple object that is duplicated en masse, like snow, rain, or dust.

**particle system**

Contains a specific type of particle, such as snow. Each particle system contains a different particle type.

**perspective**

Distortion of images taken with a wide *field of view*. Causes linear dimensions to appear larger if they are closer than similar dimensions lying at a farther distance.

**phoneme**

A single facial position that creates a sound used when speaking.

**Photoshop**

A popular image-editing software package used to create and edit images and textures; made by Adobe.

**pivot point**

The point about which transforms are applied.

**pixels**

Small, square dots that collectively make up an entire screen.

**polygon modeling**

A modeling method that creates models using attached polygonal faces that are smoothed across their edges.

**post processing**

The process of adding effects to an image after the *rendering* process is complete.

**post production**

The work that comes after a scene is ready to render. Can be used to add effects such as glows and highlights; to add transitional effects to the animation such as including a logo on the front of your animation; and to composite several images into one.

**previews**

Test animation sequences that render quickly to give you an idea of the final output.

**primitives**

Basic building block objects that are created simply and can be edited to create new objects. Typical 3D primitives include spheres, cubes, cylinders, cones, and planes.

**projection map**

A type of material map that is used with lights.

**props**

Objects within the game that the player can interact with.

**RGB**

A set of three values that define the intensity of Red, Green, and Blue colors that are mixed to determine the color of a pixel.

**radiosity**

A rendering method that creates realistic lighting by calculating how light reflects off objects.

**raytracing**

A rendering method that calculates image colors by following imaginary light rays as they move through a scene.

**reference materials**

Sample materials that are used to provide inspiration for an artist during the art design phase.

**reflection**

What you see when you look in a mirror. Reflection values control how much a material reflects its surroundings.

**refraction**

A property that defines how light bends as it moves through a transparent material. The amount of refraction a material produces depends on the *Index of Refraction.*

**rendering**

The process of computing a scene's final image taking into account the scene's geometry, lights, materials, and textures.

**rigging**

The process by which a character is endowed with a skeleton that is used to simplify the animation process.

**rigid body**

An object that is defined with the physical properties to act as a solid object when colliding with other objects like a rock or a bowling ball.

**root object**

The top *parent object* that has no parent and controls the entire *hierarchy*.

**shaders**

Algorithms used to compute how a material should look given its parameters.

**shadow**

The area behind an object where the light is obscured.

**shadow map**

A type of *shadow* that is an actual bitmap that the renderer produces and combines with the finished scene to produce an image.

**skeleton**

A system of bones that lies underneath a character's skin and is used to animate a character.

**skin**

A character mesh that is draped over a skeletal bone system. Skin deforms as the underlying bones are moved.

**skybox**

An object that surrounds the entire scene that is mapped with a background image.

**smoothing groups**

A specified region listed by a number that defines how the edges of the region should be smoothed.

**soft body**

An object that is defined with the physical properties to act as a squishy object when colliding with other objects like a pillow or a bouncy ball.

**Softimage XSI**

A 3D modeling, rendering, and animation software package made by Avid.

**software**

Computer programs that are installed and run on the computer to accomplish a specific function.

**specular highlights**

Highlights on a shiny object where the lights reflect off its surface.

**spline**

A special type of line that curves according to mathematical principles.

**storyboard**

A series of hand-drawn panels that quickly show the actions involved in an animation sequence.

**terminator**

The last object in an *inverse kinematics system* that is affected by the child's movement.

**texture**

An image that is wrapped (or mapped) about an object.

**tiling**

The process of laying texture images end to end to cover the entire surface of an object.

**trajectory**

The actual *spline* path that an object follows when it is animated.

**transforming objects**

The fundamental process of "repositioning" or changing an object's position, rotation, and scale.

**translucency**

Scatters the light passing through an object so that other objects cannot be seen through it, like frosted glass.

**transparency**

The amount of light that is allowed to pass through an object. The opposite of *opacity*.

**transparent objects**

Objects that you can see through, like glass and clear plastic.

**UI**

An acronym that stands for User Interface. A user interface consists of the controls used to interact with the game and the information that defines the game experience.

**UV Mapping**

A method of defining the position of texture maps on a 3D object.

**vertex color**

A method of coloring an object by assigning a color to a vertex. Different colors applied to adjacent vertices produce a gradient across the object face.

**volume light**

The effect of a beam of light shining through fog, smoke, or dust.

**wireframe**

A render type that displays only the lines that make up an object.

**world object**

An imaginary object that holds all objects.

# Appendix C

# Directory of Animation Schools

● ● ● ● ● ● ● ● ● ● ● ● ● ● ● ● ● ● ● ● ● ● ● ● ● ● ● ● ● ● ● ● ● ● ● ● ● ● ● ● ● ● ● ● ● ●

Although animation programs and classes can be found in universities and colleges across the country, the schools listed below are distinguished in their reputation and should be given special consideration.

To search for an animation school closer to your home, check out the list of schools on the Animation World Network Web site: `http://schools.awn.com`.

## The Art Institutes

The Art Institutes begin the list because it starts with the letter A, but also because it is one of the best schools available for 3D animation and digital art. It has locations in cities all across the country and offers an online program. It offers degrees in Game Art & Design, Media Arts & Animation, and Visual FX & Motion Graphics, among others.

The Art Institutes also has a strong placement program for helping you find your first animation job. You can learn more about The Art Institutes at `www.artinstitutes.com`.

## Ringling School of Art and Design

Located in Sarasota, Florida, Ringling School of Art and Design is a private school offering Bachelor of Fine Arts degrees in Computer Animation, Graphic & Interactive Communication, Fine Arts, Illustration, Interior Design, and Photography & Digital Imaging. You can learn about Ringling's programs at `www.rsad.edu`.

# Full Sail

Full Sail offers real-world experience through its programs. It is located near Orlando, Florida, and includes degrees in Computer Animation, Digital Media, Entertainment Business, Film, and Game Design and Development. You can learn more about Full Sail at www.fullsail.com.

# California Institute of the Arts

The California Institute of the Arts offers programs in Experimental Animation and Character Animation. Find CalArts at www.calarts.edu.

# Vancouver Film School

Located in Vancouver, British Columbia, Canada, the Vancouver Film School offers programs in 3D Animation and Visual Effects, Classical Animation, Digital Character Animation, Game Design, and more. Learn more about Vancouver Film School at www.vfs.com.

# Sheridan College

Another excellent animation school in Canada is Sheridan College, located in Toronto, Ontario, Canada. The Computer Animation program focuses on computer animation, digital effects, and character animation. Find out more about Sheridan College at www.sheridanc.on.ca.

# Savannah College of Art and Design

Located in Savannah, Georgia, with a satellite campus in Atlanta, the Savannah College of Art and Design offers numerous art-oriented programs, including animation and interactive design and game development. You can learn more about this college at www.scad.edu.

# DigiPen Institute of Technology

The DigiPen Institute of Technology, located in Redmond, Washington, offers two-year degrees in both Video Game Programming and Computer Animation. Find out more about DigiPen at www.digipen.edu.

# Parsons School of Design

Located in New York, New York, Parsons School of Design offers degrees in Character Animation, Experimental Animation, and Multimedia/Games. You can find it at www.parsons.edu.

# Digital Media Arts College

Located in Boca Raton, Florida, Digital Media Arts College offers both Bachelor and Master degrees specializing in Character Animation, Experimental Animation, Computer Animation/Digital Art, and Multimedia/Games. You can find it at www.dmac-edu.org.

# Ex'pression College for Digital Arts

The Ex'pression College for Digital Arts can be found in Emeryville, California. It offers accelerated Bachelor degree programs in Sound Arts, Digital Visual Media (including 3D Animation and Visual Effects), and Digital Graphic Design. You can learn more about its programs at www.expression.edu.

# Vancouver Institute of Media Arts

The Vancouver Institute of Media Arts, commonly referred to as VanArts, can be found in Vancouver, British Columbia. It offers certificates in Character Animation, Computer Animation/Digital Art, and Multimedia/Games. You can learn more about its programs at www.vanarts.com.

# Academy of Art University

Located in San Francisco, California, the Academy of Art University offers certificates and Bachelor and Master degrees in numerous areas, including Cartooning, Character Animation, Experimental Animation, Computer Animation/Digital Art, and Multimedia/Games. You can find it on the Web at www.academyart.edu.

# Gnomon, School of Visual Effects for Film, Television and Games

Located in Hollywood, California, Gnomon offers certificates in several different areas. It is a training facility designed to give you the skills you need to become productive quickly. You can find more information at www.gnomon3d.com.

# Oregon3D

Located in Portland, Oregon, Oregon3D is a training facility designed to give students and professionals the skills they need in focused sessions. For a complete list of upcoming courses and facilities, check out its Web site at www.oregon3d.com.

# Index

# Notes

# Notes

# Notes

# Notes

# Notes

## BUSINESS, CAREERS & PERSONAL FINANCE

0-7645-5307-0

0-7645-5331-3 *†

**Also available:**
- Accounting For Dummies †
  0-7645-5314-3
- Business Plans Kit For Dummies †
  0-7645-5365-8
- Cover Letters For Dummies
  0-7645-5224-4
- Frugal Living For Dummies
  0-7645-5403-4
- Leadership For Dummies
  0-7645-5176-0
- Managing For Dummies
  0-7645-1771-6

- Marketing For Dummies
  0-7645-5600-2
- Personal Finance For Dummies *
  0-7645-2590-5
- Project Management For Dummies
  0-7645-5283-X
- Resumes For Dummies †
  0-7645-5471-9
- Selling For Dummies
  0-7645-5363-1
- Small Business Kit For Dummies *†
  0-7645-5093-4

## HOME & BUSINESS COMPUTER BASICS

0-7645-4074-2

0-7645-3758-X

**Also available:**
- ACT! 6 For Dummies
  0-7645-2645-6
- iLife '04 All-in-One Desk Reference
  For Dummies
  0-7645-7347-0
- iPAQ For Dummies
  0-7645-6769-1
- Mac OS X Panther Timesaving
  Techniques For Dummies
  0-7645-5812-9
- Macs For Dummies
  0-7645-5656-8

- Microsoft Money 2004 For Dummies
  0-7645-4195-1
- Office 2003 All-in-One Desk Reference
  For Dummies
  0-7645-3883-7
- Outlook 2003 For Dummies
  0-7645-3759-8
- PCs For Dummies
  0-7645-4074-2
- TiVo For Dummies
  0-7645-6923-6
- Upgrading and Fixing PCs For Dummies
  0-7645-1665-5
- Windows XP Timesaving Techniques
  For Dummies
  0-7645-3748-2

## FOOD, HOME, GARDEN, HOBBIES, MUSIC & PETS

0-7645-5295-3

0-7645-5232-5

**Also available:**
- Bass Guitar For Dummies
  0-7645-2487-9
- Diabetes Cookbook For Dummies
  0-7645-5230-9
- Gardening For Dummies *
  0-7645-5130-2
- Guitar For Dummies
  0-7645-5106-X
- Holiday Decorating For Dummies
  0-7645-2570-0
- Home Improvement All-in-One
  For Dummies
  0-7645-5680-0

- Knitting For Dummies
  0-7645-5395-X
- Piano For Dummies
  0-7645-5105-1
- Puppies For Dummies
  0-7645-5255-4
- Scrapbooking For Dummies
  0-7645-7208-3
- Senior Dogs For Dummies
  0-7645-5818-8
- Singing For Dummies
  0-7645-2475-5
- 30-Minute Meals For Dummies
  0-7645-2589-1

## INTERNET & DIGITAL MEDIA

0-7645-1664-7

0-7645-6924-4

**Also available:**
- 2005 Online Shopping Directory
  For Dummies
  0-7645-7495-7
- CD & DVD Recording For Dummies
  0-7645-5956-7
- eBay For Dummies
  0-7645-5654-1
- Fighting Spam For Dummies
  0-7645-5965-6
- Genealogy Online For Dummies
  0-7645-5964-8
- Google For Dummies
  0-7645-4420-9

- Home Recording For Musicians
  For Dummies
  0-7645-1634-5
- The Internet For Dummies
  0-7645-4173-0
- iPod & iTunes For Dummies
  0-7645-7772-7
- Preventing Identity Theft For Dummies
  0-7645-7336-5
- Pro Tools All-in-One Desk Reference
  For Dummies
  0-7645-5714-9
- Roxio Easy Media Creator For Dummies
  0-7645-7131-1

* Separate Canadian edition also available
† Separate U.K. edition also available

Available wherever books are sold. For more information or to order direct: U.S. customers visit www.dummies.com or call 1-877-762-2974.
U.K. customers visit www.wileyeurope.com or call 0800 243407. Canadian customers visit www.wiley.ca or call 1-800-567-4797.

 **WILEY**

## SPORTS, FITNESS, PARENTING, RELIGION & SPIRITUALITY

0-7645-5146-9

0-7645-5418-2

**Also available:**
- Adoption For Dummies
  0-7645-5488-3
- Basketball For Dummies
  0-7645-5248-1
- The Bible For Dummies
  0-7645-5296-1
- Buddhism For Dummies
  0-7645-5359-3
- Catholicism For Dummies
  0-7645-5391-7
- Hockey For Dummies
  0-7645-5228-7

- Judaism For Dummies
  0-7645-5299-6
- Martial Arts For Dummies
  0-7645-5358-5
- Pilates For Dummies
  0-7645-5397-6
- Religion For Dummies
  0-7645-5264-3
- Teaching Kids to Read For Dummies
  0-7645-4043-2
- Weight Training For Dummies
  0-7645-5168-X
- Yoga For Dummies
  0-7645-5117-5

## TRAVEL

0-7645-5438-7

0-7645-5453-0

**Also available:**
- Alaska For Dummies
  0-7645-1761-9
- Arizona For Dummies
  0-7645-6938-4
- Cancún and the Yucatán For Dummies
  0-7645-2437-2
- Cruise Vacations For Dummies
  0-7645-6941-4
- Europe For Dummies
  0-7645-5456-5
- Ireland For Dummies
  0-7645-5455-7

- Las Vegas For Dummies
  0-7645-5448-4
- London For Dummies
  0-7645-4277-X
- New York City For Dummies
  0-7645-6945-7
- Paris For Dummies
  0-7645-5494-8
- RV Vacations For Dummies
  0-7645-5443-3
- Walt Disney World & Orlando For Dummies
  0-7645-6943-0

## GRAPHICS, DESIGN & WEB DEVELOPMENT

0-7645-4345-8

0-7645-5589-8

**Also available:**
- Adobe Acrobat 6 PDF For Dummies
  0-7645-3760-1
- Building a Web Site For Dummies
  0-7645-7144-3
- Dreamweaver MX 2004 For Dummies
  0-7645-4342-3
- FrontPage 2003 For Dummies
  0-7645-3882-9
- HTML 4 For Dummies
  0-7645-1995-6
- Illustrator CS For Dummies
  0-7645-4084-X

- Macromedia Flash MX 2004 For Dummies
  0-7645-4358-X
- Photoshop 7 All-in-One Desk Reference For Dummies
  0-7645-1667-1
- Photoshop CS Timesaving Techniques For Dummies
  0-7645-6782-9
- PHP 5 For Dummies
  0-7645-4166-8
- PowerPoint 2003 For Dummies
  0-7645-3908-6
- QuarkXPress 6 For Dummies
  0-7645-2593-X

## NETWORKING, SECURITY, PROGRAMMING & DATABASES

0-7645-6852-3

0-7645-5784-X

**Also available:**
- A+ Certification For Dummies
  0-7645-4187-0
- Access 2003 All-in-One Desk Reference For Dummies
  0-7645-3988-4
- Beginning Programming For Dummies
  0-7645-4997-9
- C For Dummies
  0-7645-7068-4
- Firewalls For Dummies
  0-7645-4048-3
- Home Networking For Dummies
  0-7645-42796

- Network Security For Dummies
  0-7645-1679-5
- Networking For Dummies
  0-7645-1677-9
- TCP/IP For Dummies
  0-7645-1760-0
- VBA For Dummies
  0-7645-3989-2
- Wireless All In-One Desk Reference For Dummies
  0-7645-7496-5
- Wireless Home Networking For Dummies
  0-7645-3910-8

## HEALTH & SELF-HELP

0-7645-6820-5 *†

0-7645-2566-2

**Also available:**

Alzheimer's For Dummies
0-7645-3899-3

Asthma For Dummies
0-7645-4233-8

Controlling Cholesterol For Dummies
0-7645-5440-9

Depression For Dummies
0-7645-3900-0

Dieting For Dummies
0-7645-4149-8

Fertility For Dummies
0-7645-2549-2

Fibromyalgia For Dummies
0-7645-5441-7

Improving Your Memory For Dummies
0-7645-5435-2

Pregnancy For Dummies †
0-7645-4483-7

Quitting Smoking For Dummies
0-7645-2629-4

Relationships For Dummies
0-7645-5384-4

Thyroid For Dummies
0-7645-5385-2

## EDUCATION, HISTORY, REFERENCE & TEST PREPARATION

0-7645-5194-9

0-7645-4186-2

**Also available:**

Algebra For Dummies
0-7645-5325-9

British History For Dummies
0-7645-7021-8

Calculus For Dummies
0-7645-2498-4

English Grammar For Dummies
0-7645-5322-4

Forensics For Dummies
0-7645-5580-4

The GMAT For Dummies
0-7645-5251-1

Inglés Para Dummies
0-7645-5427-1

Italian For Dummies
0-7645-5196-5

Latin For Dummies
0-7645-5431-X

Lewis & Clark For Dummies
0-7645-2545-X

Research Papers For Dummies
0-7645-5426-3

The SAT I For Dummies
0-7645-7193-1

Science Fair Projects For Dummies
0-7645-5460-3

U.S. History For Dummies
0-7645-5249-X

# Get smart @ dummies.com®

- **Find a full list of Dummies titles**
- **Look into loads of FREE on-site articles**
- **Sign up for FREE eTips e-mailed to you weekly**
- **See what other products carry the Dummies name**
- **Shop directly from the Dummies bookstore**
- **Enter to win new prizes every month!**

\* **Separate Canadian edition also available**
† **Separate U.K. edition also available**

Available wherever books are sold. For more information or to order direct: U.S. customers visit www.dummies.com or call 1-877-762-2974.
U.K. customers visit www.wileyeurope.com or call 0800 243407. Canadian customers visit www.wiley.ca or call 1-800-567-4797.